The Process of Change

THE GUILFORD FAMILY THERAPY SERIES
Alan S. Gurman, Editor

The Process of Change

PEGGY PAPP, ACSW

Ackerman Institute for Family Therapy

Foreword by Donald A. Bloch, MD

The Guilford Press
New York   London

Printed in the United States of America
Last digit is print number 9 8 7 6

LIBRARY OF CONGRESS CATALOGING IN PUBLICATION DATA
Papp, Peggy.
  The process of change.

  (The Guilford family therapy series)
  Bibliography: p.
  Includes index.
  1. Family psychotherapy. 2. Change (Psychology) I. Title. II. Series.
RC488.5.P36 1983   616.89′156   83-12814
ISBN 0-89862-052-X

To my children—Tony and Miranda

F O R E W O R D

Family therapy, and the changes in paradigms associated with it, has revolutionized the mental health field, redefining in the process such key concepts as resistance, change, symptomaticity, and indeed therapy itself. Over the last dozen years there has been a revolution within the revolution, sparked by the work of Jay Haley, Paul Watzlawick, Milton Erickson, and Mara Selvini Palazzoli and the Milan group. There has been a burgeoning of clinical innovation and creativity. This volume is the product of one such flowering. It reports the strategic thinking and actions of a team approach to work with seriously disordered families.

Over the years the dark and difficult path of psychotherapy has been illuminated by great clinician–teachers. Each plants a torch along the way lighting up a bit more of the shadowy darkness. What seemed baffling and unmanageable becomes accessible; in the process, artistry is transformed into teachable precepts. Peggy Papp is one of these great clinician–teachers; this volume takes us a good day's journey along that twisting road.

It is interesting to think about how different these leaders are from each other. What category system would encompass Erickson, Ackerman, Haley, Jackson, Whitaker, Minuchin, Satir, and Papp, to mention some of the most obvious members of this pantheon. Yet they share important qualities, I think. As clinicians, they are tough-minded and persistent—focused on the clinical problem at hand. They have a sense of mission about their work, of their own importance, if you will. They are almost invariably witty and humorous—idiosyncratic and quirky in a way that is not oddball but rather that creatively touches and illuminates human issues. They all, I should add, have that almost indefinable personal quality that is perhaps best spoken of as *presence*: They are not to be overlooked, in the consulting room, on the lecture platform, or in the pages of their writings. Finally, it should be mentioned, they are all hard workers—no wonder, for the work is hard indeed.

The clinician–teacher does *and* teaches. This book is highly satisfactory on both counts. The clinical examples are well presented, completely and honestly enough so that we can see how the author's thinking proceeded, and well edited so that our time and effort are conserved. There is a minimum of exposition, *no* jargon. We are told simply and directly what was done and why; both the tyro and the experienced clinician are bound to learn how to do their work better.

The cases are presented in full enough detail so that we can make up our own minds as to the correctness of the interventions that were carried out. The data are put before us completely, including the wrong moves, indecisiveness, puzzlement of the therapeutic team. We see the work, warts and all, and can only be grateful to Papp and her colleagues for their candor. At times it looks like magic, but anyone who has watched this and similar teams at work knows how much hard effort and careful thought goes into each planned intervention.

Over its history, psychotherapy has struggled with certain central ambiguities:

- People seem to cling to the very behavior that incapacitates them and makes them miserable.
- People do things that do not seem to make sense; assistance is sought from highly trained and expensive professionals so as to change these behaviors, yet the clients seem intent on actively frustrating their efforts.

It is as much the "nature" of systems to maintain dynamic equilibria as it is the "nature" of the tiger to eat the goat, or, for that matter, of the goat to be eaten. None are to be blamed, yet psychotherapists, since Freud's day, have used the pejorative word "resistance" to describe this aspect of systemic functioning. The heart of the author's work is to find ways to use this tendency to stay the same in the service of change.

The therapeutic work is carried on by a group; indeed, the virtuoso use of the group as a therapeutic tool is what this book is about to a large degree. As Papp notes, this way of proceeding builds directly on the early work of Mara Selvini Palazzoli and the Milan group. Yet, how different it is. Similar principles are at work, particularly in regard to the management of resistance and the use of tasks and rituals and ceremonials. There is a main point of divergence that represents a genuine and profound technical innovation as well as being, in appearance at least, in marked contrast to the Milanese approach. This has to do with creating a structure in the therapeutic team that is isomorphic to the nodal, symptom-related pattern in the family.

As I see it, this innovation grows out of Papp's early work with family sculpting and couples choreography and continues in a developing line through her use of the observing group as a Greek chorus. The interesting difference from the Milan practice lies in the Italian adherence to a highly formal and invariant presentation of the group (at least in their earlier work), along with a personal style that minimizes involvement and affective expression. The Americans, by contrast, are not above hyperbole and dramatic gesture in the interest of eliciting an enactment.

One of the clinical presentations aptly catches and condenses the dramatic beauty of this style. In it, an enmeshed warring and worrying mother and her children are told a fairy tale—about an enmeshed warring and worrying royal family. The tale highlights the family drama and conflict, and reframes it. One session, no more, then a later follow-up thank-you note from "The Noble Woman."

Work such as that reported here brings renewed excitement to psychotherapy. The work is hard; let no one forget that. There is something unavoidably deceptive about describing these clinical struggles in words on paper. It may look less complex and rich than it really is, and perhaps it may look easier. I have been privileged to watch the work of Peggy Papp, Olga Silverstein, and their colleagues over the years and know at first hand about its depth and difficulty.

The author is a pragmatist to the core, profoundly committed to understanding what works and is teachable and to using that as the ultimate test of the goodness of any idea. Many years ago she was a junior colleague of mine, but that relationship has long since evolved so that I can count myself among the large number who have learned from her. Those who read this book carefully and search for the special ways in which they can adapt its wisdom and insights to their own situations, their own capabilities and talents, will know the benefits that come from being among her students.

Donald A. Bloch

C O N T E N T S

The Process of Change

C H A P T E R 1

Introduction

This book is written in the hope that it will serve as a guide to those therapists who are interested in exploring paradoxical and strategic interventions with couples and families within a systems framework. Because it is meant to be a practical book it is composed mainly of case studies showing the step-by-step process by which concepts are put into practice over time. When theory is isolated from practice, the same as when behavior is isolated from context, it tends to lose its meaning through the process of disassociation. Over the years, I have observed that students learn best when concepts are directly related to clinical cases. Often after discussing theory in what I considered to be a clear and articulate manner, students asked the very same questions I thought I had just answered. Although academic definitions are useful in developing abstract concepts, they are not very helpful in knowing how to deal with the live family. "Theory is good; but it doesn't prevent things from existing" (Jean Martin Charcot, quoted in Freud, 1893/1962). Therefore, rather than defining concepts historically or academically, I have tried to limit myself to defining them according to their clinical applicability: formulating hypotheses, designing and carrying out interventions, handling the fallout from change, dealing with crises, and solidifying change. A guideline for using different types of interventions in different situations is also included.

The introduction into this country of the Milan team (Mary Selvini Palazzoli, Luigi Boscolo, Gianfranco Cecchin, and Giuliana Prata) in 1977 and the subsequent publication of their book, *Paradox and Counterparadox* (1978), shortly thereafter created a new wave of excitement and experimentation with the paradoxical approach. This excitement and curiosity was originally stimulated by Jay Haley with *Strategies of Psychotherapy*, in 1963, and *Uncommon Therapy* (based on the work of Milton Erickson), in 1973, and by Watzlawick, Weakland, and Fisch with the publication of *Change* in 1974. Although each of the above applied paradoxical concepts differently, each reported such dramatic results that more and more therapists were enticed to experiment with them.

One hub of this experimentation was the Brief Therapy Project of the Ackerman Institute for Family Therapy that was organized by Olga Silverstein and myself in 1975. The project was set up to explore the use of paradoxical and strategic interventions with families of symptomatic children. Although inspired by the work of the Milan team, which we visited in 1974, the project quickly developed its own unique characteristics. Ideas that are transported from one country to another are transformed by the style, culture, and previous training of the therapists. Just as the Milan team transformed the ideas of their predecessors, Haley, Watzlawick, Weakland, Fisch, Bateson, and Erickson, into their own special modality, so the Brief Therapy Project transformed their ideas again.

The original project was composed of eight self-selected family therapists, all trained at the Ackerman Institute.[1] The group of eight was divided into two groups of four each, Olga leading one and myself the other. We met for one full day a week, devoting mornings to discussing theory and developing concepts and afternoons to seeing families. All the sessions were video-taped and observed from behind a one-way mirror by the three remaining colleagues in each group who formed the consultation team. Over the years the team divided and re-formed, with members leaving and being added.

The title "Brief Therapy" was given to the project as our original intention was to limit the therapy to a maximum of 12 sessions. As it became clear that different families change at different rates of speed, the time limit became a hindrance

[1] Olga Silverstein, Paul DeBell, Gillian Walker, John Clarkin, Betty Lundquist, Richard Evans, Peggy Papp, and Joel Bergman; Lynn Hoffman, Anita Morawetz, Peggy Penn, Jeffrey Ross, and John Patten joined the group at a later date.

rather than a help and we abandoned it. The number of sessions has varied from 1 to 22, with the majority falling in the middle.

America is a country in which many different approaches to family therapy have burgeoned, and most therapists have been influenced by a variety of these. My own professional background includes serving on the faculty of three prestigious family practice centers (Ackerman Institute for Family Therapy, Philadelphia Child Guidance Clinic, Center for Family Learning), all employing different conceptual models. Initially trained by Nathan Ackerman, I was introduced to the field by a flamboyant pioneer whose approach was mainly psychodynamic. Later, as one of the founders of the Center for Family Learning, I learned and taught the ideas of Murray Bowen, whose concepts regarding the extended family have influenced both my professional and personal life. From 1976 to 1979, I served on the faculty of the Philadelphia Child Guidance Clinic where I was exposed to the theatrical artistry of Salvador Minuchin and to the power and clarity of Jay Haley. The writings and tapes of Haley initially aroused my interest in exploring the use of paradox. This interest was whetted by my informal conversations with him over the years in which he shared his time and thoughts most generously.

The ideas of the Mental Research Institute, as presented by Watzlawick *et al.* in *Change*, were a further stimulus for me, along with the eloquent elaboration of these ideas by Watzlawick in *How Real Is Real?* (1976) and *The Language of Change* (1978). The input of John Weakland as a friend and consultant shed light on the practical application of these ideas. The concept of applying paradoxical interventions to an entire family system and ritualizing these interventions with written messages was a development of the Milan team and added to the conceptual framework upon which the Brief Therapy Project was founded.

In 1974, I visited the Milan team at the Centro per lo Studio della Famiglia and was impressed by their rigorous, disciplined adherence to systems concepts, their creative leaps of imagination, and the adventurous and unconventional interventions that ensued. The following summer, Olga Silverstein journeyed with me to Milan; inspired by this visit we returned to set up the Brief Therapy Project.

The initial period of attempting to establish coherent concepts from such a rich assortment of ideas was challenging and required hours of experimenting, integrating, discarding, alternating, reshaping, extending, and creating new forms. Although much of this process took place in the meetings of the Brief Therapy Project, the way in which the ideas are formulated and articulated in this book is my own.

Over the years, in my search for faster and more effective ways of doing therapy, I have come to the conclusion that no one approach is right for all families and situations. Therapists need a repertoire of ideas and interventions that they can call into play to suit a particular situation. The therapist who has the flexibility of being able to choose between several different approaches to any given problem is likely to find the most creative solution.

Most of the cases presented in this book were treated in the Brief Therapy Project of the Ackerman Institute, where a consultation team was used. Olga Silverstein served as my chief consultant on the following cases: The Daughter Who Said No, Exorcising Ghosts, Don't Turn Out to Be like Father, What Price Liberation?, The Golden Thread, and The Great Mother Tradition. Although Olga has chosen not to coauthor this book with me, the ideas in it were developed in close collaboration with her. Without her ingenuity, wisdom, and creativity, the project would not have flourished in the way it has. Our method of working depends on an intimate collaboration between therapist and consultant, on the building of one idea upon the other, on the counterplay of imaginations. Much credit also goes to Stanley Siegel, director of education, who recently joined the project and whose new perspective has proven valuable both in the clinical work and in the writing of this book.

I am also indebted to my friend and colleague from Great Britain, Alan Cooklin, director of the Institute of Family Therapy in London, for his perceptive critique; to Anita Morawetz for her excellent suggestions; and to Alan S. Gurman for his editorial assistance.

It would have been impossible for this project to flourish except in the kind of atmosphere of freedom and experimentation that has been created at the Ackerman Institute by its director, Donald A. Bloch. Under his leadership, the institute has become a place where many different and often conflicting ideas can exist side by side. His insistence on this policy of open-mindedness has created a peculiarly American democratic institution that is unusual in a field which tends to polarize and adhere dogmatically to one particular modality. Over the years, he has proven a constant source of encouragement and support to those of us at Ackerman who are addicted to experimentation. He has defended our right to do this even when he did not concur with our ideas, and he has helped to pick up the pieces when we faltered. I wish to extend to him my heartfelt thanks and appreciation.

CHAPTER 2

The Dilemma
of Change

What Is a System?

The word "system" has become a cliché of family therapy—a word that has lost much of its meaning through overuse, generalization, and academic elaboration. Although "systems theory" is the cornerstone upon which family therapy is based, the diversity of clinical approaches indicates the many different ways in which a family system can be defined and treated.

Most trainees respond to an academic explanation of a family system with a dazed look, as though to say: "So what does one do with a self-corrective, homeostatic system which is error activated and regulates itself through negative and positive feedback loops in order to maintain its equilibrium?" (a cybernetic definition of a system). Or: "How does one deal with a unit with an internal design which evolves to new and unpredictable levels of organization through the process of discontinuous change and unpredictable leaps?" (an evolutionary definition of a system).

Unfortunately, these concepts are easier to define academically than they are to apply clinically. When working clinically, most therapists' definitions of a system are based on what they believe is causing the problem and how they intend to intervene. For example: Salvador Minuchin defines a system according to boundaries and hierarchical organization, as that is what he attempts to change; Murray Bowen's definition is based on a concept of triangles and degrees of differentiation, as this is his field of intervention; Jay Haley and Chloé Madanes view a system in terms of power structure and focus on altering this; Norman Paul looks for areas of unresolved mourning, Boszormenyi-Nagy for three-generational loyalties, and Selvini Palazzoli for systemic paradoxes, these being the focal points of their interventions. As Lynn Hoffman so aptly states, "Family therapy was, and still is, a wondrous Tower of Babel; people in it speak many different tongues" (1981, p. 9).

What is referred to by "systems theory" in family therapy is a loosely connected series of concepts rooted in general systems theory and cybernetics. The many different ways in which systems theory has been interpreted and applied have been written about extensively (see Watzlawick, Beavin, & Jackson, 1967; Watzlawick *et al.*, 1974; G. Bateson, 1972; Hoffman, 1981; Keeney, 1983; Paolino & McCrady, 1978; Minuchin, 1974; Bowen, 1978; Selvini Palazzoli *et al.*, 1978; Haley, 1977; and Napier & Whitaker, 1978). For the purposes of this book, I shall limit myself to describing the most basic tenets of this theory and how these are translated into clinical practice in this particular approach.

The key concepts of systems thinking have to do with wholeness, organization, and patterning. Events are studied within the context in which they are occurring, and attention is focused on connections and relationships rather than on individual characteristics. The central ideas of this theory are that the whole is considered to be greater than the sum of its parts; each part can only be understood in the context of the whole; a change in any one part will affect every other part; and the whole regulates itself through a series of feedback loops that are referred to as cybernetic circuits. Information travels back and forth within these feedback loops in order to provide stability or homeostasis for the system. The parts are constantly changing in order to keep the system balanced (as a tightrope walker constantly shifts his/her weight to preserve equilibrium). The overall system maintains its shape as the pattern of linkage between the parts changes. This concept of patterning and circular organization, as opposed to individual description and linear explanation, has become the foundation upon which family therapy rests.

Such a concept means that no one event or piece of behavior causes another but, rather, that each is linked in a circular manner to many other events and pieces of behavior. These events and behaviors form consistent, recurring patterns over time that function to balance the family and permit it to evolve from one developmental stage to another. All behavior, including the symptom, establishes and maintains these patterns. This regulatory function is considered to be more important than the behavior or symptom as an entity in and of itself. The therapist's primary concern is with the *functioning* of behavior and how the function of one piece of behavior is connected with the function of another piece of behavior in order to preserve family equilibrium.

Family members are not seen as *possessing* certain innate characteristics but *manifesting* behavior in relation to the behavior of others. Rather than attempting to understand the cause of the behavior, the therapist attempts to understand the fluctuation of the pattern from which it derives its meaning. For example: A linear cause-and-effect explanation of a problem might be that a child is withdrawn because he has a rejecting mother. The therapist would then focus on trying to get the mother to be less rejecting of the child. This linear perspective might also include a three-generational cause-and-effect description, which states that the mother is rejecting because she herself had a rejecting mother. A systemic view, on the other hand, would see the withdrawal of the child as part of a set of relationships that form a cybernetic circuit, namely, mother becomes critical of the son when father, who feels controlled by mother, undermines her authority by being overly permissive with the son. In response, the son supports father against mother, causing mother to become increasingly antagonistic toward the son.

No one person is considered to have unilateral control over any other person. The control is in the way the circuit is organized and continues to operate.

The Milan team has developed a unique way of avoiding linear thinking when forming a hypothesis by substituting the infinitive *to show* for the infinitive *to be*. For example: "The father, Mr. Franchi, shows during the session a veiled erotic interest in the designated patient, who, for her part, shows hostility and scorn toward him. Mrs. Franchi shows intense jealousy toward husband and daughter, while she shows strong affection toward her other daughter, who, in turn, shows no sign of reciprocating this affection" (Selvini Palazzoli et al., 1978, p. 28). This description does not label any of the individual members as being "jealous," "hostile," "seductive," "affectionate," or "rejecting." Rather, it describes a series of interconnected responses and relates those responses to the context in which they are being shown. They are viewed as mere moves and countermoves that are essential to the family game.

In systems thinking, there are no absolutes or certainties; reality and truth are circular. The "pragmatic truth," as it is referred to by the Milan team, is the truth that is the most "useful," that is, the truth that connects certain events and behavior in such a way as to enable the family to make constructive changes.

Symptom Formation

The question that might well be asked at this point is why, if the system constantly balances itself in order to maintain its equilibrium, should there be any problems requiring clinical help? The answer is that sometimes the family's way of balancing itself includes a symptom that is unacceptable to them and/or to society. When the symptom causes intolerable stress, either inside or outside the family, the family is compelled to seek help.

The occurrence of a symptom may be precipitated by a multitude of events. It may be triggered by a change in one of the larger systems in which the family exists, such as the social, political, cultural, or educational system. For example: an economic depression resulting in unemployment or disastrous financial losses; a political crisis that tears the family apart, either physically or ideologically; a social revolution, such as occurred during the 1960s, that overturns conventions and rigid roles; poor educational methods or facilities; and racial, social, or sexual discrimination. All are part of wider cybernetic circuits that affect those of the family. Or, the precipitating event may come from inside the family as a reaction to some life cycle occurrence, such as the death of a grandparent, the birth of a child, a debilitating illness, or the departure of children from the home. Elizabeth Carter and Monica McGoldrick (1980) have described in detail the different kinds of symptoms that are likely to emerge at different points in the life cycle.

Any one of these events may shatter the family's familiar coping patterns, and a symptom may develop as a means of establishing a different pattern. Because one particular pattern is not working in a family doesn't mean that other patterns are not working. The therapist's job is to identify the particular pattern that is related to the symptom and to find a way of changing that particular pattern.

The current controversy in the field as to whether the symptom serves a homeostatic function or an evolutionary function—that is, whether it is in the service of keeping the family the same or encouraging it to evolve to a different stage—is of little consequence in this approach, since the crucial clinical issue is that the symptom and system are *connected* and defined as *serving one another*. It is left to the therapist's discretion to define the precise nature of the reciprocity in a way that is most therapeutically useful. Since change and stability are viewed as two sides of the same coin, the choice is purely a pragmatic one. "All change can be understood as the effort to maintain some constancy, and all constancy is maintained through change" (G. Bateson, quoted in M. Bateson, 1972, p. 17).

The question is often raised as to whether a symptom always serves a function in the system or whether it may be a reaction to a situation outside the family, such as work, school, or social relationships. Although the origins of a symptom may be rooted in an outside event, its persistence would indicate it is being *used* by the family in some ongoing transaction. For example: If a husband is laid off from his job because of an economic recession, he may become depressed as a result of being unemployed. The depression will most likely disappear when he obtains another job. However, if in the meantime he begins to use this depression as a weapon in an ongoing power struggle between him and his wife, the depression is likely to become chronic, because it will be serving a function in the marital relationship. The extent to which a symptom is functional varies according to circumstances, time, and place. The symptom may serve different functions at different times for different sets of relationships. Families who do not use transitory symptoms as weapons in ongoing family transactions seldom appear for therapy.

The Dilemma of Change

The systems approach that I am describing depends on the ability of the therapist to adopt and maintain a particular attitude toward change and to use that attitude therapeutically. This attitude emerges by following systems and cybernetic thinking to their ultimate conclusion: If the family is seen as a self-regulating system and the symptom as a mechanism for regulation, and if the symptom is eliminated, then the system will be temporarily unregulated. In systemic terms, change is not a single solution to a single problem but a dilemma to be resolved. This is true whether the system is biological, ecological, psychological, social, or political. Change exacts a price and raises the question as to what the repercussions will be for the rest of the system. To ignore these repercussions is to act out of what Bradford Keeney (1983) terms "ecological ignorance." These repercussions have become strikingly evident in recent years as scientists from various fields have observed the effects of altering one part of a system. Solving an immediate problem often creates another problem in the larger ecology. For example: DDT destroyed insects but was discovered toxic to animals and humans; prohibition generated a new profession of bootleggers who acted homeostatically to maintain the supply of alcohol; killing off coyotes to protect farmers' sheep increased the rabbit supply, which in turn destroyed farmers' crops; forest fires, once considered a natural disaster, were discovered to serve long-term beneficial functions and recently have sometimes been left to burn. If solutions are to be more than transitory, they must take into account the complexity of larger systems over time. Experienced family therapists have become well aware of this as they have observed new problems emerge from the elimination of the old: parents returning after the symptom in the child has disappeared to say, "Everything is fine with Jane, but now we aren't getting along"; or an optimistic spouse becoming depressed as the depressed spouse becomes more optimistic; or a "well" sibling turning troublesome when the identified patient does better. These consequences of shifting a system are graphically illustrated in Chapter 9, "Treating Couples," when the wife declares that her husband is now everything she has ever wanted him to be, "and I just can't bear it." Or, when the pursuing wife realizes how much she liked being alone as soon as her husband begins coming home every night. The distancing of the husbands had clearly served a function in the marital relationships that was only realized once they were no longer distant. An artistic depiction of the consequences of "cure" is seen in Marco Bellocchio's remarkable film, *Leap into the Void*, in which a brother's life is shattered when the burden of his sister's illness is removed from him. It was this universal phenomenon that led George Bernard Shaw to observe that there are two tragedies in life: one is not to get your heart's desire, and the other is to get it.

This does not mean that people should not strive to get their heart's desire or to change but simply that the consequences of doing so are unpredictable, filled with unexpected twists and ironic turns. If the therapist can be aware of the rich complexities involved in changing a system, he/she can use those complexities in the service of producing change.

Some recent critics of the cybernetic model contend that this model is a theory of stability rather than of change and is therefore inadequate as a basis for therapy. "The chief demerit of the theory for therapeutic purposes is that it is not a theory of change but a theory of stability" (Haley, 1980, p. 15). This critique depends on whether or not the theory is used merely to describe the self-corrective processes in the family or used clinically to produce a therapeutic result. In the approach of the Brief Therapy Project, the theory of stability or homeostasis is used paradoxically to effect change. The concept of self-regulation is used to connect the symptom with the system and thus change one of the crucial premises under which the family is operating—the premise that the symptom is a foreign element outside the system and can be changed separately. When the family comes for therapy they have disconnected the symptom and are asking the therapist to change the symptom without changing their system. The therapist connects the symptom and the system to show that one cannot be changed without changing the other and presents the family with their own dilemma. This *dilemma* of change, and all the issues pertinent to it, becomes the focal point of therapy. The central therapeutic issue is not how to eliminate the symptom but what will happen if it is eliminated; the therapeutic argument is shifted from the problem, who has it, what caused it, and how to get rid of it, to how the family will function without it, what price will have to be paid for its removal, who will pay it, and whether it is worth it.

The reverberations of systemic change, and the dilemmas that are created by them, become the central point of a therapeutic debate between the therapist and family. This debate contains within it a series of drastic redefinitions that change the family members' perception of the problem and, consequently, their perception of the solution to the problem. During the process of debate, all the issues that are related to change and that lie on the ulterior level of the family—the secret alliances, hidden coalitions, covert contests, and disguised arrangements—are made manifest and connected with the symptom. As family members repeatedly attempt to reinstate their premise by disassociating the symptom, the therapist continues to negate their premise by connecting it. When the family accepts the new premise, it is possible for change to take place suddenly and in an undetermined direction. "Because only some of the personal characteristics of the elements are fully absorbed and utilized by the system, others remain available and can be put to use in constructing a working family system, for instance when the equilibrium of the old has been destroyed. . . . This interaction does not demand hard and protracted work on the part of the therapist but only the ability to seize the right moment and the right time" (Selvini Palazzoli et al., 1978, p. 199).

In order to fully understand the ulterior level of the family—the hidden alliances, coalitions, contests—it is helpful to understand something of the family belief system that governs this level.

Belief System

The behavioral cycles in each family are governed by a belief system that is composed of a combination of attitudes, basic assumptions, expectations, prejudices, convictions, and beliefs brought to the nuclear family by each parent from his/her family of origin. These individual beliefs interlock to form the governing premises that rule the family. Once again, it is not the individual beliefs or assumptions of either parent that the therapist considers important but how these are linked to form the operating rules of the family.

Some of these beliefs are shared; others are reciprocal and provide the basis for the parents' original attraction to one another. During courtship and the early phases of marriage, a series of negotiations takes place around these beliefs and is expressed in the form of family themes. Important behavioral sequences then become organized around these themes which often serve as metaphors for the type of symptom that is chosen. By "theme" is meant a specific emotionally laden issue around which there is a recurring conflict. Since there are many such themes in every family, the therapist looks for the one that is most relevant to the symptom. Some common family themes are: responsibility versus irresponsibility, with one spouse assuming the role of the responsible one and the other spouse assuming the role of the irresponsible one; illness versus health, with one spouse becoming emotionally or physically ill and the other spouse acting as the psychiatrist or doctor; closeness versus distance, with one spouse pursuing the other in an attempt to gain emotional closeness and the other spouse evading the pursuit in an effort to create emotional distance; teacher versus student, with one spouse assuming a position of authority and competence and the other spouse remaining helpless and incompetent. The positions may shift in different situations, but the central theme remains the same. When either spouse becomes dissatisfied with the other spouse's behavior in the service of the theme, he/she may turn to a child to enact a solution. The child comes to the aid of the parents by assuming a reciprocal position to one of the parents, thereby substituting for the position formerly taken by the other spouse.

Comprehension of these beliefs and ensuing themes cannot be arrived at through direct questioning but must be deduced. This deduction is based on listening for metaphorical language, tracking behavioral sequences, and picking up key attitudinal statements such as, "I knew all these things about him when I married him, but I thought the love of a good woman would cure him." Such a comment illuminates the repeated attempts of a wife to rescue her husband from his errant ways. She believes if she is good enough and loving enough long enough, she will save him from himself, and this will make her feel needed and important. Her husband's statement, "My wife's character is stronger than mine and her judgment is better," indicates his belief that he has a weak character and needs to be rescued from his irresponsible ways by his responsible wife. These reciprocal beliefs result in predictable behavior patterns that center on the central theme of rescuing. These patterns may be functional and asymptomatic over a long period of time. They cease to become so if either spouse escalates or changes his/her position. For example: If the husband, at some point, decides that his wife's rescue efforts are choking him rather than saving him, he might begin to try to escape from her. The wife may then turn her rescuing efforts toward their son, who obligingly develops a symptom so she can save him instead. The father may then signal their daughter to rescue him since his wife has failed, and the daughter may then begin to compete with her mother over who is the best rescuer of men in the family. The theme of rescue and escape governs the family's transactions, with each person operating from a different position in relation to the central theme.

The belief system and the themes that emerge from it have been described by different authors as family myths (Ferreira, 1966), family constructs (Reiss, 1971), family themes (Hess & Handel, 1969), and family identity (Wolin, Bennett, & Noonan, unpublished). Wolin et al., describing family identity as the family's "subjective sense of its own situation, continuity, and character," contend that this identity is a way of establishing connections between one generation and another.

Some schools of therapy concentrate only on the behavioral cycle and, while recognizing the existence of the belief system, do not use it therapeutically. "The effects of behaviors upon behaviors, the way interpersonal sequences are organized, will be carefully noted, while on the contrary, no inference will be made about the motivations of the participants" (Sluzki, 1978, p. 367). It goes without saying that change can be brought about in many different ways on many different levels. Although it is not necessary for either family members or the therapist to concern themselves with the belief system in order to effect change, a knowledge of it gives a broader context from which to intervene, particularly when a paradoxical approach is used, as these beliefs and themes lay the groundwork for intervening indirectly and metaphorically. The influence of belief systems on the ideational levels of family members will be discussed in detail in Chapter 3.

C H A P T E R 3

Forming a Hypothesis

The first step in any therapeutic approach is the formulation of a hypothesis, without which a therapist has no way to elicit or organize information. A hypothesis, according to *Webster's International Dictionary*, is "a starting point for an investigation." But the therapist must first know what he/she is investigating; otherwise, a vast amount of meaningless information is gathered. The purpose of this investigation is to define the reciprocity between the symptom and the system within the framework of time and change. The therapist needs to know the answers to such questions as: Why is the family presenting this particular problem at this particular time? Which events and behaviors have precipitated the problem? What current cycle of interaction is maintaining it? How has this cycle changed over time? How has the family's method of coping with the problem changed? How have their methods affected the problem? What will happen to the family in the future if the problem continues? If it disappears?

The initial hypothesis is necessarily speculative and is used as the basis for gathering more information that will either confirm or refute it. The therapist may modify the formulation many times as new information is gathered from the family. It is not necessary to wait for a definitive hypothesis before intervening, as many times only the interventions themselves produce crucial information. Nor is it necessary for the hypothesis to be absolutely accurate; it must only be relevant to the family and to change. The criteria for its relevance is evaluated on the basis of feedback—on the subsequent responses of the family members.

Since the major purpose of the hypothesis is to make connections, how information is gathered is extremely important. Many times, trainees gather information in such a way as to end up with isolated facts about isolated occurrences, which may be staggering in and of themselves (incest, rape, murder, suicide, etc.) but which are meaningless unless connected in a useful way with the presenting problem. The family members themselves cannot make these connections, as the continuation of a symptomatic behavior requires that they remain unaware of them.

In gathering information, the therapist takes a neutral position and tries not to imply any moral judgments or to align him/herself with any one faction of the family. To maintain neutrality, the therapist does not focus on any one person for any extended period of time to the exclusion of others, as this gives that person special status. Since all behavior is viewed as an attempt to balance the system in some way, the therapist respects the unifying intent behind it, though the behavior in and of itself may not be condoned. This neutral position is often difficult for therapists trained in a more confrontational method to comprehend. The goal of therapy is not to bring about change through small moves within a session—by the therapist's actively realigning, restructuring, or reorganizing the family through his/her authority or artistry—but rather change is brought about through the therapist's ability to stand outside the system and gain a holistic view—to comprehend, respect, and connect all family transactions and, finally, to aim an intervention at those most relevant to the presenting problem.

If the therapist were to react judgmentally to a particular behavior, it would then be inconsistent to define that piece of behavior positively as serving a function in the system.

In gathering information, it is helpful to keep the following questions in mind:

1. What function does the symptom serve in stabilizing the family?
2. How does the family function in stabilizing the symptom?
3. What is the central theme around which the problem is organized?

4. What will be the consequences of change?
5. What is the therapeutic dilemma?

In order to answer these questions, the therapist must enter the session with certain basic assumptions regarding the reciprocal relationship between the symptom and the system. In this approach, these assumptions are:

1. The occurrence of a symptom usually coincides with some change or anticipated change in the family that threatens to upset the equilibrium (such as a family member leaving home, getting married, changing jobs, starting school, getting divorced, reaching adolescence, approaching middle age, becoming ill, or dying).
2. The anxiety about this change activates conflicts that have been lying dormant, and these conflicts, rather than being resolved, are expressed through a symptom.
3. The symptom can either be a means for preventing this threatened change or providing a way for it to take place.

For example: The presenting symptom in one case was the delinquent behavior of a 16-year-old daughter who suddenly began failing in school, truanting, stealing, lying, and coming in at four in the morning. This coincided with her mother's promotion to a job that kept her away from home until late every evening. It was discovered that the maternal grandmother disapproved of the mother working and voiced this disapproval to the daughter. Whenever the daughter misbehaved, the grandmother would call the mother at her office, whereupon the mother would promptly leave work to come home and straighten out her daughter. The daughter's misbehavior served the function of preventing change by interfering with the mother's job and keeping her in the traditional role the grandmother had selected for her.

In another case, the symptom of a 26-year-old daughter was viewed as a way of provoking change in a family. A year and a half after the death of the mother, the daughter returned from abroad and began living alone in the empty family house. Her sister and brother had moved away and her father had remarried and was living with his new wife. There were many emotionally laden issues surrounding the mother's death that had never been discussed among the family members but that resulted in tense silences and awkward distancing. The daughter proceeded to shatter the silence and distance through extremely provocative behavior—starting fights, throwing the house into total disarray, indulging in drug and alcohol abuse, and publicizing her moods of depression. The father finally gathered the family together and brought them to therapy, where the daughter opened up all the unspoken issues related to the mother's death and compelled the family to deal with them. In this case, the symptom was seen as an attempt to expedite change by taking the family past the mourning stage.

In developing a hypothesis, information is gathered and integrated on three different levels: the behavioral, the emotional, and the ideational (what people do, feel, and think). In order to understand family patterns, it is important to comprehend how all three levels are connected and cross-fertilize one another.

The Behavioral Level

Detailed information regarding behavior often reveals important distortions or contradictions that are the key to understanding the functioning of that behavior. The therapist should obtain a slow-motion picture of the events leading up to, during, and after the occurrence of the problem. Therapists often have difficulty obtaining information regarding specific behavior as family members tend to talk in generalities and give highly subjective descriptions. For example, a wife may claim that she is always "reaching out" to her husband sexually. In exploring further what she actually does when she "reaches out," the therapist may discover that she attacks and criticizes his love making, causing him to recoil. This information might cause the therapist to speculate that the function of her "reaching out" is to protect herself from learning about her own sexual difficulties. Or, a husband may describe himself as becoming totally helpless in the face of his wife's anger. In actuality, what his "helplessness" entails is going from bar to bar until his wife comes looking for him. What he describes as "helplessness" is a series of activities designed to get his wife to chase him. The underlying effect of behavior on others is important to account for in assessing its function.

In order to obtain this kind of information, the therapist must be persistent in tracking a particular behavioral sequence—he/she must ask what specific actions follow other specific actions and what the specific response of others is. It is sometimes necessary to pursue this to the point of tedium in order to cut through the family's vague language. The following typical dialogue illustrates the persistence this pursuit entails:

THERAPIST: What do you do when Jimmy gets a bad report card?

MOTHER: I don't know what to do.

THERAPIST: So what do you do?

MOTHER: What can I do?

THERAPIST: I'm not sure what you can do, but what do you do?

MOTHER: I've tried everything.

THERAPIST: What have you tried?

MOTHER: Nothing works.

THERAPIST: When was the last time nothing worked?

MOTHER: Yesterday.

THERAPIST: How did it not work?

MOTHER: I just gave up.

THERAPIST: And how did you give up?

MOTHER: I ran to my room, threw myself on the bed and cried.

THERAPIST: What did the other members of your family do when you did that?

MOTHER: Jim didn't care at all; he went outside to play.

THERAPIST: What did your husband do?

MOTHER: He came in and tried to calm me down.

THERAPIST: How did he try to calm you down?

MOTHER: He assured me everything was going to be all right, and promised to spend more time with Jim and try to straighten him out.

From the description of the mother's actual behavior and the response of the husband, the therapist might hypothesize that the function of the mother's giving up was to light a fire under the father and get him more involved in the family.

The Milan team has developed a particularly useful technique for gathering information called circular questioning in which each member of the family is asked how he/she sees the relationship between two other members of the family. This is an effective way of getting information regarding differences and change in the family. For example: A child might be asked, "Do you think your parents have been getting along better or worse since grandmother died?" (Selvini Palazzoli, Boscolo, Cecchin, & Prata, 1980). Regardless of which technique is used in obtaining information, it is important that the information be connected to form a systemic hypothesis.

The Emotional Level

In observing the emotional level of the family, the therapist must focus on the *function* of feelings and the form of their expression. The expression of feelings is a powerful tool in influencing other family members. This is a difficult concept to teach as it goes against the popular notion that feelings are sacred—that they are an authentic indicator of "who we really are" and "where we're really at," and "it is good to know this and let others know it." This so-called cult of communication ignores the politics of feelings within a social context. Feelings do not emanate from the individual psyche in communion with itself but are stimulated and qualified by an audience of others, even when this audience is only anticipated or remembered. Like behavior, the expression of feelings programs, and is programmed by, *others*.

For example, a wife may be programmed by her husband to feel and express anger toward his mother so he can avoid feeling and expressing anger toward her himself; a mother may program a child to feel and act helpless so she can feel and act helpful; a wife may program her husband to feel and act jealous so she can have reason to accuse him of controlling her. It is this patterning of feelings—this system of emotions—that is important for the therapist to note in forming a hypothesis. Under what circumstances are feelings aroused and expressed? What counterfeelings and reactions do these emotional expressions stir up in others? If a mother cries in a session over the death of her father, her feelings of sadness may very well be genuine, but she cannot remain unaware of the effect of her tears on the family—perhaps her hyperactive son calms down, or her husband moves closer to her, or her daughter stops berating her. Just knowing that the mother feels sad is not particularly helpful, but knowing at what particular moment she chooses to express her sadness, how she expresses it, and how others react to it, indicates its function.

The Ideational Level

Besides knowing what every family member does and feels about the problem, the therapist must know how they perceive the problem, how they perceive its cause and its cure, and how they react to each other's perception. The ideational level is the most difficult to understand, as it often extends beyond awareness and is related to belief systems.

The key to understanding this level is likely to be revealed through content as well as process, and therefore the family's language becomes extremely important. The therapist listens for metaphors and attitudinal statements, such as, "Men love women, but women love their children," indicating the belief that a woman's primary loyalty is to her children and not to her husband. Or, "No one will ever love you as much as your family does," indicating the belief that one can never fully trust an outsider. These statements often contain the family's secret rules that maintain the symptom.

In order to have a clear understanding of this level, it is helpful for the therapist to gather information concerning each parent's family of origin. Since this is where the attitudes, perceptions, beliefs originated, a historical perspective of the extended family often sheds light on current transactions. Although it is not necessary for the family to understand the connections between the past and present, a three-generational context gives the therapist a broader gestalt from which to form a hypothesis and make interventions. Sometimes, crucial information is revealed concerning family ghosts, secrets, or myths that exert a powerful influence on family proceedings.

In gathering historical information, the therapist traces family themes, and if it appears that a certain theme has a direct bearing on the presenting problem, it is incorporated into the interventions. The following is an example of how this was done in a consultation interview. A therapist asked for a consultation with a rural, poverty-stricken family presented as "multiproblem" and "crisis prone," in which the older son had been brought to court because he drew a knife on the man his mother was living with. The mother, Pearl, a voluptuous, disheveled, and tearful young woman had had three marriages by the age of 32, with five children from three different husbands. She was currently living with a new male companion. She had a reputation in the community for discarding husbands and neglecting children and was referred to as "poor white trash."

Included in the consultation session were Pearl; her male companion, Chris; and three of the mother's children—Mike, the identified patient, 15; Jud, 14; and Mary Jo, 12. The eldest daughter, Mildred, 17, was living away from home with a young man, and the 11-year-old daughter, Cissie, had been sent away to live with an aunt when it was discovered she had a reading disability with which the mother felt she could not cope.

Pearl's parents were currently living with her maternal grandmother, who was described as an alcoholic who did nothing but drink all day and watch television. There was a great deal of friction between the maternal grandmother and the parents, and, as a result, the parents left their house early every morning and spent the day with Pearl and her family. The father used Pearl's backyard to repair old cars that he bought and sold, much to the disapproval of Chris, who experienced this as an invasion of privacy. Chris complained that he and Pearl had no time alone together because she was at her parents' beck and call and gave in to their every whim. This was the source of many arguments between the two of them. When the arguments escalated, Mike would step in to protect his mother from Chris, who would then begin to fight physically with Mike. Pearl would then step in to protect Mike from Chris, who was on the verge of leaving home as he was afraid he would eventually hurt someone. This followed the pattern of the previous three husbands' leave taking, which was always motivated by Pearl's intense involvement with her parents and her protection of Mike.

The therapist's major focus had been on trying to stop the violence and establish a semblance of order in the family. He had given innumerable concrete tasks in an effort to draw boundaries, establish hierarchy and priorities, and enforce discipline—all to no avail. Pearl continued to allow the children to do whatever they pleased and left them every night to play bingo with her mother.

During the consultation interview, it was revealed that Pearl had run away from home when she was 15 because of the constant arguing between her parents. Her mother had chased after her for years, until her legs became paralyzed and she was confined to a wheelchair. She blamed Pearl for having crippled her for life. (It was actually a tumor on her spinal cord that caused the paralysis.) However, Pearl assumed the blame for having crippled her mother, and it was clear through her behavior and certain statements she made that she had devoted her life to trying to make it up to her. Her obsession in paying back this enormous debt took precedence over every other relationship. Her mother made incessant demands on her and, although she resented them, Pearl capitulated—putting her on the toilet, preparing her meals, taking her for rides in the car, playing bingo with her, and so on.

As the theme of indebtedness and restitution was further explored, it was discovered that shortly after Pearl was born, her mother "gave away" Pearl's two older brothers to foster parents. The parents felt they were incapable of caring for them because of poor health and poverty. Pearl's father also wanted to give her away, but her mother insisted on keeping her, adding to the debt Pearl felt she owed her mother. These two brothers now lived in the neighborhood and constantly reminded Pearl in different ways how much they resented her having been the chosen child while they were sent away. (Another debt to pay.) Pearl also felt she owed a debt to her son Mike, as he was the victim of the violence and abuse that took place in her first marriages, and she therefore could not tolerate getting tough with him.

It seemed clear that until Pearl came to terms with her legacy of indebtedness, it would be difficult for her to establish boundaries either with her parents or children. This legacy made it impossible for her to allow herself to be happy with a man (how could she be happier than those she had caused to suffer?), and Mike's behavior served the function of preventing her from becoming too close to anyone.

My recommendation to the therapist was that he anchor future interventions to this powerful theme of indebtedness and restitution that ruled the family. I suggested he begin by calling a meeting of the entire extended family (including the maternal grandmother, the parents, and two brothers). In this meeting, he should continue to explore the issue of unpaid debts in the family: who else owed them, to whom, how were they being paid, at what rate of interest, and whether there was a statute of limitations. It was considered of prime importance to know how the other family members colluded with Pearl to keep the family under the shadow of the unpaid debts. (It was speculated the accounts between Pearl's mother and grandmother had not been straightened out, either.) Furthermore, upon the basis of the information gathered, the therapist was encouraged to construct a family ritual around the expiation of the debts, enabling the family to pay them off openly and officially. Since this was the kind of family that was extremely sensitive to epithets, such as "poor white trash," "weak character," and "bad blood," it was also suggested that the ritual be framed within the context of the family's being extremely responsible and honorable in their determination to fulfill their obligations to one another.

Historical data often help the therapist uncover a central theme that ties the behavioral, emotional, and ideational levels of family functioning together. This historical background is more relevant in some cases than in others, depending on the degree to which the legacy of the past is turned into rigid rules that govern the present. During the early years of the Brief Therapy Project, we tended to ignore the historical context of symptoms and focused primarily on current behavioral cycles. In some instances, however, interventions aimed only at these cycles failed to produce results as they did not change the thematic ideology behind the cycles. We now collect historical information routinely during the first session and decide later whether or not to use it therapeutically.

Setting the Terms for Therapy

After the therapist has formed a hypothesis, the next step is to establish a therapeutic contract with the family by setting the terms for therapy. This is done by defining the connection between the symptom and system and posing the dilemma of change. Whoever controls the definition of the problem controls the therapy.

If the family is allowed to set the terms through their definition of the problem, the therapist will be lost because the family's definition is maintaining the problem. If the therapist becomes involved in a linear discussion as to whether or not the mother should be less controlling, the father should be less passive, or the children should be less rebellious, the therapist has allowed the family to win the therapeutic contest. A discussion of these issues avoids the function of the behavior and ignores the fact that family members are using control, passivity, or rebelliousness as tactics in their negotiations.

In working out a therapeutic contract, the therapist must be aware of the hidden agendas and contradictions in the presenting requests and quickly redefine the problem in soluble terms. Often, the family is asking the therapist to attempt the impossible—to change past events, remake a family member, resolve an issue in a contradictory way or solve a conglomerate of individual problems. For example, a trainee asked for consultation on a case that she proceeded to describe in the following manner:

I am feeling overwhelmed by this single-parent mother and her 7-year-old boy, Tim. She is still refusing to go to work, is on welfare, and always has a new physical symptom. She is going to three different doctors who all tell her something different, and then she asks me what to do. She has alienated everyone who tries to help her, including her family and friends. She will not allow Tim's father to see him as he doesn't pick him up on time, and the father is threatening to take her to court. She is constantly fighting with him over alimony and custody. She complains therapy isn't helping her and I'm not doing enough. She seems to have enormous unmet dependency needs and involves everyone in trying to fulfill them. She is threatening to commit suicide and threatening to place Tim. What should I do?

My answer was, "What is the problem?"

The trainee was feeling overwhelmed because she had not connected any of the above facts into a systemic hypothesis and consequently was trying to resolve a dozen or more problems separately. The first crucial question was, what function did the mother's helplessness serve in maintaining which relationship system?

Further exploration in the following session revealed that the mother had functioned in a competent way until she met and married her husband, at which point she went into a decline because her husband, according to her, destroyed her confidence through his tyrannical control and incessant criticism. Although divorced, she remained in a hostile and competitive struggle with him.

In the consultation, we defined the mother's helplessness as her way of remaining intensely involved with her husband and continuing to prove him right on a daily basis by remaining incompetent in every way possible. This definition of the problem was clinically useful as it connected the symptom (the mother's helplessness) with the system that maintained it (her relationship with her husband). The new therapeutic contract was based on working out a different relationship with her husband.

In another case, a couple who was experiencing marital strife was brought in for consultation because the trainee had failed to establish a therapeutic contract with them. The husband was extremely resistant to therapy, having taken the position from the beginning that there was no need for therapy since they didn't have any problems and the ones they did have they could resolve themselves. However, his wife threatened to leave if he wasn't willing to recognize their problems and do something about them. He came reluctantly to the sessions to appease her and spent his time defending, contradicting, denying, and insisting that the only problem was that his wife manufactured problems. The trainee was attempting to do therapy without having set the terms for it.

In the consultation interview (to which the husband came a half hour late) I instructed the trainee to tell the husband that his only problem was that he couldn't convince his wife they didn't have a problem. He should try and convince her that she was happy, that they had a good relationship, and he could resolve any problems they had between them. The trainee did as instructed, the husband complied, and, as could have been anticipated, his attempts failed. At the end of the session the trainee was instructed to tell the husband to go home and continue to try and convince his wife they didn't need therapy. If he could not convince her, he was to call for an appointment. This placed the burden for the resolution of the husband's contradictory position on him rather than on the therapist. By redefining the problem, the contract was changed from the trainee trying to convince the husband they needed therapy, to the husband trying to convince his wife they didn't. The therapist had set the terms for therapy: Either the husband would have to make his wife happy or he would have to admit he couldn't and that this was a problem.

Classification of Interventions

In developing this approach, it soon became apparent that the symptom serves different functions in different situations and that some are less vital to family equilibrium than others. If the symptom is primarily a response to a crisis or a transitory event, it is not necessary for the therapist to become preoccupied with the consequences of change as the family will in all probability quickly absorb them. In such cases, a direct approach in which the therapist merely defines the problem and advises the family what to do about it is appropriate. On the other hand, if the symptom is being used as a secret weapon in a covert battle or has become embedded in a repetitious cycle of interaction, attempts to alleviate it will most likely be undermined. The therapist is then placed in a paradoxical position of being asked to eliminate a symptom that the family has an investment in keeping but cannot acknowledge openly. In such cases, an indirect or paradoxical approach that focuses on the consequences of upsetting this investment is most expedient.

The question often arises as to how the therapist can determine which type of function the symptom serves. It is sometimes impossible to do so before intervening, as only the feedback from the intervention provides the therapist with the necessary information.

During our first years of experimentation in the Brief Therapy Project, we sometimes used paradox when it was inappropriate or unnecessary. The overuse of a technique when one is first learning seems unavoidable. One of our first families was a single-parent mother who came with her uncontrollable 8-year-old son. The son started a commotion the minute he entered the room, refused to sit still, and ran around overturning furniture, banging toys, and constantly interrupting his mother. The consultation team sat on the other side of the one-way mirror, reflecting on the function of the symptom and trying to design an elaborate paradoxical intervention while the child continued to tear the place apart. The din finally became so overwhelming that the team decided to knock on the door and tell the therapist to ask the mother to control the child so the interview could be heard. The therapist complied, and the mother proceeded to plead with, placate, beg, and bribe her son to behave. The rest of the session was spent in instructing the mother how to get a clear message across to her son. This task was gradually accomplished and the son responded to the mother's increasing firmness. Since this very simple direct coaching worked in the session, the team and therapist decided to instruct the mother to continue it at home to test whether or not she could follow through on it. Specific instructions were given regarding how to handle the son under different circumstances. The mother was able to carry out the instructions and noted an immediate decrease in the child's obstreperous behavior. Whether or not the symptom was serving a function was irrelevant at this point as it was not so vital or ingrained that it could not be changed.

30   SETTING THE TERMS FOR THERAPY

However, at other times we had the experience of giving instructions over and over again that the family failed to follow through on. If the family continually fails to respond to direct interventions, it is a good sign some secret agendas or hidden transactions are blocking change. Occasionally, a symptom-producing behavior is interrupted, only to have the symptom reappear at a later date in a different form. Because it is impossible to predict if and when this will occur, and because future problems cannot be worked on before they appear, the therapist can only find solutions as the problems manifest themselves.

Certain families indicate from the beginning that logical interventions will prove futile, for example, families in which bizarre transactions take place, or in which a high degree of anxiety, defensiveness, denial, guilt, or anger prevents the family from "hearing" the therapist. In order for the therapist's suggestions to make sense, the interventions must address themselves to the premises under which the family is operating. If the family is operating from some powerful hidden belief or carrying out an injunction involving some entrenched tradition from the past, a commonsense approach is unlikely to be effective. In such cases, we use paradoxical messages that address these beliefs or injunctions. Later, direct and paradoxical interventions may be alternated, with the direct interventions used to test the family's readiness to change and the paradoxical to continually define the covert transactions that are hindering it.

There are certain crisis situations—violence, sudden grief, attempted suicide, loss of employment, or unwanted pregnancy —in which a paradox would be inappropriate as the therapist needs to move in quickly to provide structure and control. Paradoxical interventions are best reserved for those covert, long-standing, repetitious patterns of interaction that do not respond to logical explanations or rational suggestions.

In an effort to determine which type of intervention was the most appropriate to which situation, I classified them under the headings of Direct Interventions or Compliance Based, referring to the therapist's expectation that the family would comply with them, and Paradoxical Interventions or Defiance Based, referring to the therapist's expectation that the family would defy them. (These terms were coined by Rohrbaugh, Tennen, Press, White, Pickering, & Raskin, 1977.)

Direct Interventions: Compliance Based

Direct interventions—advice, explanations, suggestions, interpretations, or tasks that are meant to be taken literally and followed as prescribed—are aimed directly at changing family rules and roles. They include coaching parents on how to control children, redistributing jobs among family members, establishing disciplinary rules, regulating privacy, establishing age priority, and providing information that the family lacks, as well as promoting open communication, giving personal feedback to the family, and directly commenting on the family interactional patterns.

Following is an example of a situation in which it was decided in the first interview to use a direct intervention: The presenting problem was the incipient school phobia of a 4-year-old daughter who became hysterical every morning when her mother tried to put her on the school bus. She kicked and screamed until the mother, who had recently started back to work and was feeling guilty about sending her daughter to nursery school, took her off the bus. The mother would then be upset and resentful for the rest of the day because she had missed work. The next morning the mother would approach the bus with great apprehension, and the daughter, sensing her mother's anxiety and guilt, would throw another temper tantrum until she was removed.

The mother took responsibility for the problem, saying she knew she was not handling the situation properly and needed some guidance. The husband, a commuter who left the house very early, was supportive of his wife's working, and there seemed to be no marital problems of any significance that the daughter might be caught up in. The therapist, sensing the mother to be cooperative and motivated, coached her in taking firm, definitive action. She was advised to put her daughter on the bus, turn her back and walk away, and under no circumstances take her off the bus again. The mother was able to comply, and after three mornings of decreasing tantrums the daughter boarded the bus without a problem.

In this family, the symptom was not being used to resolve another relationship but was simply an overreaction of mother and daughter to a new life situation. If the symptom had been serving a function in the marital relationship, such as providing a way for the father to express his disapproval of the mother's working, the problem could not so easily have been resolved.

Paradoxical Interventions: Defiance Based

There are many different definitions of paradox. One of these, in *Webster's International Dictionary*, is "an assertion or sentiment seemingly contradictory, or opposed to common sense, but that may be true in fact. . . . 'This was sometime a paradox, but that may be true in fact.' Shakespeare."

The most important word in this definition as related to our clinical use of paradox is "seemingly." Our paradoxical messages only *appear* to be contradictory. They contain a double message to the family—one message implies it would be good for them to change, the other implies it would not be so good— and the messages are delivered simultaneously. The therapist is convinced both of the messages are "true" and therefore can deliver them with the utmost conviction and sincerity. For example, in "The Daughter Who Said No" (Chapter 6), I tell the daughter that the more unhappy she is now, the better it will be for her because her unhappiness is her way of saying no to her parents. I am delivering the seemingly contradictory message that the daughter must be unhappy in order to be happy. This is true because the consequence of her being happy is that she will please her parents, which will make her unhappy; but the consequence of her being unhappy is that she will displease herself.

Paradoxical messages are used in the Brief Therapy Project to define the seemingly contradictory behavior family members are actually engaged in with one another. They are not manu-factured in the therapist's head and imposed on the family. They are referred to as "defiance based," as it is hoped the family members will defy the part of the message that restrains them from changing. In this case, it was hoped that the daughter would defy my recommendation that she continue to be unhappy as a way of saying no to her parents and find other ways of differentiating herself.

In designing a systemic paradox, the therapist connects the symptom with the function it serves in the system and prescribes each in relation to the other. The consequences of eliminating the symptom are enumerated and the therapist recommends that the family continue to resolve their dilemma through the symptom. For example, in a family in which the presenting problem was the delinquent behavior of the adolescent son, the therapist determined that this behavior coincided with the father's taking on a new business and being away from the home for long periods of time. It also coincided with the older children leaving home, either going away to college or getting married. This left the mother and adolescent son alone together a great deal of the time and an overly close relationship developed between the two of them. The mother, who had looked forward to enjoying a life of ease with her husband once the children were raised, was bitterly disappointed and turned to her son for solace. She believed a good wife never complained to her husband, and she prided herself on having shielded him from the children's problems over the years.

The son, who was extremely sensitive to his mother's distress, tried to alleviate it by remaining close to her. When the burden became overwhelming, he engaged in delinquent activities. The mother took on the burden of trying to handle the son's problems by herself until they escalated beyond her ability to cope, at which point she called in her husband. The husband responded by rushing home from work and laying down the law to the son who would straighten out until the next cycle began all over again.

The therapist told the family that at the present time it seemed necessary for the son to continue his behavior because it was his way of bringing his father home to his mother. The mother was unable to do this for herself because she felt it would be a betrayal of her role as a good wife. The father was also unable to do it on his own as he wasn't as tuned in to his wife's emotional antenna as his son was and so couldn't sense when she was lonely. Since the parents were unable to solve the problem of their marriage, it seemed necessary for the son to continue to do so with his delinquent behavior.

This of course was unacceptable to each family member. The mother exclaimed, "That's ridiculous! Why should our son continue to have problems to save our marriage?" The father responded, "I certainly don't need my son to take over my job with my wife." And the son stated vehemently, "Let them solve their problems themselves. Why should they involve me?" Commonly known as a "recoil," namely, when the family rebels against the therapist's prescription by questioning it or refusing to go along with it, this is the desired response to a paradoxical intervention; it indicates the family members have begun to question their way of handling the problem. As the therapist continues to debate the family dilemma and to pose the consequences of change, the premises under which the family members are operating continue to be altered. They find it increasingly difficult to hold onto their original premise that the son is emotionally disturbed and needs psychiatric treatment and, consequently, to hold onto their solution to the problem, which is to change the son's behavior without changing their own. Each paradoxical message contains within it an implied alternative that points toward the direction of change. In the above message, the implied alternative is for the mother to find another way to bring the father home when she needs him and for the father to be more attentive to his wife's emotional needs.

This is a different approach to the use of paradox than the one commonly used in individual therapy where interventions are aimed primarily at changing specific behavior and not at changing the systemic transactions or premises governing the behavior. Only the symptom is prescribed. For example, a stutterer may be told to stutter deliberately at certain times under certain conditions. This "intentional effort," as described by Frankl, brings the symptom under the voluntary control of the patient. The symptom is not connected with any other relationship in a larger system and a perceptual change is not the goal.

Designing a Paradox

There are three major steps in designing a systemic paradox: redefining, prescribing, and restraining.

REDEFINING

Before the therapist can prescribe the symptom and the system, both must be redefined positively. A good doctor does not prescribe bad medicine. Each piece of behavior is redefined as a loving gesture in the service of preserving family stability. For example, anger may be defined as intense love, suffering as self-sacrifice, or distancing as a way of reinforcing closeness.

In cases involving violence, suicide, incest, or illegal acts, the *motivation* behind the behavior is defined positively, not the behavior itself. For example, in a single-parent family in which the maternal grandmother had recently died, the 17-year-old son (an only child) became extremely argumentative and physically abusive with his mother. The therapist hypothesized that the son's behavior was connected with the mother's grief that she had not expressed openly nor shared with her son. Instead, she withdrew to her room and remained silent for long periods of time looking sad.

The therapist defined the motivation behind the son's violence by saying it reminded her of a leading character in the play *Liliom*. Every time Liliom saw those he loved suffering and felt helpless in doing anything about it, he became violent and struck out at them physically. Like Liliom, the son tried to relieve his mother's sadness by picking fights with her. The therapist recommended that he continue to show his sympathy for his mother but in a different way so his mother could appreciate it. Since he wrote songs for a rock group, every time he saw his mother looking sad, he should write a song that he felt expressed her feelings and sing it to her—or perhaps they could sing it together. This prescription provided a way for mother and son to grieve together and dissipated the silent tension that was provoking the violence.

PRESCRIBING

Having been defined positively as serving one another, both the symptom and the system are prescribed. The wording of the prescription is extremely important. It should be brief, concise, and unacceptable to the family. If it is acceptable there will be no recoil. In order to sound sincere, rather than sarcastic or disrespectful, the therapist must have a convincing rationale for the prescription—one that he/she considers valid. It should be delivered with the utmost conviction by the therapist who then must cling tenaciously to this formulation and the rationale for it in the face of the family's attempt to invalidate it. As the family reacts, the therapist fits each piece of interaction into the conceptual framework of the prescription. (An example of this appears in Chapter 6 under "Enlisting the Sibling Subsystem.")

A common mistake made by beginners is to formulate a lengthy and elaborate message in which the symptom is not connected to any particular transaction in the system. Another common mistake is to prescribe each behavior separately without connecting them, such as "Sara, you should continue to have headaches; mother, you should continue to worry about them; father, you should continue to withdraw; and John, you should continue to fail in school." This lacks therapeutic impact as the behaviors are not connected through their functions.

RESTRAINING

If the therapist is to be consistent with the above two steps, whenever the family shows signs of changing, the therapist must restrain them. If indeed the symptom is an essential element in the functioning of the system and the therapist respects that system, he/she can only be concerned if the symptom begins to disappear.

If the family presses for change, the therapist must remain reluctant to proceed. Depending on the circumstances, the therapist may decide to schedule a small change under carefully monitored circumstances. The family is told this is to test their tolerance for change. This cautious attitude is maintained throughout therapy with the therapist worrying rather than rejoicing over progress.

If the family shows signs of reverting to their old behavior after a scheduled change, the therapist may chastise him/herself for having been swayed by the family against his/her better judgment. (There are many examples of how these techniques are applied in the following chapters.)

Reversals: Compliance and Defiance Based

A reversal is an intervention in which the therapist directs one family member to reverse his/her attitude or behavior around a crucial issue in the hope it will elicit a paradoxical response from another family member. A reversal is both defiance and compliance based. It requires the conscious cooperation of the family member who is being instructed by the therapist and the defiance of the family member who is receiving the results of the instruction.

Murray Bowen developed reversals in coaching individual family members to differentiate themselves from their families of origin. An example would be coaching a man who is an overly responsible son to go home and act irresponsibly; to lean on his family rather than allowing them to lean on him; to become helpless rather than helpful, the patient rather than the doctor.

Reversals can be used in treating families, couples, or individuals. They are likely to be most effective when the reciprocal positions in a repeated cycle of interaction are clear and the therapist can motivate at least one person in that cycle to reverse his/her position. The other persons in the cycle need not be present or even involved in the treatment.

Reversals are particularly helpful in treating individuals who live alone and have no family system available to bring to the treatment session. The presenting problem of such persons usually arises from their having taken a fixed position in regard to some life situation that escalates the problem rather than resolves it. They can be coached to change their situation by taking a different position.

If a family member refuses to come for therapy—a spouse rejects marital therapy, or a problem child boycotts family sessions—those family members present can be instructed to turn the situation around by reversing their behavior at home. Even when all family members are available for treatment, those who are on the receiving end of the reversals should not be present in the session as success depends on those persons being surprised and reacting spontaneously to an unexpected change in attitude.

There are three steps in planning and carrying out reversals: motivating, sustaining, and renegotiating.

MOTIVATING

The effectiveness of reversals depends to a large extent on the therapist's skill in motivating a family member to reverse his/her position around a toxic issue. The therapist must convince this member that what he/she considers to be his/her "authentic behavior" is in fact being programmed by others to serve the agenda of a larger system. This is difficult to do, as most people see themselves as free agents, acting on the basis of their independent choices, and do not see their behavior as conditioned by others. They are likely to perceive the therapist as asking them to give up control or let other family members "have their way."

People cannot change their way of behaving without experiencing some initial awkwardness and apprehension. Because there is an element of performance in planned behavior, it is initially experienced as unfamiliar and unnatural. Sometimes people react negatively to the suggestion that they deliberately behave in a different way responding with "I don't want to play a role" or "that would be dishonest." One way of counteracting this resistance is to point out to them that deliberately choosing to play a different role is no less authentic than continuing to play one imposed by their family system. The role they have been slotted into in their family is no more endemic to their "true nature" or "intrinsic personality" than a new role that they might choose to play.

In preparing people to perform reversals, it is advisable to impress on them ahead of time that the tasks will be extremely difficult, that they will initially feel mechanical and unnatural, and that they will undoubtedly create anxiety in themselves and others.

The question is often raised as to why it is necessary for a person to go to the opposite extreme in order to change his/her situation rather than just taking a middle position. The answer is that the family system is so powerful it rarely responds to halfway measures. Drastic action is required to upset the equilibrium of an emotional system.

SUSTAINING

Once the initial cooperation of the person has been gained, the therapist's next job is to sustain it in the face of a forceful system that constantly tries to counteract every move in an opposite direction. Occasionally, immediate results, new and gratifying responses from other family members, are achieved, but usually the family reacts by escalating their position in an attempt to reestablish the old order. The therapist should anticipate these responses with the person who is being coached to prevent discouragement when the family doesn't respond in the desired way. The first inclination is to give up, saying, "Nothing I do makes any difference," or, "I'm tired of playing a part."

At such times, the therapist may choose to revert to a paradoxical intervention, defining giving up as serving the program of others and prescribing it, such as: "You must be picking up messages from your husband that he needs you to continue to explode. If you stopped exploding he would probably get in touch with his own feelings and that might be intolerable for him. I respect your wish to continue to protect him by expressing all his angry feelings for him." Most people cannot tolerate the idea that their behavior is being programmed to serve the secret agenda of others.

RENEGOTIATING

If a person does succeed in reversing a fixed position and is able to sustain it over a period of time, a new relationship must be negotiated based on that position. Besides having to deal with the reactions of others to the shift, the person may be surprised by his/her own reactions. These sometimes involve intense feelings resulting from the new perspective or what is commonly called "insight" that is gained from the changed position. One mother, after experiencing a marked positive change in her relationship with her daughter, suffered intense remorse at the realization of "what we missed out on all those years." In another case, a daughter became very angry at her family for the first time as she moved out of the position of parenting and realized she had never been allowed to be a child. One cannot see clearly the position one has been in until one has moved out of it.

At times, a sense of loss may be experienced as a result of relinquishing whatever benefits accrued from the old position. For example, a family go-between may lose the sense of importance in giving up the role of family mediator; a problem child may miss the excitement of having the family's spotlight focused on him/her; a wife may experience a sense of boredom when she stops fighting with her husband. Although it is impossible to anticipate what each person's reactions to change will be, the therapist should be prepared for negative as well as positive reactions and help the client to negotiate relationships on different terms.

Following are some examples of reversals that were successfully used with a family, couple, and individual.

FAMILY

In this family it was clear from the first session that the school failure of a 13-year-old son was an act of rebellion against the high expectations and constant pressuring of his parents. The therapist decided to see the parents separately, believing them to be good candidates for reversals for the following reasons: The repetitious cycle of interaction that was sustaining the problem was simple and clear, the parents prided themselves on being intelligent, logical, and self-sufficient, and there were no obvious disagreements between them that would mitigate against their joining in a cooperative effort in handling their son.

The therapist prefaced the instructions by telling them she would not suggest the following approach to parents who were not as knowledgeable and sophisticated as they. She identified the problem as a power struggle that their son was winning and instructed them how to "use reverse psychology" on their son in order to win the struggle. Instead of constantly emphasizing responsibility, maturity, achievement, and living up to his high potential, they should find ways of suggesting to him that he restrain his potential, retard his growth, and put the lid on his achievements. The parents understood the rationale behind the instructions. They went home and told their son they had been doing a lot of thinking about his situation and they had come to the conclusion that it wouldn't be so terrible after all if he failed and had to repeat the same grade over again because children were growing up too fast nowadays anyway. The longer he remained a child the better because that way he would stay close to the family and if he had to attend summer school at least they would know he was safe instead of with those reckless boys in camp.

The son initially reacted with suspicion and disbelief, but as the parents persisted in maintaining their antiachievement attitude, he quickly caught up in school in order to avoid having to spend summer vacation with the family.

During the summer the parents called and requested marital therapy. No longer focused on their son's behavior, they became aware for the first time of some troublesome issues between the two of them. These issues surfaced only after the problem with their son was alleviated.

COUPLE

Reversals can be successfully alternated with either direct or paradoxical interventions. In the following case, with Olga Silverstein as the therapist and me as the consultant, reversals were used to augment a recoil from a paradoxical intervention.

This couple was engaged in a parent–child rather than a husband–wife relationship. The wife played the role of the delinquent daughter, drinking at bars until all hours of the night, attending wild parties, smoking pot, and carousing around with other men. The husband played the reciprocal role of distressed parent who tried to reform her. He waited up for her on the front steps, lectured her on the error of her ways, and called her all day long to check up on her whereabouts. He also bought all her clothes, doled out her allowance a little at a time, and treated her like a child. He complained she was irresponsible and immature while the wife complained the husband was boring and no fun.

The initial paradoxical intervention defined the behavior of each as serving the other and prescribed it. The wife was told she should continue acting like an adolescent and allow her husband to parent her because she sensed it was important for her husband to have a little girl to take care of rather than a wife. The husband was told he should continue parenting his wife because he sensed it would be frightening for her to grow up and take responsibility for herself.

The couple reacted with denial and indignation to the prescription and demanded that the therapist help them change the situation. The therapist finally allowed herself to be persuaded to do so but only on condition that they follow her instructions implicitly, which they agreed to do. These instructions were given to each separately.

The husband was told that if indeed he wanted his wife to grow up as he said he did, he must become totally unpredictable by doing the opposite of what he was doing. Rather than waiting up for her at night he should pretend to be asleep when she came in. It was suggested he leave a midnight snack and a little note saying, "Thought you might be hungry, darling. I've gone to bed. See you in the morning." If his wife turned on the lights or knocked over the furniture to awaken him, he was to open one eye, nod sleepily, mumble casually, "Oh, it's you dear," and turn over and go back to sleep. He was not to call her during the day and, instead of disapproving of her friends, suggest she see them more often as he was going to be working late at the office.

Initially, the wife reacted to her husband's detachment from her antics by escalating them. The therapist, anticipating this, rehearsed the husband in maintaining his position in the face of her escalation. As he did so, the wife began to find her husband more interesting and became curious about his comings and goings. She began staying home more often or inviting him to go with her in the evenings.

While the husband was being coached to take less responsibility for his wife's behavior, the wife was being instructed to take more responsibility for her husband. She was told if indeed she wanted her husband to stop acting like a parent as she said she did, she should smother him with mothering. This would also give him a taste of his own medicine. She was to call him many times a day at the office and become extremely concerned about his whereabouts and preoccupied with his physical and emotional well-being.

The husband, recognizing that a caricature of his own behavior was being played back to him, reacted with a combination of amusement and annoyance. Each in turn was secretly delighted by the response of the spouse to the role change, reporting to the therapist, "You should have seen the expression on her face when I said I didn't know what time I'd be home," or, "He didn't know what to do when I called him for the fifth time at the office."

Within a few months the wife proudly announced she had

obtained a job and opened her own bank account. After some initial anxiety, the husband accepted her declaration of adulthood and the relationship evolved from a parent–child to a husband–wife.

INDIVIDUAL

Reversals with the extended family were chosen as the primary mode of treatment in the following case as the presenting symptom of depression was seen as being directly related to the client's family of origin. This single woman in her thirties, though living away from home, continued to assume the emotional responsibility for her mother and sister who lived together and were in constant conflict. The client, being the oldest daughter, had been placed in a parental role at a very early age, but, with the death of her father five years earlier, her mother and sister had escalated their demands on her. She was expected not only to solve their life problems but also to mediate the many intense conflicts between the two of them. She responded by increasing her efforts to take care of them and always failed as she could never do enough. She invariably ended up feeling guilty and would withdraw in cold, resentful anger. Mother and sister, feeling abandoned, responded by frantically escalating their demands and the cycle would repeat itself.

The therapist defined the woman's depression as a result of her being in the impossible role of mothering her mother and sister rather than being a daughter and sibling to them. She was instructed to reverse this by acting helpless, demanding, and childish. Whenever her mother called to complain about being neglected, she was to develop a problem of her own and ask for help. When she was called upon to act as mediator between her mother and sister she was instructed to either disappear when they began to argue, or if this was not possible, to distract them with a more dramatic problem than theirs.

She carried out the task in the following way: On Thanksgiving day when her mother and sister began their usual fights in the kitchen just as the guests sat down to dinner, she pretended to faint in the middle of the kitchen floor. The mother and sister rushed to her aid and became so preoccupied in taking care of her they forgot their argument. She played the prima donna for the rest of the day with her mother and sister catering to her and taking care of her every whim.

On other occasions she simply walked away from the two of them saying, "There is no hope for this family," forcing them to reassure her that there was.

As she continued to change her role, she began to reap the rewards of her actions. "I feel I'm in charge of the situation now, rather than it running me, I'm running it. It's a big relief and it's fun too." As she removed herself from the role of mediator between her mother and sister, their relationship improved markedly, and the sister eventually obtained a job and moved away from home. This was more than the client could tolerate and she complained of feeling lost and lonely. "I didn't like being the parent and I'm glad I'm out of that role, but now I don't know who I am. At least I felt important and needed before."

There is a misconception in the field that everything else in one's life falls into place if one changes one's position in one's family of origin. More often than not, change is a mixed blessing accompanied by feelings of confusion and disorientation. A vacuum is left that was filled by the intense preoccupation with the family.

In the case of this young woman, once she relinquished her overinvolvement with her mother and sister, she became painfully aware that she had no family of her own to become involved with. The next stage in therapy dealt with her overcoming her tendency toward reclusiveness and seeking a more active social life for herself. The reversals were the first necessary step in this process. A three-year follow-up revealed her to be happily married.

C H A P T E R 5

Negotiating Change

Negotiating Change through a Greek Chorus[1]

A distinguishing feature of our work in the Brief Therapy Project is the use of a consultation group to assist in negotiating the dilemma of change. This consultation group is composed of several colleagues from the project who alternate in observing one another from behind the one-way mirror. The group acts as a Greek chorus, regularly sending in messages that provide a running commentary on the dilemma of change and the relationship between the family and the therapist in attempting to resolve this. Like the voice of a family prophet, the group acts as a higher authority who sees into the future and predicts the consequences of change.

The group is presented to the family in a way that invests it with the highest authority possible. The family members are told they are privileged to have this special resource available to them under the auspices of the project and that the group is composed of experts in the field who are authorities on their particular kind of problem. If the family members so desire, they are introduced to the group, but no further contact with it occurs. The group remains at a distance, an invisible eye, a prophetic voice: unapproachable, unimpeachable, and unnegotiable.

Group messages are formed in collaboration with the therapist who has the final say as to their content and who

---

[1] This section is a revised version of "The Greek Chorus and Other Techniques of Paradoxical Therapy," *Family Process*, 1980, 19(1), 45–58, and is reprinted by permission of Family Process, Inc.

decides on what position to take in relation to them. At the therapist's discretion, the group may be used to support, confront, confuse, challenge, or provoke, with the therapist free to agree or disagree with its position.

The physical procedure for using the group varies according to the therapist's preference. The most common procedure is for the therapist to excuse the family for a coffee break toward the end of the session while the group convenes in the observation room where their discussion is video-taped for future reference. The family is then reconvened, and the therapist delivers a communication from the group that can either be written and read aloud or delivered extemporaneously. This again is up to the therapist, depending on whichever form he/she is comfortable with. After delivering the communication, the therapist terminates the session, not allowing the family to dissipate the contents of the message through an intellectual discussion. Like a time bomb, the message is left to explode at a later date as the family struggles with its meaning.

The group is free to interrupt at any time during the session or call the therapist out to make suggestions. A prearranged signal may be agreed upon by the group and therapist whereby the group interrupts at a particular point in time with a particular message. If cotherapy is used (at the discretion of the therapist), a three-way strategy is worked out between the two therapists and the group.

FORMING A THERAPEUTIC TRIANGLE

One of the most potent uses of the group is the creation of a therapeutic triangle resulting from a planned, ongoing contest between the therapist and group. In this triangle, the group usually takes the position of the antagonist of change, enumerating the consequences of eliminating the symptom and cautioning against upsetting the present established stability, while the therapist takes the position of the protagonist of change, defending the family's ability to adjust and enumerating their resources. The family is put in the position of determining who is right through their subsequent behavior. If they change, they prove the therapist right; if they remain the same, they prove the group right—but they also validate the group's assertion that the price of change was too high in terms of dealing with other relationships in the family. Since this assertion is unacceptable to the family, they have an incentive to prove the group wrong and the therapist right. This triangle shifts the therapeutic contest from the dyadic struggle between the therapist and family into a three-way bargaining operation between family, therapist, and group. The group sometimes deliberately sets a high price for change in terms of other relationships. The therapist then acts as the middleman, negotiating the price on the family's behalf. There are any number of positions the therapist can take in these negotiations, such as criticizing the group for setting too high a price, proposing a compromise, or siding outright with the family against the group. For example, in the middle phases of therapy with a family in which the symptom was the inabiity of the 28-year-old daughter, Kathryn, to leave home, the group criticized the therapist for implying that Kathryn might think about leaving home now that her parents seemed to be getting along better. They sent in the following message:

> For the first time in her married life, there may be a danger of mother pinning her hopes on father to keep her from being so alone. Kathryn knows this might not be safe, since father's primary allegiance is still with his own mother. Therefore, Kathryn must remain like a watchful mother at home, expressing her doubts and disapproval of the premature union between her parents. This way she will prevent her mother from once more suffering profound disappointment.

The therapist disagreed with the group, saying that in her opinion it would be safe for Kathryn to leave home because father seemed to have convinced mother she came first. The group again chastised the therapist for being overly optimistic and challenged the parents to show more evidence that it was safe for Kathryn to leave home.

In these negotiations, the family's perception of the problem as Kathryn's disturbed psyche disappeared and was replaced with a new perception having to do with Kathryn's relationship with her mother, father, and grandmother. Any failure to change was related to this perceptual framework. Each time Kathryn hesitated on the brink of leaving home, the therapist regretfully agreed with the group. Throughout therapy, therapist and group counterpoint one another around the theme of homeostasis and change. If family members fail to change or fall back into their old positions, the therapist agrees with the group that change is too costly, too upsetting to other relationships. The group's opposition gives the therapist powerful leverage in the ongoing treatment. The family has no access to the group except through the therapist and so can never gain control over it.

The juxtaposition of the therapist and group is similar to that described by Carlos Castaneda in *Journey to Ixtlan* (1972, p. xi). Carlos has asked the Indian sorcerer Don Juan for his advice about a friend who cannot control his unruly son. Don Juan suggests that the father go to Skid Row and hire a frightening derelict, instruct the derelict to follow him and his son, and, in response to a prearranged cue after some objectionable behavior on his son's part, leap from the hiding place, pick up the child, and spank the living daylights out of him. The father must then console his son and help him regain his confidence. This should be repeated several times in different places. Don Juan assures Carlos that the boy would soon change his view of the world and advises, "If one wants to stop our fellow men one must always be outside the circle that presses them. That way one can always direct the pressure."

The consultation group serves a function similar to the derelict, as an agent "outside the circle that presses them," and the therapist functions similarly to the father who directs the pressure.

This is a different use of the group than that of the Milan team, who do not divide the positions of the group and therapists.

STAGING A FAILURE

In some cases, the therapist and group may decide to anticipate how the family will defeat the therapist and deliberately stage a failure. If the family refuses to allow access to their system by denying the existence of any problem other than the presenting one, the therapist can ostensibly accept this and attempt to eliminate the symptom in a way that is bound to fail. The group then reprimands the therapist for misperceiving the situation and comments on the reason for failure. This process dramatizes all the issues relevant to change.

An example of this appears in my article "The Family Who Had All the Answers" (Papp, 1977). The parents claimed they had a perfect marriage and the only problem was their delinquent son and quarrelsome daughter who constantly fought with her father. The parents had established a *quid pro quo* in their marriage, with the mother assuming the role of a helpless, accommodating little girl and the father the role of boss and disciplinarian. The mother acted like a peer with her children, treating her daughter like her best friend and her son as a provocative brother. Whenever the daughter was angry at the mother, she fought with the father instead as the mother was her best friend.

The children preserved the balance of power in the marriage, helping the father to maintain his image as the strong, powerful one and the mother her image as the weak, helpless one. The dilemma for the therapist was that a change in the parental relationship would create a change in the marital relationship that the parents were trying desperately to preserve.

Following a prearranged plan, the therapist attempted to reduce the tension between father and daughter by having them communicate around a hot issue. This predictably led to an escalation of attacking and defending. The group then sent in the message that the therapist was off the track in trying to get the father and the daughter to stop fighting, and that the therapist should encourage them to fight more, on the grounds that if the daughter was to grow up and establish her own identity, she had to rebel against at least one of her parents. Since mother was her best friend and she couldn't fight with her, she had to fight doubly hard with father.

The father stated he would be devastated if the fighting continued, but the therapist reported that the group felt he would be willing to tolerate a certain amount of devastation in order to protect his wife.

The therapist then turned her attention to the relationship between mother and son and tried to get the mother to be firmer with the son. This ended in a sibling quarrel between the two of them in which mother ended up stating, "If you treat me lousy, I'll treat you lousy." The group warned the therapist against trying to get the mother to be strong and firm with the son because then the father might be tempted to be soft and friendly. Since they had such a nice balance going in their marriage and their roles were clear, the therapist did not want to tamper with the balance. The group emphasized that their marriage was more important than anything else and that the few problems their children had were a small price to pay for maintaining the stability of their relationship. The therapist countered the group by taking the position that their marriage was strong enough to be able to tolerate some changes. The wife agreed and the husband wasn't sure. He asked if they could try changing their roles for a week to see what would happen. The therapist agreed to allow them to try this and instructed the mother to be firm and demand obedience from her children and the father to simply have a good time with them. The group sent a final message objecting to the task and warning the therapist and family that if the mother became firm and demanding with the children there was a danger she might become firm and demanding with the father and this would not sit well with him.

The group's prediction came true. In carrying out her task, the mother became aware for the first time how angry she was at being in the compliant role. She began expressing some of her resentment to the family, particularly to her husband, who was thoroughly intimidated by her aggressiveness. He did not appear for the next session giving his heavy work schedule as the reason for his absence. The therapist sent the following letter: "Dear Mr. W—I wish to apologize for having set a fire under your wife. I hope she's not too strong for you to handle. I am concerned about this and will be discussing it with you in the next session." The therapist also apologized to the wife for not having paid more heed to the warning of the group and instructed her to revert quickly to her old role to protect her marriage. This was, of course, unacceptable to her. Once the cat is out of the bag it is difficult to put it back. The parents requested help in negotiating a different marital relationship and the presenting problems in the children disappeared after eight sessions.

SUPPORT

The group is not always used to form a therapeutic triangle. It is sometimes used just to praise or support certain aspects of

the family that need strengthening. At these times, the therapist agrees with the group and the messages are unanimous.
For example, in a family in which the husband presented a
gruff exterior to cover a tender heart, the wife often failed to
appreciate his tenderness, as it was expressed through gestures
rather than words. The lack of appreciation discouraged him
from making further advances and he would retreat behind his
"don't give a damn" pose. When he gave her a book of her
favorite poems for her birthday, the group used the occasion to
define him as a romantic figure.

> The women in the group were touched by Tom's beautiful gift to
> Myrna. They wished their husbands would think of things like that.
> They have always felt there was a romantic side to Tom, and they are
> curious as to how it will express itself in the future. They are taking
> bets on it, but won't reveal them.

Another example of support was sent to bolster a husband's confidence in dealing with the women in his family:

> The men in the group are impressed by John's diplomacy in handling his
> mother-in-law. Since they also have difficulty with theirs, it has been a
> valuable lesson for them.

In a single-parent family in which a mother was raising six
children single-handedly under extremely adverse conditions,
a message of appreciation and encouragement was sent to
counteract her self-deprecation. She was extremely critical of
herself because her children were showing some minor problems. During the first interview, the group sent the following
message:

> The group is impressed with the strength and courage mother has
> shown in struggling against enormous odds to hold her family together.
> Her major problem is she expects herself to be wonder-woman, and
> instead she is only an unsung heroine of our time. Hopefully, the
> children will be able to help her correct this image of herself.

PUBLIC OPINION POLL

Sometimes the group is used as a public opinion poll to take
odds on the course of change. A message may be given such as:

> The group is split on this crucial issue. Half the group feels the parents
> will not be able to keep the children from sabotaging their rekindled
> romance, however, the other half believes they are now together
> enough to do this.

The therapist can side either way. As the session continues, if the parents begin to let the children stir up trouble between them, the counts can shift and the message can be sent in such as:

> The latest count from the group shows there has been a shift in opinion. All but one person believe the parents have lost the battle and have let the children take over. This one person is holding out because he believes father has the power to take charge.

Sometimes the opinion is divided along sex lines, and a message is sent in that heightens the sexual conflict, such as:

> All the women in the group predict it will be Jim [the husband] who will be responsible for creating the next crisis by drinking too much, while all the men believe Judy [the wife] will do it by involving her mother in their private affairs.

This increases the incentive of each partner to win the battle of the sexes.

Or the group may be divided along the lines of ambivalence, identifying and clarifying the contradictory alternatives. In a family in which the mother was conflicted over her own liberation, alternating between an obsessive involvement in a triangle with her husband and son, and a concerted effort to get a doctorate in literature, the group sent the following message:

> Mother's predicament has created a political division among the women in the group. One-third feels she should stay home and devote her entire time and attention to her husband and son, as this is the highest achievement a woman can aspire to; one-third feels she has already done this for 15 years with little appreciation from either her husband or her son for her efforts and that now she has a right to fulfill her own creative potential; the remaining third agree with the latter, that mother has the right to fulfill her own potential, but is worried that father and son might become totally helpless without her.

Hearing her own ambivalence stated in these terms, only the second alternative was acceptable to the wife. She got her doctorate and gave up trying to change the father and son.

SURPRISE AND CONFUSION

Since surprise and confusion are important elements of change, the group is.sometimes used to produce them. It may send in a message to arouse the family's curiosity, stir up their imaginations, or provoke them into revealing some hidden information. These messages are sometimes left deliberately unclear as an invitation to the family to fill in the gap. For example, in one family the parents were extremely closed off and secretive, creating a stilted atmosphere of vague foreboding that was difficult to decipher. Their adolescent son constantly provoked them with disruptive behavior in an effort to counteract the deadly atmosphere. This produced a round robin in which the parents engaged in a never-ending battle to quiet their son and the son engaged in a never-ending battle to disquiet his parents. The therapist and group speculated that there was some kind of well-guarded family secret that was creating this foreboding atmosphere and the concomitant turmoil. The therapist returned from a consultation with the group to deliver the following message:

> The group has the impression that this family is like a prison, but it is unclear who is the jailer and who are the prisoners. Somebody here secretly in their heart might want to escape, but this would be devastating to the family, as it is a very close family. (*Addressing the son.*) In a sense, Matthew, your job is to keep this game of jailers and prisoners going, as in reality that person might try and make a break for it.

Matthew responded, "I'm the one that's locked up." The therapist replied, "I'm not sure—Are you being locked up or locking everyone else up?"

During the next session the mother revealed she had been thinking of leaving the family for some time. Now that the issue was out in the open, it could be dealt with.

UNHOOKING THE THERAPIST

Therapists often become overly responsible with crisis-prone families, responding to their histrionics with anxiety and desperate efforts to help them. The family is quick to sense and exploit this. In such situations, the group can be used to comment on the relationship between the family and the therapist in such a way as to free the therapist.

This was demonstrated in the case of a trainee who had allowed herself to become intimidated by the extraordinary demands of a single-parent mother. When the trainee had completed her training and it became necessary to terminate therapy, the mother had an intense reaction. She spent the sessions crying and complaining that she would never be able to trust anyone again, that she would never find another therapist as helpful to her; she refused to be transferred to anyone else and threatened suicide. The trainee was advised to bring the family in for a consultation with the team. (In the training program, the team is only available for scheduled consultations.)

After a great deal of reluctance the mother finally consented to come for a consultation but stated she would not talk during the session and would not answer any questions. She adhered to her promise and sat silently crying and refusing to participate. The three children, thoroughly intimidated by the mother's mood of anger and sadness, mumbled perfunctory noncommital answers to the therapist's questions. In order to get the mother to participate in the termination process, the team decided to side with her against the therapist by criticizing the therapist's skills and her inability to terminate therapy. It was speculated that the mother would have no other recourse but to come to the therapist's rescue by cooperating with her. After a consultation with the team, the therapist returned to the session with the following message:

> The group has chastised me for pressuring you to come to this consultation against your will. They believe it shows a lack of professional judgment on my part. They think I should apologize for wasting your time and causing you all this inconvenience for nothing—you took the children out of school, paid all that money for their bus fare, took time off from your job—all this for nothing. And you had warned me beforehand you would not talk and I should have listened to you.

The mother mumbled, "How were you to know?"
The therapist continued:

> They also believe that the problem in ending therapy is not yours but mine. They noticed I am having difficulty even letting you go today. They think that because of my intense involvement with you I would find it difficult to envision you making changes with somebody else. Some of the group even suggested that I ask you to remain the same and never go beyond the level of progress we have achieved together because they think I would find that intolerable. I feel badly that they see me like this because, as you know, I am finishing my training. I don't

think they are right. I believe I can tolerate knowing you will go on to change with somebody else. And here is the name of the person who runs this single-parent group which I told you about.

She handed her the name and the mother took it reassuring her, "Nobody is perfect, you know. Everybody makes mistakes. What do they expect anyway?" The mother gradually became animated and loquacious and spent the rest of the session discussing the children, her job possibilities, and a new boy friend. She left the session smiling, having proven the group wrong and the trainee a wonderful therapist who could successfully terminate treatment.

USE OF A CONSULTATION TEAM IN TRAINING

Forming a consultation team with trainees who observe each other's work and consult on each other's cases is an excellent model for training. The formulation of hypotheses and the design and implementation of interventions becomes a group activity led by the supervisor that provides an opportunity for each trainee to have personal input into each case. The atmosphere of a think tank can be exhilarating and the interchange of ideas can lead to innovative and creative techniques. The group also serves the valuable function of disciplining trainees to think systemically as they carefully monitor each other's ideas. At the same time, the anxiety of interviewing in front of their colleagues is greatly reduced since the group shares with them the responsibility for handling the cases. As one trainee put it, "I don't feel I'm in this all alone. I know my group is thinking with me."

There are a number of ways the group can be structured, and Olga Silverstein and myself have experimented with several in our attempts to teach trainees to think creatively. Cases can be assigned to individual trainees, who then interview behind the one-way mirror with the rest of the trainees acting as a consultation team; or, the group can be divided into smaller groups of three or four trainees and cases assigned not to the individual therapist but to the group as a whole. The group then decides who will interview the family, who will act as consultants, how many therapists will be in the room, and what positions they will take around which issues. The responsibility for the family lies with the small groups, with the supervisor acting as a consultant to each group.

Negotiating Change within Different Frameworks

IN COTHERAPY

In presenting this material, the question is often asked: What does one do if one doesn't have a consultation team? The same principles may be applied without a team in a variety of ways. Cotherapists can take planned positions in relation to certain critical issues and debate these issues in front of the family, thereby introducing the therapeutic triangle into the session. The opposing faction, rather than being on the other side of the one-way mirror in the form of the consultation team, is brought into the room in the person of a cotherapist who argues with the other therapist about different aspects of change.

An example of how this approach was put to good use was illustrated in a case I supervised in one of my training groups. The marital tension centered around the husband being overweight, depressed, and currently unemployed. He had a history over the years of quitting jobs or getting fired just as he was doing well and in danger of being promoted. His history revealed an older brother, Larry, who, as the firstborn, was considered by the family to be a knight in shining armor. From his birth, he was treated as the crown prince who could do no wrong, and Charles had always lived in his shadow. At one point, when Charles began to surpass his brother in school, Larry became extremely upset and developed an illness of unknown origin. The family sent Charles to a different school, presumably to better pursue his avocation, but Charles always believed it was so he would not compete with his brother. This school had a lower academic standard, and Charles did poorly there.

The timing of Charles's request for therapy was thought to be significant. He applied to our institute for marital counseling, with his wife, Grace, shortly after Larry and his wife, Angela, began having marital problems for the first time.

After observing the first session, I suggested that the problem could best be handled by a cotherapy team who, as the first step, would connect the presenting problem with Charles's relationship with his brother and debate the advisability of changing this within the session. The male therapist who was assigned the case chose a female therapist to work with him, and, after a consultation break in the second session, the following dialogue took place:

MALE THERAPIST: I'm sorry we kept you waiting so long, but the truth is we have had a disagreement; and, rather than arguing about it between ourselves, we thought it would be more helpful for you to hear just what our disagreement was. We do agree on one thing, and that is that Charles has deliberately kept himself down all his life because he thinks he does not deserve to be happier than his brother. He has gone to great lengths to do this—losing or quitting jobs, gaining weight, getting depressed, and now having a problem with Grace. What we disagree on is whether or not he needs to keep doing this. I believe it's time for Charles to stop living in his brother's shadow and begin to seek independent happiness. I see no reason why he should continue to wipe himself out just so his brother can look good.

FEMALE THERAPIST: I disagree with that point of view because I believe if Charles sought independent happiness, he would feel he had deserted his family, and this would be intolerable to him. You are forgetting that, once before, he sought independent happiness by excelling in school, but this upset everyone terribly and Larry became ill. Charles would live under the threat that this would happen again. I think it's important for him to keep dimming his light, as he's doing, so Larry's light can shine all the brighter in contrast and preserve the family belief that Larry is special.

MALE THERAPIST: In my opinion, he has supported this belief long enough, at great cost to himself and his own family, and I say the time is ripe for him to give it up.

FEMALE THERAPIST: You make it sound so easy. It's not that simple to shake off the past—it casts a long shadow, as the saying goes. You're talking about this as though it were a rational decision he could make. It's not. It's a profound belief shared by his whole family. Just what do you think the reaction of his mother and father would be if he should, God forbid, become more successful than Larry? Or lose weight so he would look better? Or get it together with Grace so he had a better marital relationship than Larry? Not to mention what would happen to his sister, Edna, who worships the ground Larry walks on.

MALE THERAPIST: Well, that's not his problem, is it? I'm sure they would all survive. It's time Charles did something for himself, looked after his own interests for a change.

FEMALE THERAPIST: Well, I am a little more hopeful about Charles's prospects for employment since Larry did so well in business last year. However, Charles should first find out what Larry is making before he goes job hunting, so he can make sure he doesn't earn more than Larry. Charles should also check with Larry to find out if he's enjoying his work, and make sure, if he is, that he doesn't enjoy his more. Perhaps Grace could monitor that.

MALE THERAPIST: That might stir up trouble between Charles and Grace.

FEMALE THERAPIST: All the better, because Charles will not feel he is entitled to have a good relationship with Grace until Larry has a good relationship with Angela. I believe it would be a good idea if Charles sent Larry and Angela here to the Ackerman Institute for marital therapy. And, as a matter of fact, I'm beginning to wonder how wise it is to continue therapy with Charles and Grace, because what if it works? Charles could not tolerate feeling he had a better sexual or emotional relationship with Grace than Larry had with Angela.

MALE THERAPIST: Why should Charles and Grace postpone their possibility for happiness for the sake of Larry and Angela? I think you are exaggerating Charles's need to keep his family happy.

FEMALE THERAPIST: I like to err on the side of caution. Well, I'll go along with you for the time being, but in case the relationship between Charles and Grace improves here, under no circumstances should Charles let Larry know about it. And if Charles begins to feel happier than Larry, he should immediately gain weight and become heavier than Larry.

The therapists then turned to the couple, who had been excluded from this exchange but listening intently, and began negotiations with them around this highly charged issue. Through these negotiations, the absurdity of the covert rules in the family are made overt, and the couple is compelled to deal with them openly. Our speculation that Grace had been collusive in preserving these rules was made evident through the process of the negotiations.

A THREE-WAY DEBATE

The idea of a planned therapeutic debate can be expanded to include three therapists, a technique which was developed by Olga Silverstein, Stanley Siegel, and myself in the Brief Therapy Project. One therapist takes the usual homeostatic position, arguing that the family's dilemmas cannot be resolved except through the symptom. The other two therapists disagree, offering alternatives that point the direction of change. However, they disagree on the alternatives, on whose dilemma is most essential to change, what the family priorities are, and how change should come about.

The effect of this debate resembles what takes place in a court of law when lawyers, arguing for clients with conflicting interests, lay bare the essential facts of the case. By presenting the dilemmas of various family members in relation to the presenting problem, the therapists make explicit the covert rules preventing change. The family, witness to the investigation, is put in the position of having to judge the evidence as they hear their case argued. But it is not the same case they themselves presented to the jury. It is transformed through the many-sided prism of the debate and given a different meaning. The therapists never resolve the dispute, but leave the family to come up with their own conclusions and solutions based on the new evidence offered them.

The following case illustrates the way in which this approach was used with a family torn asunder by divorce. The family presented the problem as the attempted suicide of the 16-year-old son, Bruce, his continuing depression, and his hatred of his father. Through the debate, the therapists connected these symptoms with unresolved loyalty issues in both the nuclear and extended families.

During the fourth session, to which the father came for the first time, the debate was staged to dramatize the way in which Bruce protected his mother from his father's criticism. At the beginning of the session, I took Bruce on the other side of the one-way mirror to listen while Olga and Stanley debated the issues between the parents. Before leaving the session, I told Bruce that if at any point he thought his mother needed him to protect her from his father's criticism, he should enter the room and do so.

Olga, standing in for homeostasis, prescribed the system by recommending to father that he keep criticizing mother because, in that way, he would make sure Bruce would protect her. Since father felt guilty about abandoning mother, it was important for him to know his son would always stand beside her. Stanley, representing change, argued that the role of protector was detrimental to Bruce and that he should abandon it and take care of himself. I took a third position, saying the real problem was mother's emotional cutoff from her extended family, which deprived both her and Bruce of important relationships. (Mother had not spoken to her family for over a year because she felt they had sided with father, who maintained friendly relations with them.)

As I entered the room, the following exchange took place.

PEGGY: I was observing with great interest what was going on in here, particularly the debate between Olga and Stanley. And while I agree with what each of them said, I think there is a third dilemma that is even more crucial to Bruce. It's his feeling about his mother's distress over the cutoff with her own family.

I then went on to say that this put Bruce in an impossible position: Although he would have liked to repair the rift both for himself and for mother, he could not do so without feeling disloyal to her, because she would think he was siding with father, who had a friendly relationship with mother's family.

STANLEY: I think it's time that Bruce does what's right for him.

PEGGY: Well, but what's right for Bruce is connected with what's right for his mother . . .

STANLEY: I worry to what extreme Bruce will go to give his mother the loyalty he feels that she should have.

PEGGY: Well, what do you think is the alternative?

STANLEY: The alternative is for Bruce to do what is good for him—to begin to grow up, to take more responsibility outside of the house. If he wants to speak with his grandfather, he should speak with his grandfather, because I think mother can handle it. If he wants to speak with his dad, he can speak with his dad. He doesn't have to be in the middle of all this.

OLGA: Stanley, you keep saying that, you know. But Bruce is the cornerstone of this family . . .

PEGGY: Stanley, when you talk about Bruce doing his own thing, that's when I begin to worry about you. (*To mother.*) Because, with this cutoff with your family, who will you have to support you? (*Mother says she has a whole network of friends. Stanley says he doesn't understand why Bruce doesn't know this. Bruce says he does.*)

STANLEY: Then how do you get the idea, Bruce, that your mother still needs you?

OLGA: From his father. I've been telling you, but you won't listen to me. . . . Everybody's worried about Bruce and mother, you know, as though they're the most important part of the family. How about worrying about father?

PEGGY: Father? Oh, he can take care of himself, don't you think?

OLGA: Oh, no, I don't think. I think it's a package deal—a three-way package deal—and if something changes, it will change for all three of them . . .

PEGGY: You mean you think Bruce is worried about his father?

OLGA: And his mother. And grandparents. And sister. He's like that little Atlas who was holding up the whole world . . .

STANLEY: Maybe you're right, and maybe he's worried about his father, and that if he doesn't stand by his mother, his dad might get upset.

OLGA: Absolutely. I don't doubt that . . .

FATHER: My message is to take care of mom, but I also would like to talk to him.

PEGGY: That may not be possible for Bruce at this point to do both things.

STANLEY: I think it is.

FATHER: Can I vote with you?

PEGGY: How?

STANLEY: I think Bruce can honor his parents, but he doesn't have to go to such extremes. I think he can act independently.

FATHER: I think he can—that he's capable.

STANLEY: He's already telling me that he is. You know, he's doing more things outside the house, he's finding more places he's needed.

PEGGY: (*To mother.*) If Bruce had a relationship with his father, I would be very concerned about what would happen to you.

MOTHER: Why?

PEGGY: Because you have such strong feelings, and I think you would feel that he was siding with his father against you and that he had left you.

FATHER: I think Bruce has room in his heart for both of us. (*Mother says she gives the children permission to be with their father.*)

STANLEY: I think father has been important to him and he continues to need him, so I don't know how he's making these choices, but I guess that's the dilemma you two [Olga and Peggy] are pointing out . . .

OLGA: (*To father*). As loyal as Bruce is to his mother, and there's no doubt about that—it's so evident no one even has to question it—the dilemma for Bruce and the real problem for him is his loyalty to you.

FATHER: I think I can see some of that myself.

OLGA: Because, in fact, the only way he can show his loyalty to you is by cutting off from you and sticking by his mother; because I think that Bruce knows that if he were to move out of that spot and weren't there to take care of her, that you would suffer intensely—would suffer a great deal of guilt and anxiety—and, in that sense, if Bruce weren't there, you would really have abandoned her, and I don't think you would be able to tolerate that. I think Bruce thinks you couldn't tolerate that . . .

STANLEY: I have to disagree with you once again. I agree with what the problem is for Bruce, but I think you can find a way to honor your parents and also be loyal to yourself—to find little steps to take care of yourself.

PEGGY: Make sure they are little.

A mirror image reflecting the multiple aspects of change—its complexities, contradictions, ambiguities—is held up to the family, shifting their singular perception of the problem. As soon as a family member begins to consider an alternative, another therapist comes in to disqualify the alternative by remarking on the way it is connected with the symptom, with the dilemma of another family member, or with the past, which cannot be changed. It is impossible for the family to disqualify all three therapists at once since all three are taking different positions. If they disagree with one, they automatically agree with another. No matter whom they side with, they have bought into the therapists' view of change, since all the dilemmas are tied to the presenting problem.

IN SUPERVISION

Differing positions can be taken by a supervisor/supervisee without the supervisor being present in the sessions. The supervisee can convey messages periodically from the supervisor, taking any number of attitudes in relation to the messages, such as open disagreement, puzzlement, exasperation, confusion, or wholehearted endorsement. The supervisor's personality can be presented in the shape that is most expedient to the intervention: a conservative old fogy who constantly tries to put the lid on the supervisee's more optimistic and enthusiastic impulses toward change; someone who aggressively and impatiently pushes toward change while the supervisee empathically sympathizes with the family's ordeal; a fortune-teller with mysterious powers to predict the future; or a slightly daft oracle who makes outrageous suggestions that the supervisee presents with reverence. Outrageous suggestions are often more effective coming from an unseen authority outside the session than from the trainee who is then called upon to defend them. A case that seemed to call for such a suggestion was presented by a trainee whom I was supervising.

The wife was an astrologer who gave professional readings and claimed to have psychic powers. The presenting problem centered around the husband's erections. The wife was preoccupied with how many he had, how frequently he had them, how long they lasted, and the caliber of them. The wife constantly initiated sex, and if her husband was impotent or failed to perform properly, which was more frequent than the wife desired, she would explode and claim he did it to spite her. The husband, who never fought openly with his wife, kept softly insisting he had no control over his erections. The wife kept loudly insisting that he did.

The trainee was instructed to tell the wife that her supervisor was an expert in sexual problems and had recommended that since she was an astrologist she should trace her husband's sexual energy according to his astrological chart and figure out when the time was ripe for him to have an erection, what kind it would be, and how long it would last. She should initiate sex only when the stars were in the right positions in the heaven for maximum sexual excitement. She of course was not to let her husband know about this. If he failed to have an erection, she would know she had missed reading an important astrological sign and should study the chart again. The supervisor had the utmost confidence in the wife's ability to predict this. The trainee took the position that, though this request was unconventional, she knew her supervisor to have unerring judgment in such matters.

This intervention took the pressure off the husband to give command performances and put the responsibility on the wife to determine his sexual moods before demanding them of him. As the supervisee was relying on the supervisor's superior wisdom, she herself was relieved of having to discuss the reasoning behind the intervention.

IN PRIVATE PRACTICE

This approach can also be used by a single therapist working alone. The therapist divides his/her opinion along the lines of homeostasis versus change, and swings back and forth according to the way the family responds to the interventions. For example, if a husband fails to respond to the therapist's repeated suggestions that he restrain his sexual pursuit of his wife, the therapist can shift his/her position to:

> I wish to apologize for having suggested that you stop pressuring Gina to have sex with you. I'm beginning to understand and respect your reason for doing this. It puzzled me for a while because you knew for sure your pressuring was guaranteed to turn her off. But I see now that your wife's withdrawal actually excites you—makes you feel like a charged stallion, a wild bull, a Don Juan with supersexual appetite—and this is important for your image of yourself as a male. I'm not sure what would happen to you if you were to give that up. For the time being, I think it's important for you to keep pressuring Gina, and for you, Gina, to keep stimulating your husband by refusing him.

The therapist backtracks from a thrust toward change and defines the problematic behavior of the husband and wife as serving a function in their system. The reframing changes the husband's premise that he is being deliberately deprived by a cold wife to the new premise that his wife is doing him a favor by preserving his masculine image and the wife's premise that her husband is genetically oversexed to the new premise that he is being excited by her sexual rejections.

Case Presentation: The Daughter Who Said No

This case illustrates the step-by-step process of putting concepts into practice over time. It describes the treatment of a 23-year-old anorectic daughter and her family who present the classical pattern of an anorectic family: a high degree of enmeshment, covert alliances between the generations, subverted conflict, and power struggles fought with guilt and martyrdom.

The parents, in rigidly symmetrical positions, are in constant conflict and divert this conflict through Rachel, the anorectic daughter, hence isolating her from her siblings and the world of her peers. The therapeutic dilemma centers around what will happen to Rachel and the various members of her family if she gives up her symptom and becomes a full-blown woman. The consultation group is used to debate this dilemma, and the sibling subsystem is enlisted to free Rachel from her involvement in the parental generation.

Twenty sessions were held over the period of one year with a one-, two- and three-year follow-up. All sessions were video-taped and observed behind the one-way mirror by a consultation group headed by Olga Silverstein.

For the purpose of clarity, the case is broken down into stages according to the following outline. This outline was

A narrated tape of the case is available for rental through the Ackerman Institute for Family Therapy, New York, New York.

prepared after the completion of therapy and did not serve as a guide for organizing the therapy.

- Stage I: Forming a hypothesis
    - Step 1: Gathering information
    - Step 2: Connecting the symptom with the family system
- Stage II: Setting the terms for therapy
    - Step 1: Defining the therapeutic dilemma
    - Step 2: Setting the terms for change
- Stage III: Putting the therapeutic contract into operation
    - Step 1: Involving father in the therapeutic dilemma
    - Step 2: Dramatizing the therapeutic dilemma
- Stage IV: Coping with the forces of change
    - Step 1: Defining change within the therapeutic contract
- Stage V: Coping with the fallout from change
    - Step 1: Defining resistance within the therapeutic framework
    - Step 2: Shifting the definition of the problem
    - Step 3: Prescribing enmeshment
- Stage VI: Enlisting the sibling subsystem
    - Step 1: Forming a coalition with the sisters
    - Step 2: Differentiating from the sisters
- Stage VII: Saying no to therapy
    - Step 1: Pushing the prescription to the breaking point
    - Step 2: Escalating the therapeutic triangle
    - Step 3: Opposing the group
    - Step 4: Supporting autonomy
- Stage VIII: Solidifying change
    - Step 1: Anticipating and rehearsing a regression
    - Step 2: Redefining the marital relationship
- Stage IX: Prescribing a farewell ritual
- Follow-up

Stage I: Forming a Hypothesis

STEP 1: GATHERING INFORMATION

The information I obtained from the first session is here summarized since information gathering tends to make tedious reading. Rachel, 23, requested therapy for herself and her family, having been referred to our institute by her internist, who diagnosed her as anorectic. Her mother and two older sisters, Clare, 31, and Sandy, 26, agreed to participate in therapy, but her father emphatically refused. Having been pushed into various kinds of therapy by his wife for the last five years, he told Rachel in no uncertain terms she would have to solve her problem herself.

I agreed to see the family without him, believing I could involve him later. Some therapists will not see the family unless everyone is present for the first session. Since my way of dealing with resistance is indirect rather than direct, my decisions are based on an evaluation of each case. In this situation it seemed important to go along with father's resistance since it was obviously a reaction to his wife's pressure. Also, the intensity of his feelings was a good indication he could be involved at a later date.

Only mother and Rachel appeared for the first interview as Sandy was in the hospital having her first baby and Clare refused to come after a fight with Rachel.

Rachel appeared frail and flat-chested, but animated, with huge dark eyes and a thin face. She was exceptionally articulate, expressing herself in colorful language and sometimes adding a comic delivery. Her mother, a large, handsome, robust woman with short, white hair, stylishly cut, possessed the style and flair of a seasoned actress. With the exuberance of Lady Bountiful she embraced family therapy saying she "believed" family members should help one another and she would do anything to help Rachel. She tempered each criticism of her with "there's really nothing wrong with you, you're a wonderful child but—."

Rachel had begun dieting four years ago during her second year at college. Since that time she had slowly but steadily lost weight until she finally weighed 89 pounds. She had not menstruated for a year and a half. During the last three years she had made several attempts to leave home but failed, each time feeling depressed, isolated, lonely, and coming back home. She now had an interim job as a secretary but was dissatisfied with it. Although living at home, she was talking about moving into an apartment of her own.

The primary concern of Rachel and her mother was not her weight loss or her diet, but the psychological implications, which they saw in terms of Rachel's intrapsychic problems.

Rachel's previous individual therapy of one year had focused on the classical individual symptoms of anorexia—high expectations, overachievement, perfectionistic attitudes, obsessions, and control over the body—but had not connected these in any way with the family system.

The mother was interested in our helping Rachel with her high expectations of herself, describing her as being "obsessively and rigidly perfectionistic." She also stated Rachel had been a rebellious child all her life. "I have been worried about Rachel since she learned to say no. It has been no and no and no and no and no and no and no ever since then. She has not wanted to adopt any of our standards, and I question her judgment." She gave as an example of this Rachel's not wanting to join B'nai B'rith or date Jewish boys, and her tendency to pick a boy up off the street and make a date with him. Rachel accused her mother of matchmaking. "I feel like it's mating season. I'm in heat and it's time to find a male for me quick before I'm not eligible anymore. I don't enjoy that." Mother then mentioned drugs and Rachel admitted she had experimented in college with pot, speed, LSD, and mescaline and ended with, "I don't regret anything."

Mother had kept everything away from father over the years to protect Rachel and to avoid a conflict. When asked what he would have done had he known about these things, she stated "I don't know. I wasn't going to give him a chance! The girls have accused me of being manipulative and maybe I am but I have to be." She spoke of the many disagreements between her and her husband, describing a long-standing conflict because of her closeness with her parents.

At the end of the session, after consultation with the team, I told Rachel and her mother we felt we did not have enough information at this point to make any suggestions and would like to delay our comments until we had met with other members of the family. Rachel agreed to try and get Clare to come to the next session but Sandy was still recuperating from the birth of her baby.

In the following session, Clare, a thin, attractive woman, fashionably dressed, was more than happy to give her impressions of Rachel and other family members. She described Rachel as being "very difficult" and her family as being one in which it was difficult to become independent, as her mother was controlling and "throws guilt around a lot." Both she and Rachel had rebelled against her mother's control, but Sandy "is the model daughter, model sister, model grandchild and, now having had a baby, will be the model mother. She never displeases anyone. She is the buffer, the peacemaker."

Both Rachel and Clare spoke of their being afraid of their father when they were growing up. He was very conservative and strict about dates, two-piece bathing suits, boy friends, hours, and so on. The mother, more lenient, took this opportunity to say that she was also afraid of his wrath and stated pathetically, "Thank God he never hit me." She compared him unfavorably with her own father and started to cry. "I tried very hard to get my family to help me, and my father would talk to my husband in a gentle manner and say how precious a wife is, how nothing really was as precious as a wife, and really she's the only one who is most important in life. But my husband would become antagonistic toward such conversations." She went into individual therapy at the recommendation of her doctor when she developed stomach trouble, and her doctor put pressure on her husband to go with her. Both blamed him for her physical problems.

Rachel and Clare defended their father and accused their mother of being overly close to her family and rubbing the father's nose in it. Rachel then spoke of her father and her as being the "underdogs in the family. We're ostracized by the rest of them." Rachel had given me the first clue as to how she fit into the power struggle between her parents: She identified with the father's underdog position. I now wanted to know the function of this identification: how it was used in the ongoing day-to-day battle between the parents and how the sisters responded to it. The following dialogue was included to demonstrate how these questions were explored.

PEGGY: So you feel you're the bad guy and your father is the bad guy in the family. In what way do you feel you can bring comfort to your father?

RACHEL: Because I can understand his viewpoint.

CLARE: If there are two bad guys, then you both share the burden?

RACHEL: There's company.

PEGGY: How do you go about giving him company?

RACHEL: We have a lot of common interests, we both like cars and nature and the Bronx Zoo, and we have a good time. We go across the country together.

PEGGY: What do you think his life would be like if you weren't around?

RACHEL: I don't know—I guess he'd survive.

PEGGY: Do you think he'd be lonely?

RACHEL: Maybe, sometimes—I'm nice company for him.

PEGGY: Then who would there be around to really understand him?

RACHEL: (*Long pause.*) I don't know.

PEGGY: You don't think your mother could understand him?

RACHEL: She will never ever. I shouldn't say that, but as far as I can see, it'll be a very tough thing for my mother to ever understand how my father feels about her family. She will never ever see how he feels about her.

MOTHER: But who do I think of when I want somebody to make nice to me? I go right back to the womb. On Tuesday I spent the day with my mom and dad and it was a good day. It was a hard day. I took them shopping. They're very old.

PEGGY: Do you feel they're the only ones who nurture you?

MOTHER: (*Nodding.*) Who really take care of me. I don't want anyone here to feel bad, but Sandy also takes care of me.

RACHEL: But you demand too much. You're very hard to give to when you demand.

PEGGY: Let's see then. When you feel ganged up on by Rachel and your husband, you then go for nurturing to your parents. And who does your husband go to?

MOTHER: There's always been a young man in his life who treats him like God. Now it's Roy.

PEGGY: You're saying that he always finds someone who is like a son to him?

MOTHER: Yes, Roy is like a son.

PEGGY: Was he disappointed he didn't have a son?

MOTHER: (*Whispers.*) Very.

PEGGY: You whispered that "very." You don't want the girls to hear that?

MOTHER: (*Emphatically.*) *Very* displeased that he didn't have a son.

PEGGY: Do you think they don't know that?

RACHEL: I'm daddy's son.

PEGGY: In what way have you been his son?

RACHEL: Just—my interest in things which aren't typically feminine. I'm not scared of bugs, little things like that. Cars. Daddy asked me to cook hamburgers on the barbecue pit because I can handle it. (*She imitates a boy.*)

PEGGY: What's that like for you to be his son?

RACHEL: I kinda like it. (*She laughs and acts like a boy again.*) I don't mind, but I don't think he thinks of me as a boy.

PEGGY: Do you think of yourself as a boy?

RACHEL: No. I was saying that I felt so independent on this move. It always bugs me to depend on people.

PEGGY: What do you think it's going to be like for him, your moving out?

RACHEL: I think it's going to be all right for him. Already they're talking about switching homes with me.

PEGGY: Do you think he's going to miss you?

RACHEL: Maybe. He said he was going to miss some things but not others.

PEGGY: Well do you think your mother's going to be able to take care of his loneliness?

RACHEL: Not unless she starts to look at him from a more objective point of view.

PEGGY: Do you think you can teach her?

RACHEL: I try, I really try. Then she accuses me of ganging up on her.

CLARE: (*Defending mother.*) Daddy's not nice all the time, either.

STEP 2: CONNECTING THE SYMPTOM WITH THE FAMILY SYSTEM

After this exchange, the therapist left the session to have a consultation with the group. We formed a hypothesis based on answering the following questions:

What function does the symptom serve in the system? We speculated that Rachel was starving herself in order to remain a son to her father and fill up the emptiness in his life that she perceived was left by her mother. By not eating, she kept herself looking like a boy, prevented herself from maturing into womanhood, and implicitly promised to remain the guardian of her parents' marriage. The symptom served to keep her at home where she could continue to serve as her father's ally in his battle with her mother and to give her mother a reason for remaining close to her family. By identifying with her father as the underdog in the family, she formed a coalition with him in the service of fighting against her mother's control. The symptom also served the function of freeing the other sisters to establish independent lives outside the family, since Rachel had accepted the responsibility of mediating the parents' marriage.

How does the family function to stabilize the symptom? When mother and father became involved in a power struggle that they could not resolve, mother moved closer to her parents and compared father unfavorably to her own father. Father retaliated by siding with Rachel against his wife, and Rachel joined him to get back at her mother. She became involved in masculine activities to please her father, knowing he felt alienated in a family of women. She cannot give up the symptom as long as she believes she is needed to be a son to him. The power struggle between mother and Rachel has taken many forms over the years, including Rachel's taking drugs, quitting jobs, leaving school, dating non-Jewish boys, and disassociating herself from the family religious beliefs, as well as her present symptom of self-starvation.

What is the central theme around which the problem is organized? The central theme in this family seems to be control—who is going to control the beliefs and values of the others. This is a conventional family that places high value on conformity, respectability, achievement, duty, and family loyalty. Mother is less concerned about some of Rachel's other activities than she is about her not accepting the tenets of the Jewish faith. She complains that her husband rejects her father's value of a wife as being something "precious."

Since we have not yet seen father and Sandy, we are unable at this point to obtain a complete picture of the way each individual operates to maintain control around these central issues.

What will be the consequences of change? If Rachel stopped being a son to her father, she would have to abandon him to what she perceives to be an unloving wife, and she would also be robbed of her major weapon against mother. If she left home, mother and father would have to face their conflicts alone and would probably create a triangle involving Sandy or Clare. Mother might move even closer to her own parents and father closer to his surrogate son, Roy. This would widen the breach between the parents. If father agreed to come for therapy in order to try and resolve these issues, he would lose a major battle with his wife regarding the value of therapy.

Rachel would have to confront the outside world and its relationships rather than centering her life on the family. This would mean her taking responsibility for becoming an adult woman sexually, professionally, and socially.

What is the therapeutic dilemma? The family must decide between Rachel continuing to be symptomatic or facing the above consequences.

Stage II: Setting the Terms for Therapy

STEP 1: DEFINING THE THERAPEUTIC DILEMMA

Our first intervention consisted of setting the terms for the therapeutic contest that was to follow by defining the problem as a family dilemma. The family had defined the problem as an individual one—Rachel's rebelliousness, her obsessions, rigid expectations, and self-starvation all were seen as being disconnected from the family. In defining the problem as a dilemma, we connected the symptom with the system.

Peggy entered the session with the following message:

PEGGY: (*Sighs.*) We are stuck.
MOTHER: So are we.
PEGGY: We are in a bind and I don't know what to do about it except just be very honest and open and tell you what we're stuck with. Rachel, we are very hesitant to help you in the way we were planning therapy to take, which would be to help you think and feel more like a woman, to gain weight, to have curves, to menstruate, to go out with boys, and to just be yourself. Because, you see, we are

concerned about what will happen to your father, that he will become more isolated in a family of women, that he will turn more to his surrogate son, Roy, leaving your mother more alone, so that she will turn more to her own family. We are worried this will create an irreparable distance between the two of them.

CLARE: It's a vicious cycle, isn't it?

PEGGY: And, you see, we are concerned about all the members of your family, and when one person in the family changes, that changes the relationship of everybody.

RACHEL: (*Long pause.*) I don't think I want to sacrifice myself for my parents. I don't think I care that much. I want to help myself right now.

PEGGY: (*Still posing the dilemma.*) I can understand how you feel. I just want to make sure you are aware of the effect it will have. . . . Well, think about these things and decide what you want to do.

CLARE: (*Suddenly becoming aware of the implication of the terms I have set.*) I want to say that I got very angry about what the group said. That you decided to change your tack. I think that is wrong. (*She bursts into tears.*) I'm worried about Rachel and that's not the thing to do for her.

PEGGY: You feel that we should help her—?

CLARE: Yes, that's terrible! How can you say because it will affect other members of the family—what should she do—starve herself?

PEGGY: (*Puzzling over the dilemma.*) Well, you know, I think that has to be Rachel's decision and all we can do is—.

CLARE: But you function in that decision. You are here to help her.

PEGGY: Well, you see, Rachel is so close to her family that—.

CLARE: I think that's terrible! (*She strides across the room and grabs a Kleenex.*) I obviously don't understand what's behind it. I think it's awful.

PEGGY: We feel responsible—we feel obligated to let you know what we think the consequences of change will be and to prepare you for them.

There was a knock on the door and the group summoned me out for a brief consultation.

Rachel and Clare had reacted against the therapist's homeostatic position and were pressing for change. We decided to use this as an opportunity to bargain with them over the conditions of change and set the price as Rachel's agreement to turn the burden of her parents' unhappiness over to me. We were aware that the father might not agree to do this since he was boycotting therapy. However, it was our way of dramatizing the connection between Rachel's problem and her parents unhappiness.

PEGGY: (*Entering the session.*) The group wanted to let you know that they heard what you said and that they take it very seriously, and perhaps there is a way I can help you. (*Turning to Rachel.*) If you would be willing for me to see your parents together and for me to take on the responsibility of what will happen to them if you change, then perhaps you could begin to eat. Could you allow me to take on that responsibility rather than your shouldering it?

Rachel agreed to do this and mother was more than willing to have her husband brought into therapy.

PEGGY: My group feels that then it would be safe for you to become a woman. And I will handle the consequences of that with your father and mother.

I informed them I would call father and ask him to attend the next session. To summarize the terms of therapy:

1. We defined Rachel's symptom as her remaining at home and failing to become a woman in order to stabilize the relationship between her parents.
2. We defined the relationship between her parents as not being able to tolerate her absence.
3. We defined the therapeutic dilemma as having to choose between helping Rachel to become a woman and preserving the stability of her parents' relationship.
4. We defined the solution and therefore the terms for change as Rachel's agreeing to pass the responsibility for preserving her parents' relationship to us. This

CASE: THE DAUGHTER WHO SAID NO   77

set up the following situation: If the parents allowed us to help them with their relationship, thus releasing Rachel, she would be relieved of her burden and able to leave home. If they did not, we would ask someone else in the family to take on the burden, or else pass it back to Rachel. By making a hot potato of the parents' unhappiness and passing it around to various members of the family, we would dramatize the therapeutic dilemma.

Stage III: Putting the Therapeutic Contract into Operation

STEP 1: INVOLVING FATHER IN THE THERAPEUTIC DILEMMA

After this session I telephoned Sam, the father, and told him I respected his wish not to be involved in family therapy but since his wife had probably given me a one-sided view of the family situation, I would like to get his impressions over the telephone. He was more than willing to share these and spent the next half hour talking about how his wife put too many expectations on Rachel at too early an age, pushed her to leave home and go away to college at 16, and how he had nothing to say about it because his wife controlled the children and paid no attention to his opinions. He ended the conversation by saying he would be willing to come in for a session if it would help Rachel. I told him I would let him know when I thought it would be helpful, not wanting to seem overly eager about his becoming involved.

A week later Rachel moved away from home into her own apartment and I asked the father to come in for a session. He agreed, but only if Rachel and his wife were present, as he didn't want to be in a session with four women. His terms were accepted, and I began by informing him that we had discovered that Rachel was reluctant to leave home for fear he might be lonely if left alone with his wife. He initially scoffed this idea, but as I began to discuss the family dinners in which Rachel sided with him against mother and her family, he validated the hypothesis. He admitted that he and Rachel had a lot in common. "We identify in certain ways, we understand each other." Rachel agreed with this.

PEGGY: What else do you understand about each other?

Father then described a family dinner held with his wife's family at which he sat next to Rachel for comfort and mother had commented, "Like Robin Hood and his men, they gang up and snicker."

PEGGY: What will happen at these dinners when Rachel is not there anymore? I worry about what will happen to your father when you're not there. He will be losing an ally.
RACHEL: He won't assimilate.
FATHER: I don't understand what's going on. I don't think she's worried about me in every situation. Do you think about me when there's a party?
RACHEL: Of course I'm concerned about you. It makes me feel bad when you're both unhappy.
PEGGY: How do you know when either of them is unhappy? What are the signals?
RACHEL: When I speak to mother I hear about things that aren't happy in her life, and vice versa. I don't think either of you should keep me out of it, though. You shouldn't try to hide it.
PEGGY: Do you think you can be helpful to them?
RACHEL: I could be—I don't think they think I care.
MOTHER: I don't think she doesn't care about us. She cares desperately. She's been very helpful, she picks up my spirits, talks to me when I'm feeling down.
PEGGY: I guess you're not only worried about what will happen to your father when you're not there, but to your mother also.

Rachel agreed with this, and mother and father began to quarrel about their respective needs and sensitivities.

PEGGY: (*Again using parental conflict as an opportunity to define why Rachel cannot leave home.*) What will happen when Rachel is not there?
FATHER: She's not there now.
PEGGY: What is happening?
FATHER: We're having a bad time the last few months.
PEGGY: Maybe you'd better go back home, Rachel.

RACHEL: I'm not going home.

MOTHER: I don't want her home. We can straighten out our lives better without her there.

PEGGY: Can you? Can you do it?

FATHER: But if she wanted to be home—I don't think we would—I don't—right, Helen?

PEGGY: (*To Rachel.*) It's a tremendous temptation, isn't it?

RACHEL: No. I don't really want to go back there. I don't.

MOTHER: I'm glad.

PEGGY: I don't know. How are the two of you going to make it on your own?

MOTHER AND FATHER: (*Together.*) I don't know.

RACHEL: Do you think it's going to go on like this forever?

Father said again that it was no concern of hers, but Rachel kept insisting it was and that they try and work it out.

RACHEL: I'd like it if you could both be happy.

FATHER: How could we do that?

RACHEL: I don't know, but you're certainly not trying.

At this point I explained to father that during a previous session the group had counseled me not to help Rachel unless she agreed to release the responsibility of their unhappiness to me. I asked if he would be willing for me to take on that responsibility and he refused my offer. Mother then put pressure on father.

MOTHER: You see how Sam calls the shots? When you say you won't come here to help us, I'm at your mercy.

FATHER: I didn't want to start in the beginning. I've been through this and it didn't help.

PEGGY: Yes, you told me that.

MOTHER: What bothers you? Do you feel vulnerable? Do you feel it is an undue expenditure? What is more important—an undue expenditure or our happiness?

FATHER: Why do I have to be put in the position of choosing on the basis of what is important?

MOTHER: There we are!

FATHER: So it's therapy or nothing?

MOTHER: Of course. It's not important—we're not important.

PEGGY: You may be able to work it out without therapy, but what concerns me is are you going to be able to work it out without Rachel?

MOTHER: We should be able to go hang ourselves and have it not affect Rachel.

PEGGY: But how are you going to keep Rachel out of it?

The parents argued and Rachel tried to mediate. The therapist took a break to have a consultation with the group.

STEP 2: DRAMATIZING THE THERAPEUTIC DILEMMA

The group agreed that if I continued to pressure father to come into therapy I would be siding with mother and he would resist more and more. We decided the group should support his autonomy and recommended that the burden of the parents' unhappiness should be passed to Sandy. Since Sandy was considered a superhuman being and this was a superhuman job, she seemed the appropriate person. I read the following message:

> The group, not having met Sam before, is impressed with his ability to take care of himself. Somehow, the family mythology had led us to believe otherwise. We trust mother has the strength to do the same. As for Rachel, she has carried the burden of her parents' unhappiness long enough and should now pass the burden to Sandy.

All three burst into laughter. Father asked if I had met Sandy, and I replied "No, but I'm looking forward to it." Rachel said they were just talking about what a super person she was, and I replied, "Then we've chosen the right person for the job."

Father offered to keep coming to the sessions on the basis of helping Rachel but not to work on his relationship with his wife. Sandy accompanied the family to the following session.

Stage IV: Coping with the Forces of Change

STEP 1: DEFINING CHANGE WITHIN THE THERAPEUTIC CONTRACT

Rachel began the session by reporting a sudden and unexpected change. She had started menstruating for the first time in a year and a half and gained several pounds. Following through on my definition of the problem, I gave father credit for convincing Rachel he could manage his life without her.

RACHEL: I have to tell you something exciting that's happened. I got my period. It's very exciting.
PEGGY: You did?
RACHEL: Yes, at my sister's surprise party. (*Much laughter.*)
PEGGY: Is this the first time?
RACHEL: In a year and a half. I stopped expecting it.
PEGGY: You've decided to become a woman?
RACHEL: (*Laughingly.*) I'm considering it.
PEGGY: You'd better think this over carefully.
RACHEL: I know it's a big step.

PEGGY: (*To the parents.*) Well, how do the two of you feel about what's happening to her?
FATHER: Very much relieved that she's on her own path. Things are becoming more normal—not altogether, but approaching it.
PEGGY: You're not afraid you're going to lose your companion?
FATHER: No, I'm praying for it. (*Laughter.*) I was pleased that Rachel is approaching normalcy. She also said she gained three pounds. She is very happy about it. Didn't seem to worry about the three pounds.
PEGGY: I think you did a very good job.
FATHER: I did?
PEGGY: Yes, I think you did a very good job. Last time you were here you convinced Rachel you could manage your life without her, that you would be okay, that even if your marriage wasn't the greatest or if you didn't stay together that—.
FATHER: Well, we didn't tell these kids that yet. (*Referring to the other sisters.*)
PEGGY: Well, but you told that to Rachel and I think you did an excellent job in assuring her you're going to be okay and that it's okay for her to become an independent woman.
FATHER: And in the last two weeks things are even better between Helen and me.

Sandy was informed of our having designated her to relieve Rachel of the burden of the parents' unhappiness. Everyone reacted with amusement. Sandy refused, saying she had a new baby and besides the parents seemed to be handling their own burden now.

Stage V: Coping with the Fallout from Change

STEP 1: DEFINING RESISTANCE WITHIN THE
THERAPEUTIC FRAMEWORK

Neither Rachel nor her family were prepared for this amount of change and Rachel suffered a relapse. We immediately realized our mistake in not anticipating the consequences of change and predicting a relapse to lessen the chance of its occurrence. The family used the Jewish holidays as a way of recreating the family turmoil, with Rachel at the center. By refusing to go to synagogue on Passover, she created a minor crisis. Mother reacted in her characteristic fashion by provoking guilt, father tentatively supported Rachel, and Rachel became depressed to keep attention focused on her. She tearfully complained about her apartment, her job, the classes she was taking, and ended with: "There's nothing good about my life right now."

The whole family became involved in trying to analyze Rachel's depression and giving her helpful advice about how to pull herself out of it. Father brought up the inflammatory subject of Rachel not having gone to temple on Passover and asked if her depression was related to her feeling guilty. She denied this, and father stated: "That's good." Mother vehemently disagreed with him. During the following exchange they spoke simultaneously.

MOTHER: I don't think that's good, that's my problem. I see it as bad that Rachel, who loves us and whom we love, can do something to make us feel badly continuously and continuously—.
FATHER: That's something for us to get used to—.
MOTHER: When it would be good if she would do something to make us feel good.
FATHER: Helen—no—that's—(*Indecipherable.*)
RACHEL: How can you expect me to do something I don't believe?

FATHER: Helen, that's something—(*Indecipherable.*)
MOTHER: But you do believe. You've told me you believe.
FATHER: Helen, she believes in a different way . . .
RACHEL: But I don't. I believe in my fashion. I don't believe in keeping kosher, I don't believe in going to temple, I don't believe in dating Jewish boys, I don't believe that!
MOTHER: All right. And I believe, Rachel, that it is a sign of not quite loving us enough! I see it as a very selfish kind of act. You have no consideration. She's liable to do exactly what she wants to do because she doesn't want to please us. She's very rebellious.

Mother then went into a long harangue, giving a history of Rachel's rebelliousness. She ended up talking about how important the Jewish tradition was to her.

MOTHER: I've cried about the continuation of our Jewish tradition.
RACHEL: I'm sorry, mommy; you can cry and cry, but I'm not going to become more Jewish because you cry.
MOTHER: Therefore, then I don't think that you love us very much.
RACHEL: Well, mommy, if that's your criteria, then I really can't help you.
MOTHER: Okay, these are my feelings. That's my criteria. Yes.
PEGGY: If she really loved you enough, she'd believe what you believe?
MOTHER: No, dear, no; because I know she believes. She's told me she believes. She believes in God. She says the most important prayer in our religion every night of her life, which I don't do.
RACHEL: Why not? Don't you love me?
MOTHER: Rachel, stop shouting at me.
PEGGY: You didn't answer her.
MOTHER: Why don't I say that prayer? Have you ever asked me to join you in that prayer?
RACHEL: No, it's a private prayer. You're supposed to say it by yourself.
MOTHER: So why are you shouting at me?
RACHEL: Why don't you say that prayer? You love me?

Mother accused Rachel of being sarcastic. I asked father if he felt the same way as mother about Rachel's not going to temple. He said he would like her to attend but didn't feel as intensely as his wife. I then asked Clare and Sandy if they had a problem becoming independent in this family, and both answered in the affirmative, describing the pressure and guilt that were applied to them throughout their lives. Asked how they dealt with this, Clare replied she didn't let her parents know about half of what she was doing, and Sandy said she always did what she wanted to do. Both parents were attacked for their rigidity, and the session ended with everyone quarrelling over who was most to blame.

The group was not present during this session and the family was told they would receive a message from them after they had seen the tape. In a consultation with the team, I defined the relapse as a systems problem rather than an individual one and sent the following message:

> It is the conviction of the group that Rachel has wisely decided she has not yet finished her job of diverting her parents from their unhappiness. Since Sandy and Clare have refused to accept this job, she should return home until it is completed.

It was then agreed that at the next session I would take a more lenient position regarding this message, encouraging Rachel's independence in opposition to an adamant position from the group, thus intensifying the triangle between therapist, family, and group.

STEP 2: SHIFTING THE DEFINITION OF THE PROBLEM

In the following session, Rachel adamantly refused to return home and the parents insisted they did not need her anymore to solve their marital problem. Rachel reacted to this exclusion by complaining about every aspect of her life—her job, her apartment, her boss, her feelings of isolation and loneliness. As she enumerated her complaints, the family, following their characteristic pattern, gave her "helpful" advice replete with platitudes about how to pull herself up by her own bootstraps.

We saw Rachel's litany of complaints as a reaction to giving up her important job of repairing her parent's marriage and decided to ask the family to allow her to mourn her leave taking rather than trying to cheer her up. This was impossible for them to do.

PEGGY: The group has observed that Rachel's unhappiness seems to be a reproach to you and you're not allowing her to be unhappy. Rachel, they want to say that it's very important that you are unhappy and that your family allow you to be. How can you get them to allow you to be unhappy?

RACHEL: I'll just have to keep away from them, I guess.

FATHER: Then we would worry about her.

MOTHER: I worry about my children, especially when they're alone.

PEGGY: This is supposed to be a happy family, so it's difficult for you to allow anyone in the family to feel unhappy.

MOTHER: Are you speaking about a facade, Peggy?

PEGGY: All families are supposed to be happy. This is a very close family, so it is very important for you to feel that everyone's happy. And when anyone is unhappy (*mother sobs*), it's really hard, isn't it? How can you get mother to allow you to be unhappy?

RACHEL: I don't know. I can't reassure her.

MOTHER: (*Sobbing.*) I worry about you every day.

Clare then jumped in to say she never told her mother her problems because she didn't want this kind of reaction. Mother and Clare became involved in a heated argument. Mother stated she couldn't help crying over her children's problems. I then focused the issue between the parents.

PEGGY: Do you also cry over Sam's unhappiness?

MOTHER: Yes, a little bit. I do. He doesn't even know it.

FATHER: I don't believe it. I really don't believe it.

MOTHER: So I don't tell him.

FATHER: I don't believe it. (*The parents begin to argue.*)

PEGGY: When do you cry over his unhappiness?

MOTHER: When I see that he is unhappy in his business, that he's unhappy with his partners, if I see he's unhappy in community situations, when he's hurting himself and feeling terrible about it. When I see he's unhappy in relation to Clare's husband and himself, when I see he's unhappy

about his mother and sick brother-in-law, my heart hurts—
and it's very hard for me to let him know it bothers me,
and so I do it in my own little corner.

PEGGY: (*Sympathetically.*) You cry over him without letting him
know?

MOTHER: Cry tears? No. For my children I cry tears.

STEP 3: PRESCRIBING ENMESHMENT

The group discussed the futility of persuading mother to allow
any of her children to be unhappy. Worrying over her children
was an important life job. Rachel knew this and kept her
mother involved with her by continually giving her something
to worry about.

Rather than trying to diffuse this intense involvement, we
decided to prescribe the family's enmeshment—but in a way
that would involve father in the transaction. We added a task
that shifted some of mother's involvement with her children
toward her husband. Our purpose in doing this was to test the
parents' readiness to bridge the gap in their relationship left by
Rachel's departure.

PEGGY: It is the group's conviction that I am asking the impossible by asking a mother with a heart as tender as
Helen's to allow her children to suffer. (*As an aside, I say,
"There are a lot of Jewish mothers out there." Mother waves in
recognition.*) It is equally impossible for Rachel to break
her mother's heart. We, therefore, recommend that Rachel
call every day and tell her mother about her unhappiness.
Mother should then share this with Sam, who should then
comfort her. (*Mother cries, father reacts negatively.*)

FATHER: I don't want that kind of scene. I don't want her to
call every day and make Helen unhappy and I don't want
her to confide in me. I don't see anybody getting better
from a thing like that.

PEGGY: You won't do that for your wife and Rachel?

FATHER: (*Laughs.*) It's like a prescription.

PEGGY: That's exactly what it is—a doctor's prescription.

FATHER: That's terrible, that's very bitter tasting.

MOTHER: Why is it so hard to comfort me?

FATHER: Helen, the whole idea doesn't—.

MOTHER: Why, honey? The only thing that's changed is the comfort, because she does call every day and unburden herself and I do listen.

FATHER: (*Surprised.*) You do call every day?

MOTHER: And I don't share it with you because I get the . . . (*She indicates with her thumb a downward movement.*) The only difference would be you would put your arm around me. (*She caresses him.*)

CLARE: It would be nice if you were on mummy's side a little bit.

FATHER: I'm not not on her side.

PEGGY: (*Earnestly.*) Sam, this is very important. Can you do that for Rachel—and for your wife?

FATHER: Sure I can do it.

Rachel did call her mother every day as requested, but mother became bored with her complaints, stopped trying to cheer her up and give her advice, and finally told her she would have to solve her problems herself.

After this session, the parents took a month vacation, cutting the bond with Rachel more decisively. Threatened by this separation, Rachel moved back to their home where she felt isolated and lonely without her old job of mediator. She fell into a morose state and complained endlessly about her feelings of unhappiness and failure.

There is a myth in our profession that if parents get together and free the child from the position of mediator, the child will automatically spring forth mature, well adjusted, and symptom free. This rarely happens since the child's social development has been retarded through his/her preoccupation with the parents' problems. The child usually goes through a period of feeling a loss of identity as he/she relinquishes this very important family position.

Our next task was to help Rachel find a different position for herself. But this could not be done in the same way the family had tried, through encouragement and helpful advice, since she only rebelled against this. We decided instead to use her rebellious streak in the service of change and to define her unhappiness and failure as her way of differentiating herself from her family, which placed such a high premium on happiness and success. We decided to enlist her sisters in helping her to accomplish this task. Rachel had never felt supported by them in her attempts to establish her autonomy as the sisters often took the side of the parents in haranguing and pushing her. The support she received from them in this new alliance proved to be enormously beneficial.

Stage VI: Enlisting the Sibling Subsystem

STEP 1: FORMING A COALITION WITH THE SISTERS

The sisters were more than happy to continue to meet without the parents and quickly joined me in my position that Rachel needed to keep rebelling in order to establish her independence. In the following session, I continually reframed Rachel's complaints within this framework.

RACHEL: I feel sapped at this point.

PEGGY: Well, your parents certainly wouldn't approve of that.

RACHEL: No. I have to keep going.

PEGGY: That's right, and by being completely sapped you're saying no to them, which takes a lot of guts.

SANDY: (*Wistfully.*) That's really true.

RACHEL: But I have no self-respect.

PEGGY: Do your parents want you to have self-respect?

RACHEL: I think so.

PEGGY: And you're saying you don't have self-respect. You say your parents want you to be happy and you're saying, "I'm unhappy."

RACHEL: My parents want me to gain weight.

PEGGY: And you're staying thin.

RACHEL: I've gained five pounds and I'm very upset about it.

PEGGY: I can understand that because you feel you're losing ground with them, that you're doing something they'd like you to do, which makes you feel a nonperson.

RACHEL: I should move to Kalamazoo, get the hell out of New York, and not even think of pleasing my parents.

SANDY: (*Now in full support.*) Listen to what Peggy is saying. You are living your life to displease them.

RACHEL: I want to please myself.

PEGGY: Well, you are because you're displeasing them. The most important thing in your life right now is to say no to your parents, and you've found many ways of doing that.

RACHEL: I want to please me.

PEGGY: Well, you are because you're displeasing them.

The session ended with the group suggesting that Rachel enlist the sisters' help in the planned rebellion, saying it was too much of a burden for her to think up these elaborate schemes herself. The sisters eagerly agreed, with Sandy stating that it would be good training for her.

STEP 2: DIFFERENTIATING FROM THE SISTERS

We failed to anticipate that Rachel would sense her sisters' help as pressuring her to change, since it was being given within the context of therapy. Before forming an alliance with them, she made it clear that she had to first rebel against their expectations of her progress in therapy. She did this by remaining depressed and making veiled suicide threats. I defined these threats as her way of differentiating herself from her sisters' expectations.

CLARE: I feel angry. What Rachel is doing is hostility, talking about killing herself. Besides the fact I love her, I'm angry at her for doing it to me.

RACHEL: Then maybe I'll just make believe things are okay.

CLARE: Why can't I say what I feel?

RACHEL: Maybe I have to work it out away from my family. There are too many expectations and pressures.

CLARE: Who puts expectations on you?

RACHEL: You all do. You all expect me to deal with my problems in a certain way.

PEGGY: (*Supporting her attempt to differentiate from her sisters.*) I think that's true. You do expect her to deal with her problems in a particular way and Rachel is saying no to all of you. Not only no to her parents but to her sisters.

RACHEL: I don't think so—maybe if I were getting pleasure out of it, I could think so.

PEGGY: I know you're not getting pleasure out of it, that's not the purpose.

RACHEL: What is the purpose?

PEGGY: The purpose is to establish who you are, and that you are the one who says no to expectations.

90   CASE: THE DAUGHTER WHO SAID NO

CLARE: You really calm down when we get upset, don't you?

SANDY: I noticed that last time. As soon as we get upset, you sit back. Maybe this is what you want. Maybe we have to prove we're so concerned, or maybe you want to shake us up.

RACHEL: I'm not doing it for the dramatic.

CLARE: Look at you. Five minutes ago you were crying and saying how miserable you were.

RACHEL: (*Coolly.*) It doesn't take that much to make me go one way or the other. I don't know what it takes.

CLARE: (*Heatedly.*) Bullshit! (*They argue.*)

PEGGY: (*Defining this again as Rachel's way of rebelling against her sisters.*) I can understand why you're feeling better now, because you've just said no to your sisters and their expectations of you. I think you need to just keep doing that, Rachel, and to find other ways of doing it.

RACHEL: I really don't get this whole thing.

I then enlisted the sisters in trying to think of more constructive ways for Rachel to rebel and asked about some of the ways they had successfully rebelled. Clare listed her rebellious acts as going out with married men, dating non-Jewish boys, letting her parents know when she was having sex, not joining B'nai B'rith, and so on. Rachel joined in listing her accomplishments, such as going without a bra, wearing pantyhose without panties, raising her voice in public. Sandy suddenly burst out with, "I enjoy talking about these things. It makes me feel good." The tense atmosphere changed to one of comraderie and laughter as they banded together in discussing acts of "disloyalty."

Some questions might be raised as to the advisability of encouraging sisters to band together to form a coalition against parental control. The fact that the sisters were all adult rather than young children who are financially, physically, and emotionally dependent on their parents was a determining factor in this intervention. We would refrain from doing this with younger children with whom obedience to parental control is age appropriate.

Rachel's rebellious acts had always been accompanied by enormous guilt, and she therefore failed in each endeavor to become independent. By bringing her rebelliousness out into the open, planning it, condoning it, and scheduling it with the help of her sisters, we stripped off its more toxic aspects. Note that she then chose to rebel in relatively benign ways rather than those destructive to her health and well-being.

The parents returned from their vacation, and I telephoned to let them know we had not forgotten about them but had found the sessions with the sisters so helpful to Rachel we wanted to continue them for a while longer. I assured them they would be involved later on.

In the following sessions, I pushed the sibling alliance further and suggested Sandy teach Rachel how to become self-indulgent since Rachel emulated her father by being rigidly self-denying and frugal. Sandy coached her by instructing her to buy things she would never think of buying, such as expensive perfume, luxurious underwear, silk suits, jewelry, expensive cosmetics, and so on. I warned Rachel against indulging in food, however, and cautioned her against gaining too much weight. I set the limit at what Sandy weighed, nine pounds heavier, and thus, while seeming to restrain her, I actually encouraged her to gain. As they continued to discuss different modes of self-indulgence, some of the suggestions became outrageous, and I joined them in their frivolity and laughter.

The group interrupted to restrain me and to point out that the kind of rebellion I was suggesting was too enjoyable. I agreed with them that it was too soon to stop pushing the unhappiness prescription and I returned with the following message:

PEGGY: (*Looking contrite.*) I have been reprimanded by my group.
SANDY: (*With dismay.*) Again, Peggy? You're doing badly.
PEGGY: Yes, but I can see their point. They feel I got swept away in talking about things that would make Rachel happy, like being self-indulgent, buying expensive perfume, underwear, indulging in sex, because, Rachel, that would make you happy. And your parents would know you were happy.

SANDY: That makes sense to me. Does it to you, Rachel?
RACHEL: It doesn't make sense to me. How does it make sense to you?

SANDY: Because if you're happy, Mummy will do what she did to me. She'll make you want to puke. She'll make more fuss over that than she does over you now. If you're unhappy on your job, you can quit, and that will make them unhappy. As the job goes on, you make a list of all the things that you can complain about, so even if you have some happy moments, don't talk about those. Go home and tell them about all the lousy things that happened to you today, and make their evening miserable, and that will make you miserable too.

PEGGY: Good, good, very good.

At the end of the session the sisters gave the first indication of how they saw me in relation to the group. Although I had consistently told Rachel she must remain unhappy, they perceived me as being on Rachel's side. They picked up the second level of the paradoxical message.

SANDY: You have children, don't you Peggy?

PEGGY: Yes. I have a son, 17, and a daughter, 21.

SANDY: Is your daughter why you keep on wanting Rachel to be happy? Do you identify a little? The group keeps reprimanding you for being too soft-hearted.

PEGGY: I don't know. I'll think about that. It's hard for me to tell Rachel to be unhappy. (*To Rachel.*) Do you know that? (*I reach out a hand and touch her.*) It's hard for me to tell you to be unhappy—but I know they're right. When I think about it and I'm objective, I know that's what you must do.

SANDY: I guess that's what's good about having a group. They keep you objective.

PEGGY: That's right.

Stage VII: Saying No to Therapy

STEP 1: PUSHING THE PRESCRIPTION TO THE BREAKING POINT

This next session was the most crucial session in therapy, marking the turning point of a lasting change. Before Rachel could become a truly independent woman, she had to be able to say no to therapy and to the absurd task we had given her of keeping herself miserable. She had been conscientiously trying to follow it, but she was becoming more and more dissatisfied with living with her parents and remaining unhappy. During this session, I pushed the prescription to the point where Rachel said no to therapy.

PEGGY: (*To Rachel.*) Well, Rachel, are you being unhappy, covering up what is pleasurable? How well are you doing that?
RACHEL: I'm trying to cover up whatever's pleasurable.
PEGGY: Good. How well are you doing in that?
RACHEL: I'm trying to say no to all my mother's suggestions, and I hate it there. (*She cries.*)
PEGGY: You're supposed to hate it there. Of course you hate it there.
RACHEL: I feel so out of it there, I really can't stand it.
PEGGY: You're going to be unhappy as long as you're at home.
RACHEL: So why do I have to be there? I don't want to be there. I have this chance to sublease this apartment and I think I'm going to do it, if it works out.
SANDY: They're telling you to do something and if you're planning to rent an apartment in April you're just not listening again. And just like mother's going to have to be unhappy for a while until things get better, maybe you're going to have to be unhappy for a while.
RACHEL: Why can't I get out of there? I want out.
SANDY: Well, you can't. So it's just too bad.

Rachel moans and groans and ends up looking imploringly at me with big, wet eyes, asking, "Why can't I sublease the place for just six months?"

PEGGY: The harder it is for you now, the better.
RACHEL: I don't understand it and I can't go on like this.
PEGGY: You won't understand it right now.

The sisters supported me and Rachel argued, finally screaming, "I can't stand it, and why do I have to force myself to be there?"

PEGGY: (*Kindly but firmly, like a doctor administering medicine.*) For the time being, the worse it is, the better it will be. The worse it is now and the more unhappy you are, the better it is. So have your sisters been helping you with that?

RACHEL: With being unhappy? No.

SANDY: We were supposed to—if she felt guilty doing something, she would call us.

CLARE: She hasn't been calling me.

PEGGY: How come you haven't been calling your sisters?

RACHEL: Sometimes I don't feel like it because I'm frustrated and I don't like this. I feel like evaluating the situation and how to make things better, and instead I'm told to make things worse, and I can't stand that. I can't go against my instincts any longer.

PEGGY: For the time being, Rachel, you have to make things worse.

RACHEL: Well, I can't, Peggy. I want to go out and get a better job and I want to make myself happy. I can't make myself get a bad job and I can't make myself more unhappy.

SANDY: Is it necessary for her to stay with her present job to make her more unhappy?

PEGGY: She should make herself unhappy in every way possible.

SANDY: Why?

PEGGY: Because only in that way is she going to be able to find herself.

CLARE: She is making my parents so dissatisfied with her they both stood there and smiled at me like dummies, they were so happy to see me. They never did this before. I looked so good in comparison with Rachel.

PEGGY: Don't you appreciate what she's doing for you?

CLARE: Yes. I felt I didn't deserve it.

PEGGY: She's giving you a gift.

CLARE: I guess so, so I shouldn't be mad. I feel guilty when I get mad at Rachel. This is my baby sister.

PEGGY: No. Anything you can do to help Rachel be unhappy is fine.

CLARE: Rachel is so self-involved right now.

PEGGY: But she needs to be self-involved in her unhappiness. She should be totally preoccupied with it.

RACHEL: (Crying.) I can't deal with people on that basis. This totally isolates me from the entire world. It's a ridiculous request to make. How am I supposed to relate to friends when I'm unhappy? Who the hell wants to be with me?

PEGGY: (*Sympathetically.*) I know this is hard.

RACHEL: This is crazy! Not hard—crazy! This means you're asking me to exist alone, to lock myself in my parents' basement and exist alone, because no one is going to want to be with me and I don't want to be with myself when I'm like this. It doesn't give me any reason for doing anything—any purpose for wanting to exist. It's making my existence so much more miserable.

STEP 2: ESCALATING THE THERAPEUTIC TRIANGLE

PEGGY: Let me talk to my group a minute. Maybe they will allow you to do something that will relieve you a little bit. You seem to get into trouble, though, every time I relent . . .

The group decided not to relent but to take a position of consternation in relation to Rachel's rumbling of rebelliousness.

PEGGY: The group says it sounds like you're not only saying no to your mother but you're getting ready to say no to me, and they are quite appalled. Are you saying no to me?

RACHEL: (*Hesitates, and then blurts out.*) Yes, I am. (*Changes her mind.*) Not to you, to the group. (*She is not quite brave enough to risk alienating me, but she feels it's safe to take a position against the group since she knows I have sometimes disagreed with them.*) I'm fed up. I don't know what to do. My human instincts tell me to do something to make things happier, and you people are telling me to be unhappy, and I don't know how to relate to other people on basis.

PEGGY: (*Acting puzzled.*) That was the way you were relating to them for quite a while. Can't you just go back to that? Or stay there?

RACHEL: No, I can't. I can't sit around and complain.

PEGGY: But you have been doing that, so it's hard for me to understand what would be intolerable about it now, since you were doing that for quite a while. What's different about it now?

RACHEL: Because I see it differently now. I see the world is not interested in me and my problems and it's not appropriate.

I dismissed myself to talk to the group, thinking it might be time for me to take a position in favor of change. It is decided I should first explore what Rachel would do if she were allowed to change.

RACHEL: I don't know. All I know is I've really been trying the past few weeks to do what you told me to do and really work at it between sessions, and, Peggy, I can't stand it! And I can't stand living with my parents. I'm regressing.

PEGGY: (*Pursuing the question of change.*) What would happen if you said no to them and me? What would you do?

RACHEL: I'd try to do what the rest of the world does—break away from home, become an adult, get a job, find my own place to live, find my own circle of friends.

PEGGY: (*Challenging her to prove herself.*) But that's just what we're afraid of, Rachel. You know the consequences of that. You know what's happened every time you've attempted to do that. The results have been disastrous for you. You've felt you couldn't do it, felt like a failure, something has always gone wrong, you've felt lonely, isolated, that you were going crazy, the noises bothered you—it was a disaster, and we're trying to save you from that.

The group called me out and we decided it was time for me to side with Rachel against the group and push for change. When given her freedom to go forward, Rachel hesitated. The medicine I had been prescribing, despite its bad taste, was a comfort to her, giving her a sense of security. The sisters also registered some apprehension as to Rachel's ability to assume responsibility for her own happiness.

STEP 3: OPPOSING THE GROUP

I entered the room and asked Rachel to support my opposition to the group.

PEGGY: Rachel, you want to help me say no to the group? I just had a big fight with them. I can't budge them. Let's you and me say no to the group.

RACHEL: (*Tearfully.*) I was afraid when you went out there I was going to hear my sentence for the week.

PEGGY: Are you ready to say no to them with me?

RACHEL: What do they say?

PEGGY: They're adamant. I cannot budge them. They say absolutely you should stay at home. You should be unhappy, should not make your life any better, should stay miserable, isolated, complain, not look for a job.

RACHEL: Forget that. Forget that right there.

PEGGY: (*Extending her hand.*) Thanks, thanks. I told them you had suffered enough, been unhappy enough, said no to Mother enough, and enough is enough. And you have the right, if you feel you can do something different, to try. And I want to say, "Go ahead."

RACHEL: With what?

PEGGY: With whatever you want to do. Whatever you want to do to make yourself happy, and we will know whether or not I'm right or the group is right.

Rachel now had a choice of siding with me by changing or letting the group win a victory by remaining the same.

RACHEL: How about saying no to my parents?

PEGGY: I think you've had enough of that.

CLARE: Can't she say no when she wants to say no?

PEGGY: Oh, that's fine; if you want to say no or if you want to say yes, feel free at this point to do whatever you want to do.

RACHEL: (*Stunned at this sudden shift and not knowing how to respond.*) Are you sincere?

PEGGY: I am.

RACHEL: (*Apprehensively.*) What do they feel I'm going to gain from doing things their way? Because, Peggy, the only thing is that when I'm unsure and don't know what I'm doing I can say, "Well, my therapist told me to do this, so it must be what I'm supposed to do." So I just don't know.

CLARE: You're taking all the supports away from Rachel by saying do whatever you want to do.

PEGGY: You mean you feel the group is right?

CLARE: I would say it's all right to say, "Do whatever you want to do" in certain directions, but I think you're pulling all the props out from under her by putting all the responsibility on Rachel. I feel she's not ready.

PEGGY: What do you think, Sandy?

SANDY: I'm a little bit afraid for her.

PEGGY: Do you think the group's right, too?

SANDY: I think they are too extreme.

PEGGY: Maybe I just had a reaction against them.

SANDY: I think gradually. I look back on her life as being too much at one time and see her doing the same thing again. She'll have too many demands on her and expectations will be too great.

PEGGY: Actually, then, the two of you are taking a position between me and the group.

RACHEL: I'm also taking a position between the two.

STEP 4: SUPPORTING AUTONOMY

I then took the position that Rachel had the right to decide on her own how fast she should change.

PEGGY: I think you're right. My position is extreme. I lost my head and got angry. I admire the fact that you were able to say no to the group and also to me just now, and to stop me from going too far. I think your judgment will guide you now as to how much pleasure and progress you allow yourself.

Her task had been changed from being unhappy and saying no to deciding on how rapidly to say yes. Thus, she was placed in charge of her own change.

Stage VIII: Solidifying Change

STEP 1: ANTICIPATING AND REHEARSING A REGRESSION

Having defied the therapists, Rachel took a giant step toward independence and in the following session described her new life. The group reminded me to schedule a regression in order to solidify change.

Clare and Sandy arrived for the session without Rachel, who was late for the first time having gone for a job interview. Sandy burst out with: "She's so happy. She's always happy. I've been under pressure lately, I've had a lot on my mind, and there's Rachel off being so happy, and I'm saying to myself, 'Goddammit, enough of this already with the smile.'"

PEGGY: That must be quite an adjustment for you.
CLARE: Even my mother and father commented on how happy Rachel is. I'm giving my parents problems now, so it takes the pressure off Rachel.
PEGGY: That's terrific. What kind of problems?

Rachel entered, elegantly dressed and looking radiant.

RACHEL: (*Glowingly.*) I'm having such a good time, Peggy. I can't believe it. I bought myself this silk suit. (*Proudly shows off an elegant and stylish suit.*) A hundred and fourteen bucks. I want to start being really good to myself.
PEGGY: (*Cautiously.*) I'm afraid to be too enthusiastic because of my group.
RACHEL: I'm afraid to be too enthusiastic too. I'm so happy I began to be afraid it wouldn't last. I don't want to be devastated. I haven't been this happy in years.
PEGGY: What's making you so happy?

Rachel spoke excitedly about her new life. She was working on a magazine, getting published, meeting famous people, and doing something for the first time in her life that she really enjoyed. She had a chance to sublet an apartment for six months and was thinking about taking it. She felt she was making less frantic decisions, but looked apprehensively toward the mirror as she said, "I know the group won't like my moving." I said maybe they would change their minds now. She spoke about a new interesting man she was dating who looked like Woody Allen. I asked if her parents would approve of him and she said she was afraid they would. She discussed her problem of saying no to men for fear of hurting their feelings, and I asked her sisters to help her with this since they had had more experience. As I joined them in a humorous and intimate conversation, the group interrupted with a knock on the door and called me out to say they would like to take a position counter to the merriment and begin instead to worry about a regression. Passover was coming up and would probably create tension and conflict as it had last year. Also, Rachel was planning to move again and we could anticipate a recurrence of the former problems.

PEGGY: The group is critical of me again. They feel we're having too good a time. (*The sisters boo.*) They are worried about what is going to happen on Passover or if you attempt to move again.

Rachel said she had already told her mother that she was not going to go to Seder on Passover. I asked her to anticipate her parents' reactions so she could be prepared for the worst. How might they draw her back into the fight between them? How could she deal with her guilt? How would she keep from siding with one against the other? What would happen to father at the dinners when she wasn't there to side with him against mother's family? Rachel replied, "I'll just have to give up that quest to please him." We went over all the possibilities carefully and Rachel said she was confident she could handle them.

Before the session ended I came back with one last warning from the group against premature optimism.

PEGGY: The group is not as optimistic as we are. They anticipate you will get depressed again, and this will probably occur around Passover or if you move. They recommend, therefore, that you deliberately allow yourself to get depressed on those two occasions.
RACHEL: What if I'm not?
PEGGY: Try to feel that way. Try to go back to the way you were feeling or—(*Loud groans and laughter from everyone.*) You don't have to go all the way back.
RACHEL: You don't know what you're asking. I want to be able to deal with these times.
PEGGY: Then practice them.
RACHEL: Okay.

We decided it was time now to involve the parents again as we anticipated they would have a reaction to the new Rachel.

The whole family was convened for this session. Rachel looked stunning with a new hairstyle, new clothes, new makeup, and a radiant expression on her face. She began the interview with:

RACHEL: I'm great. I've never been greater.
PEGGY: Tell me about it.
RACHEL: Number one—I'm in love.
PEGGY: In love? Not with a man? (*Laughter.*)
RACHEL: Yes, with a man—with a really nice man.
PEGGY: Jewish?
RACHEL: (*Chagrined.*) Yes. That's his only drawback, but he didn't want a Jewish woman either, so we decided we'd overlook it. We don't have those attributes we were trying to avoid.
PEGGY: Well, at least it's equal.
FATHER: Maybe you'll both convert. (*Much laughter.*)
RACHEL: He's the one who looks like Woody Allen. Things are working out nicely. He's very kind and sensitive. Lots of fun. He loves me, and I'm living in Manhattan doing publicity work and I have a lot of promising job prospects.

Both parents expressed their pleasure over the changes in Rachel and only once attempted to use her new romance as a focal point for an old argument between the two of them.

STEP 2: REDEFINING THE MARITAL RELATIONSHIP

It was quite clear now that the parents would never have a tranquil relationship but would probably go on fighting for the rest of their days. The important thing was that Rachel was no longer involved in their battles. She managed to stay out of this one and I described the parents' relationship as a profound and lasting bond between two stalwart, equally matched opponents who had strong and differing points of view and felt free to express them on every subject. Since it was their way of making love, they certainly didn't need any interference from anyone outside. Father, surprisingly, agreed, saying, "After all is said and done, we are meant for each other." And mother conceded that there must be something they enjoyed about fighting since they were always doing it.

An appointment was made for one month later, and I stated this would give us time to see if Rachel could stay out of her parents' love making. If she felt her parents needed a third party, she should call one of her sisters and ask them to be the third member. The sisters vociferously declined.

Stage IX: Prescribing a Farewell Ritual

In a presession discussion we decided that if Rachel had managed to maintain her gains, we would ceremonialize her leave taking by prescribing a farewell ritual.

The family reported things were going well and the parents declared it was a relief to have Rachel out of the home as it was more peaceful. The session was spent giving the family credit for the changes that had been made, anticipating future trouble spots, and making some suggestions as to how to avoid them. The session ended with my suggesting they plan a farewell party to celebrate Rachel's becoming a woman and leaving home, and that father should propose a toast to send her on her way. They responded positively and Sandy suggested they have a broomstick for Rachel to jump over, as in Jewish weddings, symbolizing the beginning of a new life.

Follow-Up

A one-, two-, and three-year follow-up revealed Rachel still in good spirits, living alone in her own apartment and loving it, excited about her new career, and dating several different men. The parents were still making love in their characteristic way, but the three sisters were staying out of it.

C H A P T E R 7

Variations on the Style and Form of Interventions

Every family dilemma is different, and the therapist should attempt to match the method of intervening with the particular form of the dilemma. This form is shaped by the special processes that create it, by the system of beliefs that govern it, and by the style and personality of the individuals participating in it.

Although there are broad general categories under which family problems can be classified, each has its own unique set of circumstances. This uniqueness should guide the therapist in designing interventions so that each is custom-tailored to suit the particular form of the problem. For example, a common family constellation is an overly involved mother, a distant father, and a problem child who acts as mediator between the parents. No standard or routine solution for this problem exists. The solution can only emerge from the specific details of how these three individuals come together to enact the scenario. A brilliant hypothesis or an ingenious intervention is of little value if the therapist fails to communicate in a style that is compatible with the family. The importance of speaking to the family in their own vernacular is emphasized by Watzlawick *et al.* (1974) in *Change*: "And the tactic chosen has to be translated into the person's own 'language'; that is, it must be presented to him in a form which utilizes his own way of conceptualizing 'reality'" (p. 113).

Each family's conception of reality is made up of a different mixture of customs, manners, values, and beliefs that distinguishes it from every other family. A literary example of the process an author goes through in attempting to delineate the distinguishing features of a character is portrayed by Virginia Woolf in *To the Lighthouse*. In attempting to describe Mrs. Ramsay, Lily asks herself, "How did she differ? What was the spirit in her, the essential thing, by which, had you found a glove in the corner of a sofa, you would have know it, from its twisted finger, hers indisputable?" (1964, p. 57).

It is this "twisted finger" of family character, the special way in which family members coalesce around a central theme, that is the preoccupation of the therapist in planning solutions. The following three cases illustrate how interventions were chosen to reflect the character, style, and beliefs of the family.

Use of a Fairy Tale

HAPPINESS IS EARNED THROUGH SUFFERING

This is a case in which the therapeutic prescription was given to the family in the form of a fairy tale as this was decided to be the best form for replicating the melodramatic style of the family. Through this make-believe vehicle the therapist mirrored the moral fervor with which the themes of guilt, penance, and suffering were being enacted in the family.

Mrs. Q telephoned our agency requesting help with Robin, her 15-year-old daughter, "because she hates me." Of secondary importance, she also mentioned that Robin was failing in school, suffered from insomnia, threw temper tantrums, and was depressed and generally obstreperous.

In the first session Mrs. Q, accompanied by Robin and her 11-year-old son, Peter, expressed herself in a flamboyant and theatrical manner, complaining she was a nervous wreck because Robin kept her awake all night. Robin claimed she couldn't go to sleep unless her mother was awake because she had nightmares and consequently mother stayed awake until all hours of the night waiting for Robin to fall asleep. If mother fell asleep first, Robin would awaken her. Since Robin was afraid to sleep alone she insisted on sharing her mother's bed with her. Although Mrs. Q believed this was wrong and resented it, she allowed it because otherwise Robin wouldn't be able to get up in the mornings and would fail in school.

Robin constantly attacked her mother during the session, accusing her of being a "bad mother." She blamed her for the divorce, for having robbed her of a father, for having neglected her and her brother by going back to work, and, her latest crime, for getting engaged to a man whom Robin vociferously disapproved of because he was of a different religion. Robin quoted her father frequently to support her complaints against her mother. He had opposed the divorce and constantly implied to the children that Mrs. Q was a bad mother and an immoral woman for having broken up the home. There was a quality of self-righteousness in Robin's complaints, and Mrs. Q defended herself in a way that was tantamount to pleading guilty. Peter periodically tried to support his mother against Robin's attacks but retreated when drowned out.

It soon became clear that the mother had assumed the burden of guilt for all the girl's charges and believed she could only redeem herself by constantly appeasing Robin. In exploring this, it seemed there were no limits to which she would not go. She waited on Robin hand and foot, drew her bath, manicured her nails, did her laundry, straightened her drawers, lavished gifts on her, and so on. The more she tried to atone for what she accepted as her "sins," the more demands Robin made on her, until she would finally explode and either hurl invectives at Robin or strike her physically. At this point, Robin would point an accusing finger, having proven her point that she was a bad mother.

When mother's fiancé, who lived in a neighboring city, came to visit on weekends, Robin forbade her mother to allow him into her bedroom. The fiancé slept on the couch while Robin slept in her mother's room. The fiancé quite naturally resented Robin's control over her mother and was threatening to leave the relationship. The mother was distraught at the thought of losing him, as he was "everything I've ever wanted in a man."

In our group discussion, we all agreed that mother shared the conviction with Robin and her exhusband that she had transgressed and should suffer for her sins. Robin's behavior served the function of providing her with a way of doing penance. We speculated that Mrs. Q could not accept the happiness her fiancé was offering her until she had atoned in some way. Her actions seemed to indicate a profound belief that her happiness had to be earned through suffering. If Robin had stopped provoking her, she would have had no way of earning her happiness since Peter was taking a supportive position in relation to her.

We agreed that a direct approach, such as instructing mother to stop trying to placate her daughter, would probably fail since we would be flying in the face of a treasured belief. It was decided, instead, that we would articulate this belief, the way each family member perpetuated it, and prescribe it through a ritual. We searched for a way to do this within the family's personal universe and hit on the idea of presenting it in the form of a fairy tale. The histrionic style of the family, the absurd way in which penance was being imposed and accepted, the tone of moral rectitude were all reminiscent of the themes running through fairy tales. The therapist told the family that their situation reminded her of a fairy tale her grandmother used to tell her and recited the following story:

> Once upon a time, there was a kingdom by the sea that was ruled over by a wise and just monarch. Now this monarch set very high standards and values for himself and his people and everyone was expected to abide by them. The main rule in this kingdom was that happiness was not free, people had to pay a price for it. The way one paid this price was through suffering, and the suffering had to equal the happiness one was seeking. Everyone honored the law.
>
> Now in this kingdom lived a beautiful woman of royal blood whose husband had gone away to battle and never returned. She was left to raise her son and daughter by herself and she taught them the same high moral values she practiced and believed in. (*Mother begins to cry.*)
>
> One day a prince from a neighboring kingdom came to visit. When he saw the noble woman, he fell in love with her instantly. He wooed her and asked for her hand. She granted it, but told him they must first seek the king's permission. When they went before the king, he said to the noblewoman: "I can see you love this man very much, but before I grant permission to marry him, you must answer one question. Do you deserve this happiness? Have you suffered enough to earn it? The

happiness you envision seems splendid and glorious and your suffering must equal in depth the heights of your happiness." And the noble woman searching in her heart of hearts had to admit that she had not suffered enough to earn her happiness. The king then told her to go home and during the following week find a way to suffer further.

The noble woman returned home and told her children of her plight. She was in great despair as she couldn't think of any way to suffer enough to pay for such great happiness and would have to forego it. But her daughter came to her rescue. She knew that the most terrible thing that her mother could feel was that she had been a bad mother. That night at midnight the daughter pretended that she was a ghost and dressed in a sheet walked back and forth in front of her mother's bedroom wailing, tearing her hair and crying "You have been a bad mother! You have destroyed your children!" (*Robin looks embarrassed and begins biting her nails.*) "If you marry the prince you will abandon your children forever."

The wailing awakened the son who ran to the daughter exclaiming, "How can you do such a thing? You know our mother loves us deeply and has taken wonderful care of us." The daughter whispered, "Hush don't you understand. I'm saving our mother by giving her a way to earn her happiness through suffering." (*Peter and Robin join mother in laughter.*) And the son replied, "What a wonderful daughter you are to do this for mother." The mother, driven to distraction, ran to the window and beat her breasts and screamed into the night "I am a bad mother. I have destroyed my children."

The king upon hearing her screams summoned her to the castle and declared, "At last you have suffered enough. The worst thing a mother can feel is that she has been a bad mother. You have won your happiness and are free to marry the prince." (*Mother is alternately laughing and crying. Robin smiles nervously and bites her nails some more and Peter looks on with amused confusion.*)

The therapist ended by saying that Robin was like the daughter in the fairy tale and seemed to feel her mother had not suffered enough to earn a new chance at happiness. Therefore, Robin should dress in a sheet every night to resemble a ghost and parade up and down in front of her mother's room wailing, moaning, tearing her hair, and berating her mother for having been a bad mother. She should make sure her mother never slept and in the morning her mother should thank her for having made her suffer so she could earn her happiness. Peter should make sure Robin didn't forget.

After a moment's thought Robin responded with, "But then I wouldn't sleep all night." To which her mother replied, "You don't sleep anyway. This would give you something to do."

As the session was ending Robin stated, "I've decided I

don't want to keep my mother awake by walking up and down in front of her door." The therapist asked, "Then how will you make her suffer?" After a moment's careful consideration Robin replied, "I'll just be awful." The therapist asked, "How will you be awful?" She answered, "I don't know." And then earnestly, "I'll make her buy me things—especially, I'll ask her for things she can't afford to give me." Her face lit up with an inspired thought, "I could get sick and I can whine a lot too." The therapist thought that wasn't enough and she should do all those things besides walk up and down. The more the therapist pushed the task the more Robin rebelled. After back and forth negotiations the therapist settled on her parading one night a week.

Before she left Robin reneged on this again saying, "I don't want to do that because I'm so tired now and I'll be too tired because I'm going out Monday." Mother seriously admonished her with, "You're not doing this for yourself, you're doing it for me." To which Robin defiantly responded, "I don't want to do it for you, why should I sacrifice myself for her?" The therapist responded, "Because that is the job of a good daughter."

An appointment was made for a month later, but within three weeks, the therapist received a letter from Mrs. Q informing her that Robin did not want to return for any more family sessions. She stated Robin was suddenly very busy with her boy friend and she hardly ever saw her. She seemed quite happy and was even pleasant to be with sometimes. Mrs. Q ended the letter by saying she and her fiancé were getting married. It was signed, "The Noble Woman."

This is a rare example of a family having instant recoil and not needing follow-up on a paradoxical intervention. We can only speculate that hearing their own story played back to them in an exaggerated form broke the spell that the family had cast upon themselves.

Use of Ceremony

EXORCISING GHOSTS

In the following family, it was not clear until well into the therapy that the theme most relevant to the presenting problem was the presence of ghosts from the past. One of the reasons we missed this initially was because the problem was an ordinary one, common to blended families, and we assumed it would respond to the usual approach of realigning the central triangle. When the family did not respond to this, we realized we had not picked up on the important clues they had given us relating to the past. In exploring this area, we discovered it was a family haunted by two ghosts: one in the form of a dead husband/father, the other in the form of the specter of homesickness. These became forbidden subjects around which secret fantasies, myths, and conjectures were built over the years. Although they were never spoken about, these ghosts exerted a powerful and silent influence on daily interactions and resulted in the presenting symptom. Two ceremonies were used as a means of uniting the family in symbolic acts that demystified the secret fantasies: one, a mourning ceremony given to exorcise the ghost of the dead husband/father, and the other a celebration ceremony given to vanquish the specter of homesickness.

The new husband, Mr. H, requested therapy because of an intense conflict between him and his wife over the handling of Lee, the 13-year-old son of Mrs. H from a previous marriage. In the first session, Mr. H, a tall, imposing black man, stated that he and his wife, Sonia, a Nordic beauty with long blonde hair, loved each other very much and were very happy together except they had disagreed over the disciplining of Lee since the beginning of their marriage. Mr. H felt Mrs. H spoiled Lee and Mrs. H felt that Mr. H was too strict with him. As time went on, each rigidified his/her position, and Mrs. H rushed in to protect Lee whenever she felt Mr. H might harm him either emotionally or physically. This escalated the anger and frustration of Mr. H to the point where he often became physically abusive with Lee. He had no difficulty with Lamarr, Lee's 11-year-old brother. There was a striking difference in the appearance between the two brothers. Lamarr, resembling his mother, was pale-skinned and blue-eyed, while Lee, in sharp contrast, was dark-skinned, with curly black hair.

In gathering their history it was learned that Mrs. H had come to this country from Norway when she was 19 and met and married Leopold, a black man. When Lamarr was 1 and Lee was 3, Leopold joined the merchant marines and several months later was reported missing at sea. He disappeared from the ship and no one found the body. The official report listed his death as "accidental" but from the description of Mrs. H, there was every indication it was a suicide. He was described as being extremely depressed and had been writing letters home about death and the day of judgment. Mrs. H could not accept the idea of suicide and had given herself and the children the explanation that he had blacked out during one of his fits of depression, fallen overboard and hit his head on the side of the ship. Mr. H, Leopold's best friend, came to console Mrs. H and they married a year later.

Mrs. H looked upset when she spoke about these events, and Mr. H reprimanded her for talking about them, telling the therapist, "She wasn't going to come because she knew she would be asked about all this and she didn't want to talk about it again." Mrs. H explained that the years following her husband's death had been extremely traumatic for her as she was left all alone with two young children in a foreign country. She suffered a severe depression and was treated by a psychiatrist for several years. Claiming she had resolved her feelings about the past, she said that it had nothing to do with her present problem and that she would like to deal with that. Mr. H concurred, and although the therapist and group noted the intensity of feelings regarding the past, they decided to respect the couples' wishes for the present and focus on realigning the triangle between Mr. and Mrs. H and Lee. The problem of a natural parent protecting a child from a stepparent is a common one and often responds to direct coaching. Mrs. H was directed to stay out of the arguments between Lee and Mr. H and let them settle them without her interference. Both parents agreed on a disciplinary plan and were more consistent in setting rules and following through on them. However, this had little effect on the intensity of Mr. H's negative feelings toward Lee. He seemed obsessed with criticizing and punishing him.

The team speculated that Mr. H's behavior might be connected in some way with the ghost of Leopold, and the therapist returned to explore this in a session with the parents alone. (It was felt they would feel freer to talk about the incident without the children present.)

In this session, it was discovered that Mr. H believed that Mrs. H was still in love with Leopold, that he was possibly still alive (having swum to an island), and that he might one day knock on their door. If he did, Mr. H believed Mrs. H would go off with him. He felt she was fascinated by the "dark side" of his personality and had been attracted to him because he "crushed" her. Mrs. H was astonished to learn of his fantasies and said they were totally unfounded, that she no longer had any feelings for Leopold, never thought about him, and certainly would never go off with him were he to appear, which she considered an impossibility. Mr. H seemed greatly relieved and said he very much needed to hear all these things. Further questioning of the couples' marital relationship was carefully warded off as they colluded to preserve privacy in this area.

In discussing Lee, the therapist learned that he was the spitting image of Leopold and possessed many of his qualities. This explained the intensity of Mr. H's feelings toward Lee, whom he undoubtedly saw as a reincarnation of Leopold and a threatening rival for his wife's love.

The therapist asked the parents' permission to have a session with the children to explore their thoughts and feelings surrounding their father's death; both agreed.

In this session with the children, it was learned that they too thought their father might still be alive and might look them up one day through the telephone book. They did not think, however, that their mother would go back to him; they hoped she would not, as that would break up the family, in which they were happy.

In a consultation, the therapist and group agreed that the family was still haunted by the ghost of Leopold and that the function this ghost served was to cover up some unaired relationship issues between Mr. and Mrs. H. Mrs. H must be sending Mr. H messages that he was in some way inadequate as a husband, and Mr. H was perceiving this as her carrying a torch for Leopold. His allusion to her being fascinated by the "dark side" of Leopold's personality indicated he felt he lacked a certain fascination that Leopold had held. Mrs. H sounded convincing in her denial of this, but because of her desire to avoid talking about this period of her life as well as her general tendency to avoid painful issues, Mr. H assumed she was still in love with him. He had kept the secret fantasy to himself, and Lee, who resembled Leopold, had borne the brunt of his wrath. The first therapeutic task was to lay the ghost of Leopold to rest, as all other issues were eclipsed by his shadow. Accordingly, a mourning ceremony was designed that involved the entire family. Since the anniversary of Leopold's death fell on Memorial Day, we chose that day for the ceremony. The therapist read the following message to the family:

> The group believes the ghost of Leopold is still very much alive in this family. Since Lee so closely resembles Leopold and is a constant reminder of him, it is little wonder that this causes a problem between Mr. and Mrs. H. We believe that it is important for this family to bury their dead so that they can live in the present, and so Lee can be relieved of his intolerable burden.
>
> We, therefore, suggest that they lay a wreath on the tomb of the Unknown Soldier on Memorial Day and say goodbye to Leopold in a proper ceremony, and that on the anniversary of Leopold's death they commemorate it with a moment of silence.

There was a long pause after which Mr. H said, "My thoughts on this tell me there is some truth in it, and perhaps, this would be very nice. We might even set aside a day every year—sort of an anniversary type thing if you would like and, as I stated before, Leopold is my friend."

The two boys smiled and Mrs. H looked relieved.

The family followed through on the ceremony, elaborating on it in their own way, lighting candles, saying prayers, and recalling fond memories of Leopold on the anniversary of his death.

This ceremony shifted the focus off Leopold and Lee and onto the marital relationship, which, it was discovered, was haunted by yet another ghost—the ghost of homesickness. The therapist learned that Mrs. H had been homesick for her native land, Norway, for many years, and Mr. H harbored a secret fear she would one day return there to live with the children. They had never discussed this openly but it was an ever-present, unspoken issue between them. Mrs. H denied she had any intentions of returning to Norway to live but admitted she had been homesick since coming to this country. She had returned once, found everything changed, and did not want to remain. However, she missed her family, the culture, the music, the food, and customs and was always comparing them unfavorably with those of this country. Mr. H and the children were threatened by her attachment to her homeland

and tried to keep her from talking about it. This prohibition made her feel even more isolated and cut off from her roots, which she deeply resented.

In order to release her from this prohibition, we prescribed another ceremony. We suggested to Mr. H and the children that since mother wasn't going to go back to Norway they must bring Norway to her. We explained that this was likely to make her less homesick rather than more homesick. We recommended that on her birthday, three weeks away, they surprise her by declaring it "Norway Day" and planning a day of Norwegian festivities. The children responded with excitement and delight and Mr. H amicably agreed to oversee the celebration.

The three went all out in their efforts, preparing Norwegian food, decorations, dances, and music, bringing out old records and photograph albums, inviting in Norwegian friends, and arranging a long distance telephone call to mother's family in Norway.

Mrs. H was enormously moved by having her native land honored and her feelings for it acknowledged and condoned by those closest to her. Mr. H and the sons were instructed to continue to allow her to indulge them.

These ceremonies in and of themselves did not solve all the problems between Mr. and Mrs. H, who continued in marital therapy, but they provided a way of bringing the ghosts out of the closet and uniting the family in symbolic acts that banished them. As stated by Selvini Palazzoli et al., "a ritual is meant not only to avoid the verbal comment on the norms that at that moment perpetuate the family play, but to introduce in the system a ritualized prescription of a play whose norms silently take the place of the old ones" (1978, p. 96).

Altering the Invisible Triangle

DON'T TURN OUT TO BE LIKE FATHER

In the following case of a divorced family, the unspoken injunction of the absent mother and the way in which the various family members related to this were chosen as the central focus for the interventions. The group became the medium through which the absent mother's injunction to the 17-year-old son was voiced. The son, by carrying out the injunction, through his provocative behavior had been preventing the family from making a transition from a predivorced state to a postdivorced state. The group, acting as the mother's surrogate, elaborated and prescribed the injunction, while the therapist supported the father in working against it. This planned split between the therapist and group mirrored the split in the family. It escalated the existing triangle to the point where the participants were compelled to realign themselves differently.

The father, Mr. Z, requested help with his son Gordon, because he was uncontrollable and disrespectful, stole money from him, refused to study, and constantly fought with his 22-year-old brother, Stewart.

In the first session, Mr. Z reported that he and his wife had divorced two years earlier and that she had since remarried and moved to California. The two sons had elected to remain with Mr. Z in order to continue their schooling and work without interruption.

Stewart had gone into business with his father and closely resembled him in appearance. Both were respectably dressed, with small trimmed beards and carefully groomed hair. Gordon, in sharp contrast, was sloppily dressed, with long, unkempt hair and a defiant manner. He spoke contemptuously of his father's business, values, and life-style throughout the session.

Stewart assumed the parental role in relation to Gordon and was critical of his father's inconsistent disciplining of him. Mr. Z admitted that he was unable to handle Gordon, knew he was inconsistent, but for some unknown reason couldn't follow through on his disciplining. He constantly abdicated his role as parent, calling his exwife long distance whenever Gordon presented a problem and even enlisting her help in persuading Gordon to come for therapy.

According to Mr. Z, this pattern had taken place during their 20 years of marriage. Mrs. Z had disciplined the children, Mr. Z had "stuck my head in the sand," and Mrs. Z had complained about his noninvolvement. When he did get involved, she criticized his ineptness with statements such as

"You just don't know how to handle Gordon" to which Mr. Z would agree.

Our first hypothesis, formed at the end of the first session, was that Gordon's behavior served the purpose of keeping everyone in the family in their familiar roles around the themes of competence and incompetence. By behaving provocatively, he kept mother in her position as the competent one, father in his position as the incompetent one, and Stewart in his position as the older responsible brother. If Gordon stopped misbehaving they would all have to give up their roles from the family of the past and take on new ones based on the separated family of the present.

If father were to become consistent, Gordon would no doubt respond by respecting him more, but this would affect the way both father and Gordon related to mother, who obviously remained intensely involved in the family. The exact nature of her involvement was unknown at this time, but we speculated she would become upset if the relationship between father and Gordon changed. Our dilemma was reflected in the group's first message:

> Your problem poses a dilemma and has split me from my group. I believe the answer to your problem is a simple one—father, you should assume your role as head of the house, be consistent in your disciplining and follow through with a firm hand. If you did this, I'm reasonably sure that Gordon would respond by giving up his provocative behavior and would grow up to become a mature adult. The group agrees this would be effective and probably produce the desired change but they are afraid there would be consequences which they are not sure you would consider worthwhile. If you did this Gordon would have to give up his job of trying to repair the broken family. Through his misbehavior he keeps everybody in the family as in the past: mother as the strong one who guides father, father as the softhearted one who needs her guidance, and Stewart as Gordon's responsible older brother. This would be a great deal for everyone to give up. Thus the group believes that you, Mr. Z, should continue to be inconsistent so that Gordon can continue to recreate the family from the past.

Mr. Z, who dabbled in psychology and philosophy, was fascinated by the message and after a long silence stated, "That's very deep thinking." The therapist asked him to keep thinking about it and decide whether the group or the therapist was right.

The message reverberated throughout the system and immediately heightened the triangle between mother, father, and Gordon. Father was tougher on Gordon who complained to mother. Mother reprimanded father, who replied by sending a copy of our message to her. Mother responded by taking it to her psychiatrist because she didn't understand it.

Gordon, astounded that his father dared to take action, came to the next session visibly angry and demanded to see the group because he didn't agree with the message. The family was taken behind the one-way mirror and introduced to group. Gordon told them they didn't know enough about the family on such short notice to make such a statement. "I think you are right in a way but you don't know enough about us to make that decision." The group nodded silently in acknowledgment of his feelings.

Back in the interviewing room he asked the therapist if he had to come back for therapy and she referred him to his father who kept turning him back to the therapist who persisted until father finally gave an emphatic yes.

Gordon said he would like to ask his mother if he had to come and reported his many conversations with her since Father cracked down on him. We discovered that not only did Gordon report everything to his mother that father did and said, but mother then passed judgment on his behavior. For many years she had disapproved of the way he ran his business, of his relationship with his extended family, of what she considered to be his conservative and moralistic views on life, and of the way he conducted himself in general.

It became more and more clear that for Gordon to have respect for his father he would have to betray his mother's most cherished beliefs about him. He chose instead to remain his mother's spokesman in the family through his contemptuous attitude toward his father and brother.

Elaborating on the definition of Gordon's behavior as serving to keep everyone in the family in their old familiar roles, the group added a new dimension by stating that it was also his way of reassuring mother he would not turn out to be like father. The therapist entered the session with a suggestion from the group that he call mother every time he misbehaved and tell her about it so she wouldn't worry he was going to follow in father's footsteps and become a conservative. Father was asked not to discuss Gordon's behavior with mother but to leave that entirely up to Gordon as they were sure he could be trusted to report to her accurately. This task put Gordon in charge of reporting his own misbehavior under the positive reframing that it was serving mother and it blocked father from constantly turning to her for advice. The therapist, in opposition to the group, took the position that father should continue to discipline Gordon so he wouldn't need to call mother.

Stewart was astounded at the perceptiveness of the group exclaiming, "That's amazing! Because our mother is always telling us not to turn out to be like father. How did they know?"

The opening dialogue from the next session is reported verbatim to convey the precise affect of the task.

THERAPIST: Well, Gordon, the group would like to know how many times you had to call your mother during this month?

GORDON: I spoke to her a couple of times.

THERAPIST: That's all you misbehaved?

GORDON: I didn't call because I misbehaved. I just called to talk to her.

THERAPIST: You were supposed to call and tell her when you misbehaved.

GORDON: I know but I didn't think I misbehaved.

THERAPIST: (*Incredulous.*) You didn't think you misbehaved since you were last here? (*To father.*) What do you think about that?

FATHER: I'll buy that. (*Stewart supports father with,* "Nothing major.")

GORDON: (*Beaming.*) You perform miracles here! I didn't do anything bad. I tried to behave so I wouldn't have to call my mother.

THERAPIST: But how will she know that you are not going to turn out to be like father then? (*All three laugh.*)

GORDON: Well, he's not that bad—I mean—well, sometimes he's okay. (*He blushes and laughs an embarrassed laugh and then quickly goes on to criticize father.*)

An animated discussion followed in which Gordon alternately admired, condoned, criticized, and condemned his father. Mr. Z managed to hold his own and not back down or apologize.

Once Gordon was more respectful of his father, he was in danger of proving mother wrong and the group decided to address this dilemma with the following message:

> The group wishes to say that now that you are respecting your father more you need to call your mother more often so you can assure her you are still faithful to her. But under no circumstances are you to let her know that father has changed. That would be very upsetting to her because that would mean she was mistaken about him.

Shortly after this session, the therapist received a long-distance telephone call from mother. This had been anticipated as the father had stopped calling her for advice, and Gordon was calling her less frequently to report on the details of his father's life. She stated she wanted to know what was going on because Gordon had reported that his father was treating him unfairly. The therapist explained to her our goal was to help father to take a firm position with Gordon in order to relieve her of the burden she had carried all these years. She said if we could do that it was more than she could ever do but she was afraid he was going too far. The therapist assured her she would try and keep father under control.

In the following session, Mr. Z reported that a new problem had arisen. Although Gordon had been very well behaved in general—had done his chores, been respectful, listened to him, and so on—he was constantly fighting with Stewart. He provoked him by interrupting his telephone conversations, criticizing his appearance, playing his stereo loud when Stewart was trying to sleep, and in every way making Stewart's life miserable.

The therapist and group speculated that since Gordon was respecting his father more he had intensified his feelings of disrespect for his brother. The group commented:

> Since Gordon has given up trying to prove to mother he is not going to turn out like father, he is trying to prove he's not going to turn out to be like Stewart. He should call mother everytime he and Stewart have a fight and tell her how much he disrespects him. This way he will keep the flame of his loyalty burning.

The therapist, disagreeing, stated she thought it was very important for Gordon to respect both his father and older brother, and Gordon stood up and bowed to them with a mock gesture of servitude. The father pretended to be king and the therapist handed him an imaginary scepter and crown saying, "You are indeed the king of the family and should act like one." Much merriment accompanied the play acting.

Father opened the last session with a glowing report on Gordon, using words such as, "unbelievably good," "perfect," "great," "just wonderful." Gordon beamed at the praise and Stewart concurred.

Gordon was about to leave to visit his mother for spring vacation and the final message from the group was that they hoped he would not feel he had to misbehave with mother in order to prove his loyalty to father. Father assured him this would not be necessary.

If the therapist had merely coached father on taking a firm stand with Gordon without dealing with the unspoken injunction, it is doubtful Gordon would have responded to therapy in the way he did. We believe that change was brought about by the combination of supporting father and at the same time voicing the message that undermined his discipline.

C H A P T E R 8

The Use of Paradox in a Medical Setting

ANDREW G. WEINSTEIN, MD

This case was selected for inclusion in this book for two reasons: first, because it deals with an important aspect of medical practice—the non-compliant patient who refuses to follow medical advice; second, because it is an example of how structural and paradoxical interventions can be successfully combined in a pediatric setting. Dr. Weinstein was trained in a structural approach at the Philadelphia Child Guidance Clinic before being assigned to my training group there.

The structural approach, as developed by Salvador Minuchin, is a body of theory and techniques directed toward strengthening the boundaries between the family subsystems: child and parent, parent and grandparent, younger and older siblings. The emphasis is on establishing a family hierarchy, which is accomplished through the active intervention of the therapist within the session. This contrasts with the outside position generally assumed by the therapist in a paradoxical approach, which depends on change taking place outside the session.

With the help of the consultation team, Dr. Weinstein managed to skillfully alternate, and at times combine, the structural and paradoxical approaches, at one point prescribing homeostasis in such a way as to change the hierarchy in the family.

This case is also in answer to the frequently asked question, "Can paradox be used with poor minority families?" The successful use of paradox

Andrew G. Weinstein. Attending Physician, Department of Pediatrics, Division of Allergy and Clinical Immunology, Wilmington Medical Center, Wilmington, Delaware.

depends upon the ability of the therapist to present the intervention within the idiomatic reference of each family. Since this family came to a hospital setting for treatment of a physical illness, Dr. Weinstein wrote a prescription for the symptomatic behavior between the mother and asthmatic son as though it were a medical prescription. All interventions are delivered in the frank, concrete style that characterizes the family.

The successful practice of medicine emphasizes several basic skills. First is the ability to recognize specific disease entities. Second is the matching of the disease state with effective treatment modalities. Third is the ability to help the patient follow through with the above recommendation. Although medical schools are very effective in presenting the first two principles, the third is frequently understated or not even approached. Frequently a patient's symptom persists despite correct diagnostic and therapeutic selections. Patients fail to improve because of a variety of factors. Some may not recognize that they are ill at all. Others prefer not to take medications because they may not believe in them, or they fear toxicity or dependency, doubt efficacy, or lack the funds to purchase them. Still other individuals prefer to maintain the ill state because of secondary gains that may accrue to them. In such cases clinicians are unable to effectively prescribe the most appropriate medical treatment to improve a patient's health.

When dealing with sick children, the clinician not only has to convince the parent (usually the mother) but the child as well to follow medical advice. It is quite common to observe parent–child relationships that have been nurtured during disease and are reluctant to unwind in the presence of help. These cases try the patience of the well-meaning clinician and are frequently referred for psychological counseling. Psychiatrists, psychologists, and social workers often fare no better than the physicians since these families do not follow their directives as well. In such cases paradoxical interventions have been demonstrated to be effective in changing behavior that runs contrary to medical advice.

This chapter will review the course of a family that included a boy with severe chronic asthma. When straight interventions were rejected by the family, a paradoxical approach successfully shifted family relationships that contributed to the illness.

The family to be discussed will be called Smith for reasons of confidentiality. They were black, urban dwellers, and welfare recipients. Mrs. Smith, 32 years old, was separated from her husband, who had disappeared from her life. Her sons, Raymond, 11, and Jeffrey, 15, attended local schools and Raymond was failing. Raymond, the asthmatic patient, earned the respect of the two leading pediatric hospitals in the metropolitan Philadelphia area, where he had accumulated more than 40 hospital admissions for severe asthma. Six months prior to the family interviews, the family enrolled Raymond in the Children's Hospital of Philadelphia Allergy Clinic where I did my fellowship training. I was also enrolled in the extern program, a family therapy training program at the Philadelphia Child Guidance Clinic (PCGC) where I was supervised by Peggy Papp. A total of five family interviews were conducted between December 12, 1977, and June 12, 1980, with Peggy Papp and five fellow trainees observing and commenting from behind the one-way mirror.

First Session

PRESENTING PROBLEM

The Smith family made an appointment to PCGC because Raymond had demonstrated immature behavior in school. His teacher was concerned about his inattentiveness and playfulness in class. Mrs. Smith had been aware of this babyish behavior at home for many years. However she was not certain of its etiology. Until shortly before seeking therapy she had believed that Raymond's symptoms were related to the medication and illness itself. She had been told by many physicians that the medication prescribed for Raymond caused shakiness and/or hyperactivity, and she had initially accepted these behaviors as an unpleasant trade-off for the benefits of the medicine. But she began to question this interpretation when she found out that he wasn't taking the medication and his behavior persisted.

During our first session she stated:

I can't use his asthma as a crutch any longer. I can't. I've done it until I'm just fed up. I've used excuses, excuses not only to him but to other people and myself.

Now the doctor put me on tranquilizers again Saturday and I'm up to here with it. This has got to stop. And I can't blame it on nothing but him.

DR. W: What do you think is going on?

MRS. S: Like, he take advantage of his asthma. Like, he know he can get sick. If he don't want to do something, he'll probably take advantage of his sickness and go ahead and do it.

DR. W: What do you mean? He knows that he can get sick?

MRS. S: Yes, to get what he want.

DR. W: What do you think he wants?

MRS. S: When I don't give him a lot of attention, he get sick.

DR. W: How is that?

MRS. S: He just get sick.

DR. W: In the room? In the house without a cold?

MRS. S: Yes.

DR. W: Without a dog running in front of his nose?

MRS. S: We don't have a dog or cat. We don't have no cats, no dogs, no dust.

DR. W: So, nothing will provoke it you think except if you don't give him attention?

MRS. S: Most of it's attention. Psychological.

DR. W: Have you noticed that too, Jeffrey? Do you feel if you ignore him he'll get sick? Is that what you're concerned about?

JEFFREY: Uh-huh.

DR. W: And you feel compelled to spend a lot of time with him as a result of that?

MRS. S: I feel I should.

It is well known that wheezing symptoms can be deliberately induced by the patients themselves. This is frequently seen in infants with asthma who provoke wheezing after crying. The severity of the symptom is based on the degree of allergenicity of the child. These children learn at a very young age their ability to control the family with their wheezing. The family, when confronted with such blackmail, usually backs down for fear of making the child ill. Such was the situation in this family.

It was clear that Raymond's brother, Jeffrey, had been given parental status in the Smith family. Mrs. S divided responsibility in caring for Raymond between herself and Jeffrey. His responsibility extended to nearly all phases of family life, including medication administration. The family was strained financially and short of manpower. When asked whether he liked caring for Raymond's health, Jeffrey replied no! However, Mrs. S interrupted him:

> Well, see whether Jeffrey like it or not, this is a fact. That we know that if he don't take his medicine, he's going to get sick. He knows it and I know it. I can't be there all the time. I have to go to the store, I go to church on Sundays, sometimes he goes with me sometimes he don't. If I am going somewhere at night and I am not going to be back at nine I say Jeffrey make sure he takes his medicine. Now Jeffrey it's like a job to him. He'll even say, "Raymond better take your medicine." . . . How do you think I feel. I go to bed, I have to make sure he takes it at nine, do you know that automatically I jump up the second time at night to make sure he has his medicine? Then I get up at six in the morning because I have to get them ready for school. My rest is broken completely around the clock. I don't go back to bed and take naps. So he has to learn and he has to realize that it's not just him. It's everybody.

The family schedule was organized around Raymond taking his medicine. However it was discovered that despite the family's effort, Raymond was not taking his medicine. Following a prescribed treatment plan is an essential component for successful management of an illness. It is not unusual for individuals to maintain their symptoms by neglecting to take their medication. But it is important for the clinician to know whether the persistence of the symptom is secondary to allergy or is the result of noncompliance with the drug regimen. Mrs. S continued:

> Let me tell you what he did. Oh I really went off. This morning I wasn't in the room when he took his medication and I said, "Jeffrey, make sure Raymond takes his pills." He caught him putting his medicine in his pocket, so a few weeks ago, I was washing the clothes. I usually unload his pockets because he brings things to the washing machine—you

know cars and different things, so I started going in his pockets and I found pills in his pockets, so I put them on the table and asked him, "Why are these pills in your pocket?" He said he didn't know.

I excused myself from the family to have a consultation with my training group and we discussed the following pertinent points:

1. Raymond had not been taking his medicine on a regular basis and this could account for persistent wheezing symptoms.
2. Both his mother and Jeffrey were overprotective toward Raymond because of fear of sudden and severe asthma attacks.
3. Raymond has the ability to bring on wheezing symptoms at will and thus controls the family.
4. The continuance of Raymond's infantile behavior is thought to be related to the function it serves in the family and is not secondary to the disease itself or the medications taken.

On the basis of this information we formulated the following hypothesis: Raymond's asthma was serving to keep him close to his mother and providing him with a reason for not growing up; it kept mother constantly involved with him, giving her a reason for not working and establishing a life of her own; and it kept Jeffrey in the role of father rather than brother and ensured his continuing presence in a tight-knit threesome.

The group thought it important to know what the repercussions would be if any of these positions were changed. Together we discussed an intervention to test this. It was decided to use Jeffrey to get Raymond out of the house and to loosen the bond with his mother. Since Jeffrey was interested in sports, he could take Raymond with him and slowly initiate him into his games.

When this was suggested to the family, Mrs. S rejected the idea vehemently, saying that this approach would result in more wheezing. Jeffrey, on the other hand, supported the intervention, stressing the need for Raymond to be out of the house more. Raymond was ambivalent. Following my suggestion, the interchange went as follows:

DR. W: I was thinking along the lines of the two brothers getting together.

JEFFREY: You see what he trying to say.

MRS. S: No, but see if he got sick, then I wouldn't be there.

JEFFREY: It sounds like the doctor is saying get out there and play like everybody else. That's what wrong with you. Don't worry about it too much.

MRS. S: I worry too much.

JEFFREY: You have to slow down and let him go ahead and do things.

RAYMOND: I'm always resting.

JEFFREY: You all fear too much.

RAYMOND: Yeah, I'm always resting, resting. She don't let me get into that active stuff. I ain't used to it and I get sick. Like I rest, I rest, I rest, but if I get active—maybe I get used to it.

I interrupted and requested an exercise challenge supervised by myself in the hospital to concretely determine its effect on his asthma. This demonstration would definitely define Raymond's capabilities to run and would be done in the safest of environs. Mrs. S reacted negatively to the suggestion.

I returned to the consultation group somewhat disappointed with the family's reaction to my suggestions. Mrs. S had blocked me at every turn. In discussing the family's response with the team we hypothesized that Mrs. S was afraid of being left alone if Raymond went with Jeffrey. Since Mrs. S had not responded to the direct approach of attempting to defuse her relationship with Raymond, we decided to give the family a paradoxical message.

Returning to the session, I told them that after meeting with my colleagues, I had decided that my idea of having Jeffrey initiate Raymond into sports was not a good one because Raymond would no longer be tied to his mother's apron strings and there was every indication that both mother and Raymond felt he was too young not to be tied to his mother's apron strings. I wrote a prescription on a pad and handed it to Raymond. The prescription read: "Raymond is to have no exercise and is to remain very close to mother." All three looked dumbfounded. Jeffrey was the first to respond: "What about school gym?" I replied, "No exercise and stay as close to mother as possible, O.K.?" I made an appointment for a month hence and ended the session.

Second Session

Four months passed before the second family session was conducted. Appointments were broken either because of weather, flu, or on one occasion because Mrs. S had a miscarriage. During this time I spoke with Mrs. S several times on the telephone and learned that Raymond defied my prescription by exercising at school during recess and gym. I asked Mrs. S to have him return to my plan.

I saw Raymond once in January at the Allergy Clinic. He had had only two mild wheezing episodes, neither necessitating emergency care. He had had no school absence since December.

The family came to the clinic on April 10 because his teacher again had complained that he was inattentive in school and had shown poor self-control. I had spoken with his teacher several times and she described his behavior as immature, nothing to indicate brain damage or learning disability. Mrs. S was reluctant to accept immaturity as the only explanation. She wondered if he had a learning problem. Jeffrey on the other hand supported my definition and I used him as an advocate for more independence for Raymond.

DR. W: Look, Jeffrey, you think your brother has a problem with self-control?

JEFFREY: Nope.

DR. W: O.K. Why do you think that?

JEFFREY: Because, he knows how to use self-control. He just play a lot, that's all.

DR. W: He plays a lot?

JEFFREY: She always make it sound like there's something wrong with him. There ain't nothing wrong with him.

DR. W: So, he doesn't have a learning problem or learning disturbance or anything like that?

JEFFREY: Nope.

DR. W: He just likes to play.

JEFFREY: Yeah, yeah.

DR. W: Right, so he can learn just as well as anybody else can learn.

JEFFREY: That's right.

Turning to Raymond I asked if he had followed my prescription of no exercise. He stated he had not.

RAYMOND: One thing went wrong.

DR. W: One thing went wrong?

RAYMOND: I couldn't stay in the house.

DR. W: You mean you didn't follow the directions?

RAYMOND: Only one direction I didn't follow.

DR. W: What direction was that?

RAYMOND: Staying with my momma and stay around the house.

Raymond had persuaded his mother to let him play outside and subsequently convinced his teacher that he was permitted to go to recess and gym. Mrs. S had tried to follow my instructions of keeping Raymond from exercising, but Raymond and Jeffrey had rebelled. The result was that Raymond began spending more time away from his mother and became physically more active. I supported Mrs. S and scolded Raymond for not following my prescription. This aroused Jeffrey's anger and he opposed me openly and defended his brother. I used his opposition to debate the issues of change versus homeostasis within the family. I continued to defend Mrs. S's right to infantilize Raymond against Jeffrey's insistence that he be allowed to grow up. The debate that follows points out the family issues involved in Raymond's acting more normally. Mrs. S continued to reprimand Raymond for disobeying doctor's orders despite the fact that she herself had reneged one day and allowed him outside.

MRS. S: I said no, the doctor said no until he sees you again. One day I did it. And then you went to school and told the teacher you could have recess.

DR. W: He said he could do what?

RAYMOND: She let me go outside.

MRS. S: When she said Raymond are you sure that your mother said you could have recess, you said yeah. I didn't tell you you could go to school and go outside. I told you that the doctor said no. I made a mistake, but I told him I let you go outside and he told me that I shouldn't have did that. And I didn't do it no more and that was it.

DR. W: Did he go outside?

JEFFREY: I don't know.

MRS. S: You remember that nice day it was real nice out.

RAYMOND: That hot, hot, hot day.

MRS. S: It was on a Saturday.

DR. W: Oh, you went outside that day?

JEFFREY: Yah. What's wrong with that?

MRS. S: That one day, but the rest of the days he wasn't permitted out.

DR. W: He's not supposed to do that.

JEFFREY: Why?

DR. W: Your mother is very concerned and she needs to see him to make sure that he won't run and wheeze.

JEFFREY: Well, he was alright in front of me.

DR. W: No, she didn't want that to happen. You remember she wouldn't even want him to run in the hospital. Do you remember that?

JEFFREY: Who said he's going to run? He can go outside and play. He can't stay in the house all the time.

DR. W: He was not allowed to go outside and play.

JEFFREY: Why not?

DR. W: Because if he plays, then he might wheeze and go to the emergency room. You know how concerned your mother is. If anything happens to him, how much she's easily upset.

JEFFREY: He should know when he ought to stop.

DR. W: He's too young.

JEFFREY: He ain't too young.

DR. W: He is too young. He can't even behave in school.

JEFFREY: I know. I tell him, I tell him. I tell him myself.

DR. W: It's not your job. It's your mother's job.

MRS. S: I'm sorry, but I'll tell him.

DR. W: It's your mother's problem.

JEFFREY: No. Why can't he play?

DR. W: Because. Ask your mother why he can't play.

JEFFREY: No, I ain't going to ask her.

DR. W: Ask her. She's your mother.

RAYMOND: My mother said it's really up to me.

DR. W: She said it was up to you? Are you speaking up? I mean, your brother has been doing all your talking up to now, and I think that the reason he was doing all your talking for you is because you're too young to speak up for yourself. How old are you?

JEFFREY: Eleven.

DR. W: You see, just like that he answers for you.

RAYMOND: Eleven and a half.

I continued to insist that the decision for Raymond's well-being lay solely with Mrs. S and since she needed Raymond to remain young everyone, including myself, had to bow to her authority. By taking this homeostatic position I changed the hierarchical organization of the family, establishing Mrs. S as the parental authority and Jeffrey as an older brother rather than the father.

DR. W: It's your mother's responsibility. She is very concerned about your brother's illness. She feels that it's very important that she and Raymond stay together. In fact (to Raymond), I want you to move your chair closer to your mother right now.

JEFFREY: Hold on.

DR. W: No, not till he moves his chair.

JEFFREY: You move the chair. That's what's wrong with you all. Know what's wrong with you?

DR. W: No.

JEFFREY: You all baby him too much, can't do this. What are you saying?

DR. W: That's your mother's problem. You are strictly the older brother.

JEFFREY: That's right I'm older.

DR. W: O.K. It really doesn't matter what you say at all.

JEFFREY: If it don't matter why am I here?

DR. W: (*To Mrs. S.*) Why don't you tell him who is the head of the family?

MRS. S: We all are.

JEFFREY: Well if it don't matter to me, what am I doing here? You got to discuss the whole thing.

DR. W: Well, I'm sorry. A parent decides what's appropriate and passes it along to the little children.

JEFFREY: Yeah, and I'm just giving a little advice that's all.

DR. W: You can give advice, but it's her decision. And right now, your mother is most comfortable with having Raymond as close to her as possible.

JEFFREY: Yeah, but he wants to change.

DR. W: No, I'm serious. I'm concerned about how your mother feels.

JEFFREY: That's dumb.

DR. W: It's not dumb.

JEFFREY: If it ain't dumb, saying something like you stay in the house all day.

DR. W: He can walk around outside, but he is not permitted to play unless it is O.K. with his mother. (*To Mrs. S.*) This is not Jeffrey's job.

MRS. S: Jeffrey's the father.

DR. W: He's the father?

MRS. S: (*Laughing.*) All right, stop, stop, all of you stop. But he is, he is.

DR. W: Is he the biological father?

MRS. S: No, he's just the father of the house, O.K.

JEFFREY: Why are you putting all this pressure on her?

DR. W: Am I putting pressure on you?

JEFFREY: I'm just saying, you putting a lot . . .

DR. W: Is this pressure to you?

MRS. S: I don't know, I don't know.

DR. W: Your mother doesn't look like she's withering.

Jeffrey was reluctant to let go of his parenting status whereas Mrs. S was reluctant to assume hers. She was also reluctant to let go of Jeffrey as her principal helper. She had been listening to the dialogue between Jeffrey and myself with comprehension and amusement and in the following excerpt indicated she had received the message and asked for guidance.

MRS. S: No, what I'm trying to say is, if you have a problem and someone knows what the problem is, I mean, then the next step is to deal with it. Like if you do wrong and you get caught, don't tell me what I done wrong. I know what I did wrong. Tell me how to get out of what I done. Now, that's what I want to know here. I want to know what to do with him.

This was a direct request for advice and I responded accordingly with direct advice.

DR. W: All right, I want you to tell Jeffrey right now you can handle Raymond and things will be O.K. Could you do that? Go ahead.

MRS. S: I can handle it. Wait a minute. I can handle it and Raymond will be alright before you know that.

I congratulated her and ended the session.

Third Session

The third session focused more on Jeffrey than Raymond. Since Raymond had had no wheezing for the past two weeks the group was uncertain what Jeffrey would do once he had lost his job as father. Mrs. S stated there had been ongoing discussions of Jeffrey's role at home since their last visit. She described him as having now taken on the job of father to the younger children on the block who played in the street.

During a break in the interview, while I discussed the case with the consultation group, Mrs. S began cautioning Jeffrey about getting serious with a neighborhood girl. It was clear that she feared an early marriage. The hidden message was that she wanted Jeffrey to remain close to her. At an earlier meeting, Mrs. S was distressed that he might go to college out of state in three years. Once she had released him from his job of parenting, she was afraid he might leave home altogether. Since she was letting go of Raymond she feared abandonment by both her sons. The group responded to her plight by suggesting that Jeffrey act the age of Raymond so Mrs. S could continue in her role as a mother.

DR. W: The group was listening to the conversation between the two of you and they're worried about what will happen to you, Mrs. S, if both boys begin to move away from home. And their suggestion is directed toward you, Jeffrey. They felt that since Raymond is growing up, getting closer to his peers, and getting away from mother they think it might be best for Jeffrey to act Raymond's age—11—so mother will have someone to take care of.

JEFFREY: Get out of here!

DR. W: (*To Mrs. S.*) Because it seems that you like to be very close to your family maybe it would be best for him to act younger so he could stay close to you. Since he's been like a father to Raymond this would be his last act of helping him.

The reaction of the family members ranged from confusion on Raymond's part, to indignation on Jeffrey's part, to amusement on Mrs. S's part. She indicated she got the message by declaring through her laughter, "All right, All right, you made your point, now stop."

I then discussed alternate ways for Mrs. S to preoccupy herself, such as spending more time with her boy friend, getting a job, making friends, finishing her education. She claimed she would enjoy having more time to herself and could find plenty of things to do with it. "I don't have a lonely problem." To prove this she began to assert herself concerning an after-school program for Raymond at the clinic. Raymond was ambivalent and Jeffrey was against it. She acted in favor of the program, shutting Jeffrey out of the conversation. She then began to follow my lead, putting pressure on Raymond to give up his immature behavior.

DR. W: So, I think we should try it once again. Ask him how old he is and then ask whether he is ready now to attend the after-school program.

MRS. S: How old are you?

RAYMOND: Eleven.

MRS. S: How old do you think you are?

RAYMOND: Eleven.

MRS. S: You want to get into this program?

RAYMOND: Yes.

MRS. S: Tell the doctor that.

RAYMOND: I want to get into the program.

MRS. S: No, no, take your hands off your face and look him in the face and tell him.

RAYMOND: I want to go to the child guidance program.

MRS. S: I can't hear you and I don't understand you because you got your throat clogged up. Talk like you would talk when you want something from the store.

RAYMOND: I want to join the child guidance program.

DR. W: I think my friends [referring to the group] are doubtful whether you really mean it, Raymond, but we'll see.

Fourth Session

The fourth session took place one month later. There was a backlash to the changes taking place in the family. Raymond had been hospitalized for severe wheezing two weeks earlier. At this session a blood drug level determination was done and a few days later the result showed Raymond to have asthma medication in his system. Noncompliance with the treatment regimen was not a factor at this time.

In consultation with the training team we concluded Raymond's recurrence of asthma was a reaction to loosening the bond with his mother and that both had become anxious about this. The team instructed me to define the problem as Raymond's worrying about his mother's mental health now that he was acting 11 years old.

DR. W: But what they're really concerned about is how you're going to feel when Raymond assumes his 11-year-old role.

MRS. S: I just have to deal with it. Like I deal with everything else.

DR. W: Can you tell him that so he understands that and he doesn't have to worry? Because I'm sure he's doing a lot of worrying about you.

MRS. S: You shouldn't worry about me. You shouldn't because see you got to hurry up and grow up so you get married and have some kids.

She strikes a bargain with Raymond: It will be O.K. for you to leave me if you provide me with grandchildren to take your place.

Fifth Session

The last session took place three weeks later. Raymond had no wheezing symptoms. He was given more responsibility for his medication and began checking off the times he had taken it on the calendar. Mrs. S was responsible for auditing the calendar. This was significant progress from the former method of standing over him and watching him swallow. At the beginning of the session a drug level was taken. It was later found to be present.

The family was brighter in appearance. Jeffrey had become less involved with family life and had returned to his girl friend. Mrs. S had begun to spend more time with her boy friend. She now perceived Raymond as being 11 years old. So did I.

Dr. W: How old do you see him?

Mrs. S: Well, I don't know because now I don't see him that much. He don't spend nearly as much time with me anymore. Now he tapes, he has a tape recorder, he tapes. He's an artist you know. He does that. I don't see him that much.

I left the Children's Hospital of Philadelphia in July 1978. As of September 1980, Raymond had continued to do well at the Allergy Clinic. He was hospitalized only one time, again in May. During this two-year period he had two emergency care visits for wheezing. He missed 10 days of school. There was only one theophylline level measurement in 1980 and that clearly demonstrated that he had been fully compliant. I was unable to arrange a follow-up family interview, so I have no information about the family situation. However, the above data do support the thesis that behavioral interventions can have persistent benefit after they are withdrawn.

In summary, there are many reasons patients don't follow medical advice. Through understanding the family relationships surrounding the individual, strategies can be devised to promote adaptive change. Paradoxical interventions can be effective when straight directives are not followed. Behavioral skills can greatly enhance the quality of medical practice.

C H A P T E R 9

Treating Couples

The criteria used to decide when to see a couple rather than the entire family vary widely among therapists. Some systems therapists such as Murray Bowen prefer to work only with the couple even when a child is problematic, believing he has more leverage in changing the system through the parents and that this change will automatically filter down to the children. Other therapists, such as Donald Bloch, include the children for at least several sessions in marital therapy using the interactions with the children to illuminate the problems in the marriage.

Most therapists base their decision on the circumstances of each individual case, on their evaluation of the problem and the best way to approach it. It is impossible to do marital therapy with two people who do not want to explore their relationship, though the therapist may believe the problem in the child is inextricably connected with the marital strife. Beginning therapists often reinforce resistance by prematurely attempting to focus on the marriage when the primary concern of the parents is still that of the child. Until the couple can see how the marital problem is connected with the symptomatic behavior they have no incentive to examine their relationship.

It is not unusual, however, for parents to request couples counseling at the end of family therapy after the smoke created by the children dies down and their own problems come into sharper focus. Occasionally, but less frequently, a couple will request marital therapy, even though the children are having problems, as they feel incapable of dealing with them while they themselves are unable to communicate with one another.

The children may then be brought in at a later date when the tension between the couple has been reduced. Family and marital sessions are sometimes alternated, thus widening or narrowing the therapeutic focus according to the size of the system under observation.

In the couples therapy that will be described here, the presenting request was for marital therapy, and the therapist and couple agreed that the marital problem took precedence over any other family problem. No children or in-laws were included in the sessions.

The concepts and techniques involved in this treatment are illustrated through the presentation of three cases from a couples group and one case from the Brief Therapy Project.[1] Although all of the concepts and techniques that follow may be used effectively with individual couples and families in different settings, I have chosen to write about them within a context of a couples group and the Brief Therapy Project where they are highly structured and easier to describe.

In forming a couples group, the major criteria for selection are a definition of the presenting problem as a marital problem and a commitment and ability on the part of the couple to work on their marriage for 12 sessions without any foreseeable interruptions. Couples not included are those who might need emergency care, namely, those for whom acute alcoholism might necessitate a detoxification program; those prone to physical violence who might require police protection; those whose extreme antisocial behavior might require a possible court referral or hospitalization, and so on. These cases require the therapist to keep options open for a high degree of maneuverability with respect to time and the use of other agencies.

Couples who are separated or actively considering separation are not included as their motivation for examining their marriage is fitful and would be disruptive to a group. Although it is true that most couples entering therapy have some doubts about continuing their relationship, the degree of uncertainty and how it is handled is important.

---

[1] The description of the couples group is revised from "Staging Reciprocal Metaphors in a Couples Group," *Family Process*, 1982, *21*, 453–467, and is reprinted by permission of Family Process, Inc.

The group is mainly composed of couples with ingrained, long-standing, repetitive patterns of interaction, such as constant tension and fighting, lack of communication, unbridgeable distance, chronic jealousy, infidelity, sexual problems, or symptomatic behaviors, such as recurring bouts of depression, phobias, or psychosomatic complaints.

Regardless of what form the problem takes the therapist looks for the reciprocity in the relationship and the central theme around which it is organized. Reciprocal arrangements in marital relationships have been observed and written about extensively for many years by therapists of diverse persuasions. The phenomenon of the hysterical wife married to an obsessional husband or the overly responsible husband married to the irresponsible wife or the mentally or physically ill wife relying on the strong healthy husband has been variously described as "interlocking collusion" (Winch, Ktones, & Ktones, 1954), "bilateral reciprocity" (Dicks, 1959), "need complementarity" (Mittelmann, 1944), "hidden contracts" (Sager, 1976), "patterns of reciprocal overadequacy and inadequacy" (Bowen, 1978), or "unconscious deals" (Framo, 1982). The genesis of the reciprocity is attributed to different sources depending on the therapist's theoretical orientation. Mittelman, coming from a psychoanalytic perspective, has classified marital relationships based on complementary interaction of mates as follows (described by Nadelson, 1978): "The patterns include: one partner emotionally detached, the other craving affection; rivalry between the partners for aggressive dominance; one partner helpless, the other ostensibly strong, but in reality seeking the dependent role." He postulates that the dependent spouse "feels safer with a strong mate while the 'stronger' supporting partner allies his or her unconscious fear of helplessness and abandonment by helping" (p. 112).

The same form of reciprocity has been described in systems terms by Haley and Madanes as one spouse taking the helpless position in order to control the other spouse and balance the hierarchical power structure.

Bowen and Framo see the reciprocity in a historical context, with Bowen ascribing it to levels of immaturity. According to Bowen, individuals tend to choose marital partners who have achieved an equivalent level of immaturity, and their relationships fall into patterns of reciprocal overadequacy and inadequacy. Framo ascribes the reciprocity to collusive mate selection: "I have postulated that mate selections are made with profound accuracy and, collusively, in two-way fashion. The partners carry psychic functions for each other, and they make unconscious deals: 'I will be your conscience if you will act out my impulses'" (1982, p. 124).

This reciprocity is not always problematic and indeed a certain degree is necessary for a complementary coexistence. It only becomes problematic when the reciprocal arrangement is thrown off balance in some way. The triggers for upsetting this balance are numerous and may come from either inside or outside the marital system. For example: A husband may be transferred by his business firm to another city, necessitating the wife's moving away from her extended family. The reciprocal arrangement of "I will be a good wife to you as long as you allow me to remain a good daughter to my parents" is no longer viable. The unspoken agreement has been broken and tension escalates around the theme of family loyalties.

Or the escalation may come from within the relationship, as one or the other spouse becomes dissatisfied with the way the reciprocity is being negotiated. For example: The original arrangement of student versus teacher may be upset if the spouse who is assuming the role of the student begins to resent the authority of the teacher. The teacher's characteristic reaction is to increase his/her efforts to restore authority, which increases the student's rebellion and an escalating cycle of interaction occurs. The couple usually seeks therapy when the cycle has escalated beyond the point of endurance for one or the other or both.

In this approach to couples therapy the therapist is not concerned with the genesis of the reciprocity but with the central emotional theme around which it is currently organized and with how the couple negotiates to maintain their reciprocal positioning. By "central theme" is meant a highly charged emotional issue that is shared by the couple and around which their most problematic transactions occur. Most of these transactions do not take place on the apparent or verbal level of the relationship but on the ulterior level.

Over the years in my search to comprehend this level I have experimented with defining the marital relationship metaphorically rather than literally. Metaphors provide a gestalt in which disassociated facts and events can be seen in relation to one another. Explanatory language tends to isolate and fragment, to describe one event followed by another in a linear fashion. Figurative language tends to synthesize and combine, uniting different levels of thought, feeling, and behavior in a holistic picture that gives the therapist a circular perspective. Watzlawick describes the language of change as "the language of imagery, of metaphors, of *pars pro toto*, perhaps of symbols, but certainly of synthesis and totality and not of the analytical dissection" (1978, p. 15).

In the following format for a couples group, metaphors are projected into concrete forms and staged so that perceptions, behaviors, and interaction are linked simultaneously. The staging of the metaphors is called couples choreography and is a derivative of sculpting, which has been written about extensively in family literature (Duhl, Duhl, & Kantor, 1973; Papp, Silverstein, & Carter, 1973; Papp, 1976a, 1976b, 1980; Simon, 1972; Satir, 1972).

Couples Choreography

The choreography is introduced in the following manner: The couples are asked to close their eyes and have a dream or fantasy about their spouse and to visualize him/her in whatever symbolic form he/she would take in a dream or fantasy. They are then asked to visualize what form they themselves would take in relation to their partner's form to assure that the fantasy will be systemic as well as symbolic. Next they are asked to imagine what movement or dance would take place between these two forms, given the problems they have described. Following this, they are asked to enact the fantasy physically with one another. The therapist guides them through the enactment, asking them to particularize the details of time, setting, mood, and movement. As the picture unfolds, the therapist keeps in mind the following four questions:

1. What is the central theme around which the problem is organized?
2. What are the reciprocal perceptions and positions of each spouse in relation to this theme?

3. What is the cycle of interaction that results from their negotiations to maintain their reciprocal positions?
4. What will be the consequences of change?

The choreography robs the couple of their familiar verbal cues by changing the medium of expression from words to images, movements, space, and physical positioning. It penetrates the confusing morass of verbiage that often sidetracks both couple and therapist—the superficial details, irrelevant facts, and repetitious recountings—and reveals the ulterior level of the relationship. (Gregory Bateson states, "A dream is the only part of you that cannot lie.") What emerges is a living, moving picture in which complex relationships are condensed into simple, eloquent images uncensored by logic. The images, beyond barren explanation and causal links, are highly idiosyncratic and invariably complementary (King Kong and Fay Wray, David and Goliath, a cop and a criminal, a log and a fire). Physical enactments of the fantasies put the relationship into motion. The true nature of a relationship can be seen only in terms of movement as it is always in flux.

The choreography is not only used in the first session as a diagnostic tool but throughout therapy as a barometer of of change. When the fantasies are seen sequentially and compared, they reveal more precisely than words how positions and perceptions have shifted.

The Structure and Use of the Group

Each couple is seen for one evaluation interview prior to admission to the group to determine if the presenting problem is primarily a marital problem (as opposed to one involving a symptomatic child or other family member). If they qualify, they are told the group will meet for 12 sessions, that it will be problem focused, action oriented, that tasks to do at home will be given, and that the sessions will be video-taped and occasionally played back. The group is composed of three or four couples and the membership remains consistent for the 12 sessions. No new couples are added once the group begins.

The first session begins with a brief getting acquainted period in which each spouse gives a verbal description of the problem as he/she sees it. The rest of the two-hour session is devoted to the enactment of the fantasies, and each person is requested to participate in their spouse's fantasy whether they agree with it or not.

The therapist does not comment on the choreography or give any tasks at the end of the first session but waits to review the video tape with an eye toward understanding the connections between the fantasies. During the second session excerpts from the video tape are played back to the group. This video replay is not for the purpose of gaining "insight"; rather it serves to further familiarize the couples with their reciprocal images so the therapist can speak to them in the language of their own metaphors.

Group interaction is kept focused on the marital relationships and is not allowed to become confrontational or interpretive as in conventional group therapy. Relationships between unrelated individuals are not explored or analyzed. The therapist focuses on one couple at a time, dividing the time equally each session and does not encourage group comment or interaction until the end of the session.

The group serves primarily as a theatrical setting in which participants are alternately audience and performers in their own Pirandello-like play. As the fantasies of one spouse are connected with those of another, the group is witness to the dual descriptions that emerge. These dual descriptions make it clear that the problem does not lie in the isolated fantasy of either spouse but in how they are *connected*. Because the fantasies caricature the relationships into absurd images, an atmosphere of humor, curiosity, and experimentation develops that provides the appropriate context for examining the many different sides of reality.

Prechange Tests

Prechange tests are used to further define the reciprocity by focusing on the consequences of either spouse changing their positions. Because each position defines the other, a change in one spouse inevitably changes the position of the other. For example: If the husband's position is defined as a "cop" who tries to reform his wife, and the wife's position is defined as a "criminal" who indulges in "delinquent" behavior, when the "criminal" reforms, then the "cop" is left, at least temporarily, without his familiar position. This transition is likely to arouse discomfort and anxiety.

In order to alleviate some of this initial anxiety, the couples are told that their first tasks will not be for the purpose of changing anything but will simply provide the therapist with a measuring rod to answer such questions as: "How fast should change take place, and in what areas?" "Which spouse should change first?" "How much tolerance have each for change in the other?" "What will be the consequences of change for both?"

These prechange tests serve several purposes at once. They dramatize the reciprocity of the relationship by assuming change in one will be likely to upset the other; they imply that change is inevitable rather than unattainable; and they reduce resistance since each is doing the task not because his/her own behavior needs changing but to test the ability of the spouse to tolerate change. The prechange tests also provide the therapist with valuable information regarding the couples' flexibility and motivation.

On the basis of the feedback from the test, the couples are told whether or not it is safe for them to proceed with change, or whether it would be wiser for them to retreat or remain the same. Throughout the remainder of the therapy, this attitude of awe and respect toward change is maintained by the therapist. Change is approached as something not to be taken lightly but to be regulated, monitored, scheduled, and restrained. Although this attitude is based on the therapist's legitimate concern regarding the consequences of changing reciprocal arrangements, it is used clinically as a connecting technique (defining the behavior of each as serving a function for the other) and as a paradoxical restraining technique (prescribing no change as a spur to change).

The therapist evaluates the performance of each task as an indication of whether or not it would be safe for the couple to proceed with change, to retreat, or to stay the same. If it appears that the couple can incorporate change into their relationship, an intervention is given that is aimed directly at changing their positions. If, however, it appears there are hidden agendas operating that would undermine the intervention and prevent change, an indirect or paradoxical intervention is made that is aimed at connecting their positions with those hidden agendas.

Over the years in which this format has been used, a predictable pattern of change has been observed by the therapist. Most couples shift their positions within the first several sessions as a result of the choreography and tasks. This shift is almost invariably followed by an adverse reaction by one or both in the middle phase of therapy—the fifth, sixth, or seventh session. The rest of therapy is devoted to helping them renegotiate their relationship around the new positioning.

The following three cases will demonstrate this process and will show three different methods, based on a differential diagnosis, of putting the above techniques into practice.

David and Goliath

This couple initially presented their problem as a power struggle over their apartment. The following two sets of dialogue illustrate the different kind of information that is revealed through a verbal discussion and through the choreography respectively.

Although it is clear from the discussion that they are engaged in a power struggle, the choreography clarifies the central issue around which it is organized, their positions in relation to it, and how they negotiate these.

The wife responded to the therapist's question concerning the presenting problem as follows:

WIFE: There is so much hostility and tension in the apartment. A lot of the surfacing of our problems came from when we started renovating our apartment.
HUSBAND: We seem to be taking turns, in terms of the apartment, where it became critical to have the place finished for her, now she doesn't care and doesn't do anything about it, it becomes critical for me to have it finished.
WIFE: We have this expensive wallpaper sitting around in boxes and every once in a while I start talking to him about

the wallpapering and getting it up, and he always comes up with an excuse, and now his latest excuse is that there is a little bit of wallpaper left on the wall and it has to be steamed off first.

HUSBAND: I feel Heather is bent on using the apartment— using it as she wants to use it, despite what I have to say about it, and she is, in fact, doing it. She is winning each of these things.

WIFE: That's not true. I have my desk set up in the hallway and I'm afraid of using it because of him. I feel it's a locked situation. Nobody wins.

The couples were asked to have a fantasy and the wife described hers as follows:

WIFE: It was like a Bible story—John is the giant, and I'm the little boy with the slingshot. This was over something in the kitchen like putting up the wallpaper—I was real little and sort of weak, except I had this slingshot and I knew I could kill him because I have such good aim, except for the fact that, though he was a giant, he needed all kinds of reassurance. I can't kill somebody who needs so much reassurance, even though I'm in danger.

THERAPIST: (*Asking the husband to assume the position of the giant.*) What's the expression on the giant's face?

WIFE: Just kind of hostile and gruff and menacing. (*The husband looks menacing and climbs upon a chair, assuming the pose of the giant.*) I have a way to get to him. I know just where to aim, but I am powerless because I see that he is really weak. He needs all this reassurance—I think the giant is just giantism, it's not real strength—it's somehow—from knowing him before—I'm smarter than him—I think I know what he's about, and I think he is easily destroyed and very frightened, and therefore I can't use my slingshot to get rid of the giant.

THERAPIST: Would you show us the other part of him, when he is—how did you describe it?—"scared and weak and needs reassurance?" Tell him what to do when he's looking like that.

WIFE: He'll be slumping in a chair in very bad posture, with his stomach sticking out, with his head down, and looking very depressed and like—somebody has done something really wrong to him, and—but there is no way it can be corrected, and yet he needs a lot of attention—he needs some help with this and yet the help won't do any good.

THERAPIST: What's your reaction to his helplessness?

WIFE: Sometimes I feel obligated to it, to take care of it. (*The wife is asked to do this without words. She strokes his hair, pats his head, caresses his shoulder.*) I cling to him.

THERAPIST: Hoping that will help you or him?

WIFE: Sometimes that comes out of my fear of walking out of the apartment and doing something on my own—maybe I cling to his depression.

THERAPIST: To keep yourself from going out?

WIFE: Yeah—first of all because of the fear that—of what it might do to him if I walked out, and secondly maybe because I have some fear to—of ah—you know of going out into the world.

The therapist then asked the wife to have a fantasy of what might happen to her if she did go out into the world. She enacted this with other members of the group and described it as a total contrast to staying home and nursing her husband's depression.

WIFE: It would be going out and risking my own existential fear of relating to people in my field.

THERAPIST: What would happen if you did? What is your nightmare—the worst thing that could happen?

WIFE: That people wouldn't listen, or that somehow I would feel insignificant. Maybe I feel like a grand poet if I don't go out and test it.

The therapist asked her to pretend to read her poem and asked the others to give a negative reaction. She ended up saying, "It's terrifying finding out that I'm just one of the crowd."

THERAPIST: I can understand that. You had better go back and cling to your husband.

WIFE: [In doing so] I've built up a lot of resentment toward him because I feel that he is holding me back. I feel his depression grows and I'm worried about how to change him—whew!

THERAPIST: You feel that it is safer and easier for you to stay and try to change him rather than risk reading your poetry? (*The wife agrees.*)

The therapist then asked her to show what she imagined would happen if she used her slingshot.

WIFE: That leading my own life and following my own interests is what he would conceive of as a weapon against him in some way.

THERAPIST: You feel your secret weapon is fulfilling yourself?

WIFE: Yes—and that would somehow destroy him.

The husband expressed surprise at his wife's perception of him, denying any negative reaction toward her self-fulfillment. "I would be very happy to see her succeed with her writing."

The therapist asked the wife when he became the giant in their daily life and she replied it was when he criticized her or became depressed. He overwhelmed her with his nagging, complaining, and various reform programs, and when she didn't toe the line he became depressed.

The husband was then asked to show his fantasy.

HUSBAND: She is naked. I am a gaucho—a Rudolph Valentino kind of character. We're moving in a semicircle, circling one another in a kind of dance, like Japanese wrestlers. (*They circle each other warily.*)

HUSBAND: She doesn't know what I am going to do. I have her on guard.

THERAPIST: Are you controlling the dance?

HUSBAND: Yeah—right—evidently.

THERAPIST: How do you control it?

HUSBAND: I might change directions—yes—it is controlling, I'm leading. (*He tries to trip her up, goes past her, changes directions suddenly, whirls around.*)

THERAPIST: She has to be more and more on her toes then?

HUSBAND: Yes, yes.

THERAPIST: At any point would you grab her?

HUSBAND: That's not the idea of the dance. I'm very involved in this game which has nothing to do with one's real life. It has to do with an artificial game and I'm really very involved with it.

THERAPIST: Show what would happen if you lost and she got control.

HUSBAND: (*To wife.*) Keep circling and then you'd have to instead of going away from me go towards me, or stay in this pattern of retreating. (*She takes the initiative and starts pursuing him. He is startled, laughs.*)

HUSBAND: I want to say, "Stop! What are you doing? This is my game! I'm the Pied Piper calling the tune. I don't want to play. It's my ball."

The therapist asked the husband at what point in their daily life he felt he most needed to control the dance and he stated it was when his wife became totally disorganized—when she flung her clothes and papers about the apartment, left dirty dishes piled in the sink for days, forgot important appointments that affected them both, and acted like she was on cloud nine.

THERAPIST: What would she do if she were in charge? Show us your nightmare.

HUSBAND: Well, it's really out of control—if we're doing what she wants to do—if she's leading I don't feel confident enough to follow her. We won't end up where we're supposed to end up—living like my parents, living in a middle-class existence with everything in the right place, neat, and orderly, and life all laid out. Knowing just where we're going to end up when we reach 65. But I am thinking she might be right and that her instincts may be very good for what she expounds for us as a way of life. But I don't really trust—that I could be happy.

The therapist then asked them to set up that way of life and show us a picture of it. He sat them both down cross-legged on the floor.

HUSBAND: Here are some friends. We're not worried about tomorrow or if we have to pay the rent. Just having a good time, talking, touching, very relaxed. All those problems that weigh on me every day, I'm not worried about. Not worried about paying the rent, phone bill, getting my daughter through school, not worried about my work because Heather doesn't worry about that. We're having a good time and we're just enjoying each day.

THERAPIST: That's your nightmare? (*Laughter.*)

HUSBAND: My nightmare is that I don't believe that it could be that good.

THERAPIST: Sometimes you would like to go with Heather into that other world?

HUSBAND: Yes, intellectually I know she's right. But I feel the consequences would be that I would end up begging on the streets.

Based on the two choreographies, the therapist developed the following hypothesis: The central issue around which the power struggle is organized is control versus creativity, with the husband taking the position of the controlling one and the wife taking the position of the creative one. But their positions are filled with ambiguity, contradiction, and illusion. The husband, as the giant and Pied Piper, only appears to be in control as his control depends on his wife's allowing him to lead her. The wife as David only appears to hold the ultimate weapon as her slingshot of self-fulfillment is rendered useless. She cannot kill "someone who needs so much reassurance."

Her slingshot is also rendered useless by her own "existential fear" of discovering she is "just one of the crowd." Her husband's giantism serves to keep her from recognizing this fear. Just as her creative disorganization serves to keep her husband from facing his own fear of becoming creatively disorganized.

When contradictions and hidden agendas such as these are apparent, a useful approach is to define the reciprocal positions as serving a necessary function for one another and to give a prechange test that determines the ability of either to give up that function.

The therapist told the couple it would be extremely difficult to change their situation because they were preserving each other's illusions. The husband was preserving his wife's illusion that her slingshot of self-fulfillment would destroy him because he knew that otherwise she would have to face her fear of being "one of the crowd." In order to protect her from this fear, the husband kept control of the dance with his criticism and depression.

The wife preserved her husband's illusion of being the giant and the Pied Piper because she knew this kept him from facing his impulse to abandon the values of his parents and follow her into an unknown world of unpredictability and pleasure. She protected him from dealing with his wayward impulses by constantly keeping him involved with her own. The following prechange test was given: In order to know whether either was capable of giving up their protective positions, they were to conduct an experiment. The husband was to choose one day on which he would neither get depressed nor criticize his wife and observe whether or not she developed an "existential fear." If she did he was to quickly involve her with an inconsolable depression so she could avoid facing it. The wife was to choose one day on which she would behave in an organized way and observe whether or not her husband showed any signs of giving vent to a pleasurable impulse. If so she was to "space out" so he could become involved in organizing her and thus forget about his impulse. This defined the position of each as serving the other so they could no longer be perceived as disconnected.

The following session the husband stated he had not been critical or depressed for a whole week and if this had aroused the wife's existential fear it was not evident. She had begun to write and had retrieved a manuscript from a bottom drawer and sent it to a publisher. He reiterated how happy he would be if she were to succeed at her writing.

The wife confirmed her husband's impression that neither his new behavior nor her burst of creativity had made her nervous. In fact, she was feeling elated. But she reported her organized behavior did compel her husband to give vent to a pleasurable impulse. He agreed to her choice of a vacation spot even though he considered it extravagant. The husband stated it remained to be seen whether or not he would get nervous about this.

The therapist reacted with caution saying it was really too soon to tell if they could tolerate changes in one another. They were instructed to continue in the same direction but always with an eye on the other person's reaction.

With some minor setbacks, change continued steadily until the seventh session when the husband complained his wife had fallen back into her old ways. She was scattering her papers all over the apartment, littering the bedroom, keeping him awake until all hours of the night typing, and being totally disorganized again. The wife accused her husband of being critical, moody, and constantly nagging her. The therapist interpreted their behavior as trying to protect one another again, but the wife blurted out she was more concerned about herself than her husband. She had continued to write steadily and had received some positive comments from agents and publishers. She was now confronted with her perception of a successful woman, who was someone who was "selfish," "cold," "self-centered," and "uncaring." All her life she had been afraid that if she really succeeded at anything God would punish her—she would be struck down by some terrible fate. She conceded she might have been deliberately provoking her husband into stopping her.

When the therapist suggested that the husband have an inconsolable depression to circumvent his wife's terrible fate, he vehemently refused, saying, "It's her problem, she's going to have to deal with it herself."

Once either spouse emphatically refuses to serve the other, the therapist accepts this and gives a differentiating task. It was now clear why David could not use the slingshot of self-fulfillment. David was a woman and the wife believed a woman would be punished for being "selfish."

In order to detoxify this belief she was given a ritual that compelled her to enact it in an exaggerated form. She was told that since she felt she must pay a price for success, she should pay it as she went along and then God would not have to collect it from her at some future date. Every time she felt selfish over her writing she should pay a penalty to her husband. The penalty should be equal to her selfishness. Since she was convinced her achievement would not only destroy her but would "shrink" her husband she should compensate by doing something that would build him up, something that would benefit him at her expense. The therapist assured her this pay-as-you-go plan was the only way to alleviate her guilt over success. The wife took the proposal very seriously and agreed to carry out the task, much to the husband's delight.

For a period of time the wife dutifully paid the penalty to her husband for her creativity (making his favorite meals, picking up his cleaning, cleaning up her mess, catering to his whims), but gradually she rebelled against it and blurted out in the 11th session, "I'm sick and tired of this. Why should I pay for something that is rightly mine? And besides I don't feel guilty anymore." She did not back down from this position even when she sold her first article to a magazine.

The choreography was not performed in the last session as this group predated the therapist's more extensive use of it. However, it was clear at the end of therapy that this couple's positions around the issue of control versus creativity had markedly changed. As a result of the wife assuming the responsibility for her own achievement she no longer needed to provoke her husband into stopping her by becoming disorganized. Since the husband's depression and criticism ceased to serve a function in the relationship, it was greatly reduced.

The Phantom and the Rock

When interventions are not aimed at the issue that is most central to maintaining the problem, change, if it occurs at all, tends to be peripheral or temporary. The reason the couple is in therapy is because they have avoided dealing with this issue and they are reluctant to risk unbalancing their relationship by doing so. They protect this homeostatic balance in many different ways—denying, blaming, intellectualizing, rationalizing, and confusing the therapist with irrelevant details. It is not uncommon for the therapist to focus on issues other than the one from which the basic problem stems. The following is a case in point.

The couple was seen privately for six sessions before being placed in a couples group. During the private sessions they were given several tasks that failed to produce any sustained change as they were not connected to the most relevant issue. The choreography in the couples group provided the key to a meaningful series of interventions.

Several weeks prior to the first session, the husband had revealed to his wife that for the five years in which they had been married he had been leading a secret life that consisted of his going to the office every morning and having a cup of coffee and smoking a cigarette. This was forbidden by the fundamentalist religion in which they had both been raised and in which they had married. The husband had been following this same routine while living with his parents before he married, but his wife had not known about it. She had married him under the assumption that he was as devout as she.

A few months earlier he had stopped going to church and told his wife he didn't know what he believed. All his life he had pretended to believe what others wanted him to and now he wanted to get to know himself.

The husband was the youngest of seven sons and had been raised in a household where no one ever dared question the tenets of their religion. His six older brothers had all followed the path of righteousness and were presently active in church activities. Although the husband had served the church faithfully, a gnawing doubt began to enter his mind while in his teens and had grown to great proportions. To express this doubt would have been unthinkable and so he suppressed it.

The revelation of his disbelief left the wife in a quandary. When would he know what he believed? And what would he know? Would she want to spend the rest of her life with him if he left the church? When she pressed him to come to a decision, he felt trapped as he had all his life. If she didn't press him, she felt adrift and didn't know how to relate to him.

The therapist speculated that the religious issue was a reflection of a problem in their marriage, that the husband had substituted his wife for his parents as an authority figure against whom he was rebelling, and the wife was assuming this position. The therapist told them that the religious issue was too important for them to resolve at the moment and that they should give themselves a period of three months during which neither of them should think about it. In the meantime, the therapist would work on the other issues in their marriage that they had mentioned, the husband's withdrawal and the wife's frigidity. The wife thought of sex as a duty rather than something to be enjoyed and her performance was perfunctory. She was shy about her figure, thinking it unattractive, and never undressed in front of her husband. When asked what turned her on sexually, she stated she didn't know and had never thought about it. She guessed it might be helpful if her husband romanced her or at least talked to her before going to bed.

Some simple Masters-and-Johnson-type behavioral tasks were given around the area of sex and communication. The therapist alluded to the wife's body as an unexplored country and suggested they explore together what gave her sensual pleasure. This was to be done gently, slowly without intercourse.

With the pressure of duty removed and the husband more involved in communicating with his wife in a tender way, the wife responded immediately, and, to the surprise and delight of both, began to enjoy sex. However, this initial excitement and involvement lasted only several weeks and the sense of awkwardness and distance reappeared. The therapist had not connected communication, sex, and religion to the primary relationship issue.

In the couples group the husband choreographed the following fantasy: He saw his wife as a fleeting person in a fog—a disappearing phantom. He would try to follow her and capture her but she was always just out of his reach. When asked what would happen if he should capture her and turn her around, he stated, "I would want to look at her and see her face, and allow her to see me." Asked what his worst fear would be in capturing the phantom, he said, "If she really saw me, she would run away and start to vanish again."

This sentence provided the core of a new hypothesis. The husband was afraid he would lose his wife if she ever saw him for what he really was. He wanted her to know the worst about him and to be able to forgive him. He had been testing her by smoking cigarettes, drinking coffee, and leaving the church as if asking, "Will you still love me if you know who I am?"

In the wife's choreography, she saw her husband as a 200-pound rock. She was autumn rain, which gently pattered against the rock in the hope of drawing him out. She wanted him to "stop being a rock and open up and become a flower." When asked what she would do if she found something inside the rock other than a flower, she replied that she wouldn't know what to do. "I might be scared and run away."

The wife validated her husband's perception that she was afraid to see him for what he really was. If she didn't find a flower inside she might disappear into the fog. Her avoidance of confrontation was evidenced by her use of soft autumn rain, rather than a hammer and chisel to open up the rock, guaranteeing that her mission would never be accomplished. In both fantasies, the ambiance of fog, soft autumn rain, and a disappearing phantom all suggested avoidance and cover-up.

Around the central theme of self-revelation the husband's position seemed to be "I want you to see me," and the wife's reciprocal position was "I'm afraid to look." The more the husband tried to get the wife to look, the more afraid she was to see, and the more afraid she was to see, the more the husband tried to get her to look. Over the years he had probably tried in many ways to reveal his "shadier side" to her, but she had given him the message that she could not tolerate it. Now he had been forced to go to the extreme of leaving the church and becoming a disbeliever.

The prechange test provided the couple with a structured and protected setting within which they could begin to reveal themselves to one another. The therapist told them that their problem was that they didn't know each other, and they didn't know whether it was safe to get to know each other, and, as a matter of fact, the therapist didn't know if it was safe either. In order to test this, the husband was to whisper a secret about himself into his wife's ear before going to bed each night. This was to be done in an atmosphere conducive to secrets—secluded, private, the lights turned down low. The secrets could be anything about his life, past or present, but they had to be something that she didn't know about him.

The wife was not to respond immediately but to think about what her husband had told her and to let him know the following night whether or not she could accept it. She was then to whisper a secret about herself into his ear. This gave the husband a way of letting his wife "see" him but in stages that he could control. It gave the wife an opportunity to get to know him a little at a time and to be able to reflect without pressure. It also implied that the wife might have an interesting secret life herself.

In the following session, the wife described her first reaction to the task as one of extreme apprehension and not wanting to know. However, after her initial shock and disgust wore off, she began to find the exercise "interesting" and "fun." She became intrigued by the secrets and asked to hear "all the gory details." Their discussion would continue long into the night. The wife stated: "I began to feel that my husband trusted me enough to confide these things in me, and I also thought that no matter how disgusting and outrageous they were, I could still accept him: and—it was like—so, that the main thing I learned was that I still love him."

The prechange test indicated the couple was capable of responding to direct interventions and the therapist told them it seemed safe for them to continue to get to know one another. Since they were going away on vacation without their child, this would be an ideal time to do so. In order to clear their minds of their preconceived notions about one another, they should pretend that they were courting and find out about one another as newly infatuated people do.

When they returned from vacation, the wife reported that during one of the secret telling periods, she had confided to her husband that all her life she had harbored a secret desire to get drunk (a heavy breach of their religious practices). The husband brought home some champagne and they got drunk together. This had a profound effect on the husband, who stated, "I have always felt she was sitting in judgment of me. It made me feel uncomfortable. After we got drunk together I felt we were on the same level."

Several weeks later, the wife had an anxiety reaction to the dramatic change in her husband. In one of the separate wive's groups, she reported that her husband had become everything she had always wanted him to be. He was now attentive to her, involved with their child, loving, warm, and affectionate, and "I just can't bear it! For a whole week, he has been—just sitting around and adoring me. I'll turn around to look at him and he'll just be sitting there smiling at me, and I don't know—what to do. I thought about what you said about changing too fast, and I started to fight with him, and later wondered if it was not done to gain some distance and to stop him from thinking that I was so wonderful."

The therapist supported the wife's view that change had taken place too quickly for her but pointed out that she herself had found a way of controlling it—she could always start a fight. At some future date, she might feel it was safe to reveal her greatest secret to her husband: that she had a hard time accepting the image of herself as being "wonderful."

The couple continued the process of getting to know one another, and the more they came to know one another, the more they liked each other. The religious issue resolved itself. The husband was asked by his church to accept a high position, but he refused the offer, feeling he was not worthy. However, he was extremely humbled by having been asked and began preparing himself to be worthy at some time in the future. He gave up smoking and drinking voluntarily.

In the final choreography the husband's fantasy was heavily laden with images indicating the change in their sexual relationship: "We are either stones or pieces of drift wood lying on the beach, half buried by the sand. We are peeking out so we can see the beautiful ocean. The waves come in and crash over us—they are constantly rolling in and rolling out and rolling in and rolling out. We are enjoying it together. It is a peaceful feeling. I particularly like the rhythmic envelopment of the waves."

As compared with his first fantasy of fog and a disappearing phantom, this fantasy conveyed a sense of earthiness and sensual pleasure. He had caught the phantom and they had bedded down together.

The wife's fantasy took place in a park on a windy, sunny day. They were two balloons tied together with a string: "We've been let go. We bob up and down with the wind, but we've been tied together. It's a free-floating feeling."

The frustration of trying to open up a rock with soft autumn rain had been replaced by an image of fun and freedom. Both fantasies conveyed a sense of pleasure and relatedness.

Danger in the Forest: The Fox and the Satyr

One of the most common forms of reciprocal positioning is that of the pursuing wife and the distancing husband. Usually both have a problem with the demands of closeness. The husband handles his by closing off emotionally and withdrawing, the wife by becoming preoccupied with pursuing her husband and prying him open.

Therapists sometimes get trapped in joining the wife and trying to break through the husband's shell, with the result that he closes it ever more tightly. Since he has spent his life thwarting the efforts of those who try to open him up, including family, friends, mothers, sisters, teachers, wives, psychiatrists, and society at large, he has developed ingenious ploys for evading them. A more productive approach is one based on an old Russian proverb: If one wishes to catch a squirrel one does not chase it, but instead, one lies down in the sun with a nut in an outstretched hand and falls asleep.

In the following case, the wife initiated therapy and the husband came reluctantly to the sessions, assuming the same wary stance with the therapist as with his wife.

The couple described their problem in vague terms such as, "We are always communicating on two different levels"; "Every time we discuss anything important, we wind up not understanding anything the other person has said"; "Nothing ever gets resolved."

The husband's resistance was immediately apparent as he refused to have a fantasy, saying that his mind was a total blank. The therapist did not challenge his refusal but instead said perhaps he needed a week to think about it.

In her fantasy, the wife saw herself as a fox, who was barking, gnashing her teeth, and pawing the ground trying to get her husband, who was a satyr, to come down out of a tree. The satyr was sitting on a branch in the tree, blissfully playing his flute, oblivious to the fox on the ground. The fox was trying to warn the satyr of some approaching danger in the forest but the satyr kept ignoring the fox until, finally, it ran off frantically through the forest. The wife stated these positions paralleled those at home when she was trying to get her husband to become more involved with her and the children.

The husband participated in acting out his wife's fantasy in a very constricted inhibited manner, looking more scared than blissful.

The therapist hypothesized that the key issue in their relationship was the danger in the forest and that this danger had something to do with distance and closeness and who was going to control it. The wife frantically pursued in order to establish closeness; the husband determinedly eluded her to preserve distance. The therapist speculated that it was extremely important for the husband to control this distance and that he would sabotage any effort made by the therapist or the wife to bridge it. Therefore, the prechange test was given to the wife only and the husband was directed to do nothing.

The couple was told that their problem had to do with the danger in the forest but that the therapist didn't know what that was. The prechange test would indicate whether or not it was safe to explore the danger or whether they should leave well enough alone. The husband seemed to be the most frightened of it since he had climbed the tree to stay out of its reach. The wife was told to try and find a way of luring him down so they could explore the danger together. The husband was supposed to remain in the tree until his wife had convinced him it would be reasonably safe for him to venture forth. If he came down, it would indicate it was safe to explore the danger and we could proceed with the therapy. If he didn't, it would indicate it was not safe and we should not proceed. (This put the control of the therapy in the hands of the husband. We would only move forward on a signal from him.)

At the following session the wife was asked to demonstrate what happened when she attempted the assignment by choreographing it. She assumed the position of the fox and jumped halfway up the tree three times, reported that she got no response from the satyr, and finally gave up in defeat and went sulking into the forest.

It was clear she had not changed her tactics but only modified her old ones, continuing in the position of the pursuer. The husband had remained oblivious to what was happening, not even recognizing his wife's attempt to do anything different. He stated he was waiting for his wife to lure him down but she hadn't found a way to do this. The wife admitted her attempts were only halfhearted because she resented having to take responsibility for changing the relationship since that was the role she always played.

Since the husband refused to come down out of the tree and the wife refused to move until he did, therapy was stalemated. The therapist decided to respond to the stalemate by prescribing it. She told them that the choreography and pre-change tests had indicated that they had managed to strike just the right balance of closeness and distance in their relationship and they should preserve it. At this point it would be dangerous to tamper with the delicate balance. But since they were both coming to therapy, one or the other might get impatient and think they should try and change something by getting closer. This would be a grave error. In order to avoid this, they should monitor each other very carefully during the next period of time, and if either of them made an attempt to move closer the other should thwart it instantly.

The husband accepted this prescription stoically. The wife was puzzled and thought it odd but agreed to go along with it.

At our next meeting, the couple reported that they had had a very good two weeks. The wife stated "A peculiar thing happened. We got closer to each other by trying not to—we talked more, but it wasn't the same. I tried deliberately not to ask questions, and he talked more to me about himself than I have ever experienced. I suddenly realized my asking so many questions used to shut him up."

The therapist voiced her concern about the danger in the forest—the possibility of closeness. The wife admitted, "It did frighten me a little, because inadvertently, it seemed the opposite happened from what we were doing. We got closer to each other and it was scary."

The husband claimed he didn't get nervous: "I felt in control. Perhaps since I opened up on my own terms, I felt more at ease than when I am being prodded or whatever. I set the thing in motion."

The therapist predicted the change wouldn't last because it had occurred too quickly before either of them was ready for it. This put the husband in the position of having to disprove the therapist's prediction in order to remain in control—which he proceeded to do. Each session, as improvement continued, the husband proudly announced that the therapist's predictions had been wrong. The therapist acted perplexed and wondered what exceptional characteristics they possessed that made this possible.

It was not until the ninth session that the backlash from change occurred. The wife admitted that she was having difficulty handling the new closeness. Although she had complained for years about her husband's unavailability, his new and sudden emotional involvement was making her nervous. She felt overwhelmed by the demands of his openness and began to realize how much she had enjoyed being alone.

The therapist shifted the focus of therapy to the wife's problem with closeness and enlisted the husband in helping his wife to cope with this problem. He was instructed to control his openness, not threaten her with too much intimacy, and withdraw from time to time for her sake. This reversed their original position and defined the husband as the pursuer and the wife as the distancer. The husband seemed pleased and proud of his new position as the guardian of his wife's problem, and the wife appreciated the irony of the situation.

In the wife's final choreography, she envisioned them as two small fluttery birds building a nest in a tree. "Each flies away and picks up bits of stuff to build the nest with and then returns to the other. We are chattering the whole time. We occasionally prick each other with our beaks, but it's nothing serious. At the end of the dream, we fly away together."

She no longer saw herself as a barking fox but as a bird who joined her husband, another bird, up in the tree. They occasionally pricked each other with their beaks in order to regulate the closeness as they engaged in the domestic activity of building a nest.

The husband was not asked to have a fantasy but he did volunteer that he shared his wife's.

Summary

The technique of couples choreography defines the marital relationship in metaphorical terms. When the metaphors are acted out, the reciprocity in the relationship is translated into concrete images that provide the basis for systemic interventions aimed at disrupting the escalating reciprocity. Prechange tests are used to regulate the speed of change in relation to the reciprocal positions. Change is viewed as an unsettling phenomenon that temporarily unbalances the marital relationship. The group serves as a theatrical setting in which the marital relationships are "staged" and examined with humor and objectivity. An atmosphere of experimentation is created that is necessary for carrying out the unconventional tasks.

Use of the Extended Family in Couples Therapy

WHAT PRICE LIBERATION?

The following case was included as an example of how extended family issues are dealt with when they are considered an integral part of the presenting problem. In this case, the over-involvement of the wife with her family of origin is connected with the marital strife and becomes part of the dilemma around which the therapeutic debate takes place. Mother–daughter issues are connected with husband–wife issues as three-generational themes are traced and then paradoxically used to entangle the couple in double binds from which they can only escape through alternate routes. An intense contest is set up between the group and the therapist over the wife's liberation that mirrors the positions of husband–wife–grandmother. In the last session an intervention is used that ties the issues of differentiation from both extended families together.

The wife, Marsha, a social worker, dragged her husband, Amer, to therapy after seven years of trying to break through "his block of not being in touch with his emotions." Having failed, she now wanted to hand the job over to the therapist. In her desperation to unblock him, she analyzed his every thought, action, feeling, and mood, and tried to organize them according to her standards. Besides complaining that he withdrew from her and didn't communicate, she accused him of escaping from his life—"He never sits and thinks about himself—about what life is, who he is, where he's going, and how he should get there. He has perceptions, but he hasn't gotten in touch with them. The depth of his still waters is not very deep." Although the husband was highly successful as a research chemist, she didn't approve of the way he managed his professional or social life—"He glides with his talent and doesn't make the most of it—doesn't read books, doesn't do art work, doesn't know what to do in his social life. He can't manage money and people take advantage of him because he is politically unaware."

The wife spoke of her own professional work, saying she was not where she wanted to be. She was taking more classes instead of working because, "I have a fear of getting to where I should be professionally which would be assuming adulthood by committing myself to my profession." She had had some bad experiences in the professional world that had left her extremely insecure.

The husband, who never spoke unless spoken to, and then barely above a whisper, quietly stated that the difficulty in their marriage didn't bother him as much as his wife. He felt the only problem was that his wife tried to make him think and feel the way she did and this caused clashes between them. He agreed that he needed her guidance because, "She knows more about the world than I do. Her perceptions are better and deeper than mine." He confessed he didn't express his feelings very much because he had been quiet all his life. It was clear that the husband gave his wife cues that he needed her to tell him what to do—how to think and how to behave and then resented her for doing it.

In the initial interview, the wife also spoke of the difficulty with her family of origin. "My mother and I have changed roles. She looks to me to take care of her—leans on me. In fact, my whole family gave me the message they couldn't survive without me. I'm the bright part of their lives—particularly now the baby is born. What I need is reassurance. I want Amer to make up for them and give it to me."

Her 33-year-old brother still lived at home and she had spent the last 15 years trying to get him into therapy. He had always had "emotional problems" and she was his only friend.

Although she felt at times she would like to have less contact with her family they always managed to keep her intensely involved with their problems. She acted as a mediator between her parents. "My friendship is very important to my mother. It keeps her away from my father."

While the wife was extremely enmeshed with her family, the husband was in a distant relationship with his. He had come to the United States as a foreign exchange student from a Latin country and they had met in graduate school. He was the fourth of nine children and had been left mostly to his own devices. His closest relationship was with his next older brother who was, "a rebel, the black sheep of the family who was always opening his mouth and getting into trouble while I kept mine closed and stayed out of trouble"—a habit that he obviously practiced to this day.

In consultation, the group and therapist agreed that the first intervention should be aimed at the three-generational theme of enmeshment. Clearly Marsha had taken on the role of caretaker both in her family of origin and in her present family. Amer played the reciprocal role of the helpless one who could not exist without her caretaking but resented it when she gave it. Marsha's preoccupation with her husband and family served the function of distracting her from her doubts and fears regarding her own professional development. We therefore advised Amer against having perceptions of his own because that would deprive his wife of having them for him and she might then begin to have perceptions about herself and her own life. The group expressed their concerns that these new perceptions might lead her to premature liberation, and they worried about what would happen to Amer and her family if she liberated herself. She would no longer be able to take care of them in the way in which they had become accustomed.

In opposition to the group, the therapist took the side of the wife's liberation, stating the husband and family should learn to grow up and take care of themselves and that the wife had a right to liberate herself and fulfill her potential as a woman regardless of the price her husband and family would have to pay.

This controversy between the therapist and group was escalated from session to session with the group elaborating on the conservative position that the first job of a woman was to be a good wife and daughter, that personal or professional concerns should take second place, and that it was her natural profession to change her husband and family. The therapist became more eloquent in defense of liberation, saying the wife had served as earth mother to everyone long enough and should not sacrifice her intellect and talent any longer on a cause for which she received so little appreciation.

The wife became more and more upset with the group's statements and began to fight them openly saying, "I'm fed up with their trying to keep me in my place. I'm the one to decide where my place is. Why do they keep trying to push me back when I'm trying to move ahead?"

The more the group recommended the wife think only of others, the more she began to think of herself, and the more they recommended that the husband remain helpless, the more assertive he became. This new assertiveness was extremely threatening to the wife, who initially responded by trying to wipe it out. She insisted the thoughts he was expressing were not really his "true" thoughts and his way of expressing them were not natural to him. When he expressed anger toward her she insisted he was not angry at her but at other things in his life. The group kept supporting the husband's new assertiveness by continuing to recommend that he remain limp and blank.

A major crisis came when the wife took a job and became obsessed with fears about professional advancement. "I'm afraid I will get involved in the politics of work and that will make me less important to others. I am driven to places in my work where I don't know things. This is frightening to me and makes me feel inferior. At home I have all the answers and it's safe."

The husband expressed his conflict over her new job by stating, "On the one hand I want to see her successful and on the other hand I will have to give up a lot. She might begin to think it might be more interesting to solve a puzzle at work rather than trying to solve the puzzle of me."

The group recommended again and again that the husband escalate his helpless behavior so his wife could not focus on anything but serving him, and the therapist in opposition encouraged the wife to go full steam ahead.

The wife's family reacted to her increased independence by making more demands on her and developing new problems. "They cannot tolerate seeing me move ahead professionally. I would be successful in a family who had failed. I would be showing them up, particularly my mother who is jealous of me. She's terribly afraid I'll discover where she went wrong and see her as less than adequate. Especially in relation to my brother. If I raise my son so he is in a better place than my brother she will be jealous. She's afraid I'll discover who is more feminine, who can do the womanly things better. I spend a lot of time keeping myself from knowing I'm better than she is."

She told of how her mother never had an opportunity to go to college, having had to support her family when her father died. She had always resented having to work to send her brothers and sisters through school. When Marsha had been about to graduate from college she had developed a high fever of unknown origin during exam week that had nearly prevented her from graduating.

At this point it was decided to shift the focus to the mother–daughter relationship as it was preempting all the wife's other concerns. The therapist joined the group in giving this relationship priority over the husband and wife relationship. The husband was asked to help his wife differentiate herself by giving her a reason to desert her mother.

> The group is more worried about your mother now than your husband. They think your husband might be able to tolerate your being a changed woman but that your mother couldn't. She would never be able to tolerate what she would consider to be a selfish woman, one who takes care of herself, devotes less time to her husband, her baby, her brother, her father, her mother. And you wouldn't be able to handle her disapproval. (*The wife nods and agrees.*)
>
> After a long discussion we have decided there is only one way you would be able to tolerate her disapproval. Your husband must help you in this. He must become even more demanding, helpless, and needy than your mother so you can give yourself a reason why you're taking care of him rather than her.
>
> The group pointed out to me that I have been trying to help you become independent of your mother and husband at the same time and I now realize this is impossible. A daughter must first be able to become independent of her mother before she can become independent of her husband. Amer, every time you see your wife becoming anxious about leaving her mother, you must give her a signal that you can't function without her.

During the next session, the wife proudly reported her declaration of independence from her family. She had refused to give them any more advice about her brother, had side-stepped an argument between her parents, and had gone to the country with her husband and baby for the weekend rather than spending it at their home, as was the custom.

This led to more interaction between the husband and wife that consisted of more love making as well as more open fighting. The wife responded to the change in their relationship with, "Something is coming up now that scares me—our real feelings for one another—positive as well as negative. We've been alienated and now we're being asked to trust one another a little more and that's scary. I can't leave my family until I'm sure my husband will be there for me but he's resistant. The more the group tells him to go prone, the more he stands up to me."

The group connected the wife's fear of getting closer to her husband with the fear of leaving her family and instructed her to trust her husband to regulate the closeness and distance.

> The group believes you have a right to be concerned about the danger of getting closer to one another because getting close means, Marsha, you would have to separate from your family and they know this would cause you a great deal of anxiety and stress. They feel that you, Amer, in your infinite wisdom have understood this. Every time you sensed the two of you were getting closer, you asserted yourself, knowing this would start a fight. This interrupted the closeness so that Marsha would not separate from her family too quickly. The group believes you should trust all of Amer's wisdom and put blind faith in him. They think he has an uncanny instinct for what is needed in this situation.

The therapist equivocated with the group's position, saying it was asking a lot of a woman to trust her husband blindly but perhaps she could trust him a little. They were given an appointment for two months hence after summer vacation.

During the session following summer vacation, the couple reported they had gone away on a trip together and their relationship was more harmonious than ever before. The therapist commented that Amer must have felt it was safe for Marsha to get closer to him and he confirmed this. The wife reported she was trusting her husband, "I found I wasn't measuring every minute to see if it was intense enough." She also stated she was refraining from organizing her life around being a good daughter and was spending more time thinking about herself and what to do with her life. She then expressed her anger toward the group.

> I think there is a tremendous contradiction in the group's position because they are professional women and they have a double standard. They are telling me to keep my place but they are not keeping theirs, obviously. This whole thing of telling me to give up my life for Amer and my family is not for me. I have come back with a firm stand—don't define my place for me.

The therapist agreed with her about the group and then wondered how her family was reacting to her new declaration of independence. She reported her mother had escalated her competitiveness with her. Both she and Amer were on a diet and mother kept trying to persuade them to eat. "She's afraid of my being a beautiful woman and so am I." She went on to say how shocking it would be for her to change her image of herself by becoming slender because "sexuality is involved. Our sex life has become much better lately. I'm afraid to be that person I have avoided all my life—being attractive." Amer stated he had no difficulty accepting his new image because it gave him more confidence and helped make a good first impression.

The group called the therapist out and sent back a message that connected the couple's beautification program with the group's concern about Marsha's leaving home.

> The group is worried that if the two of you get beautiful and slender together you will be so attractive to one another you will go zwash!— like two magnets and then what is going to happen to your mother? Then you will definitely leave your mother. (*Hearty laughter.*) If just one of you get slender and beautiful that would be alright but if both of you get that way you would be so enamored of one another and so turned on that you will totally abandon your mother—and they worry about her.

The wife responded after a long pause, "I think I'm going to have to let her go and do what she has to do. We're going back to Amer's country in May and she's going to have to be second fiddle."

In connection with returning to Amer's native land, Marsha discussed the problems of his family. "They are always asking for favors, making demands and Amer gives into them." Amer said apologetically that his family, particularly his father, resented their independence and that they had abandoned family values. The family kept trying to get them back into the fold.

We designed an intervention connecting the problems of Amer's family with those of Marsha's. It was given in the form of a reversal that was aimed at further differentiating Marsha from her mother and at the same time defining the problem in both families as similar. Marsha was asked to reverse her role of mother to her mother and take the position of a daughter seeking her advice.

The therapist entered the session to say she had a final showdown with her group over who was in charge of therapy and she had won. She was going to give Marsha a task over their objections—a task that would further liberate her from her mother. It was then suggested that she go to her mother as a helpless daughter and ask her advice about how to deal with her husband's family when they returned to his home. She should tell her mother about all her husband's problems with his family—how he allowed them to take advantage of him in order to remain the good son, how he didn't protect his own family from their demands, and how he kept giving into their requests. She was told it didn't matter what kind of advice her mother gave her, she didn't have to follow it, but just thank her for it. The therapist explained, "You can't leave your mother while you are mothering her, you can only leave when you become her daughter." She was told the reason the group was opposed to the task was because they knew that once she was in the position of a daughter in relation to her mother she would definitely be able to separate from her. "But most of the group wasn't too worried because they felt the task was too difficult and you wouldn't be able to do it anyway." The therapist took the position that she could do it with her husband's help. He should continue to regulate the distance and closeness.

Marsha proved the group wrong by following through on the task. "Asking for my mother's advice reduced the competitiveness between us. It wasn't very good advice but there was a good feeling between us." The relationship between the couple was going smoothly except for some minor complaints and at the end of the session, the therapist and group discussed the issue of termination. There was an actual disagreement over this with the therapist believing they should continue for a few more sessions in order to solidify the changes and the group believing they were now capable of dealing with their problems on their own. The decision was made to convey the disagreement to the couple but with a rationale that was consistent with the positions of the therapist and group in relation to change.

> The group is concerned that now that Marsha is achieving some independence from her mother, she might dare to move toward more independence in her relationship with Amer. She would do this by becoming less involved in trying to aid his emotional growth and development. If this happened she would be in danger of becoming a successful and competent woman and might worry about her mother's disapproval. Therefore, the group recommends we terminate therapy because any further therapy puts Marsha in danger of changing too much.

Marsha's mouth literally fell open and she exclaimed, "Wow! I'm getting too well, is that what they're afraid of?" The therapist took exception to the message saying she thought both had shown they could tolerate change. Marsha had been able to tolerate her mother's disapproval and Amer to tolerate Marsha's independence. However, since they had been doing very well on their own she would give them an appointment for two months from now. (Appointments were usually scheduled every two or three weeks.)

Amer telephoned two weeks before the appointment to say they would like to cancel it: Everything was going so well they didn't need it. Marsha concurred but requested that I inform the group the cancellation was not due to her fear of further change but was evidence of her ability to handle change. She had at last won a victory over the group.

Case Presentation: Anatomy of Violence

JOEL BERGMAN, PHD

GILLIAN WALKER, MSW

The following case has been included to illustrate how the approach described here can be applied to a family whose members habitually engage in bizarre and violent behavior.

Emphasis is placed on the contest between the therapist and family over control of the therapy. The therapists deliberately create a series of crises within the family by taking a metaposition to this contest. They avoid entering into a symmetrical struggle with the family by commenting only at the level of systems organization that includes the family and therapist. This master strategy forces the stress back into the family. The family keeps trying to dilute the stress through external stabilizers but the therapists eventually compel the family to handle it differently.

During the course of therapy, the family confronts the therapeutic team with an ingenious assortment of ploys to block change, including, among others, threats of murder and suicide, psychotic behavior, extreme symbiosis, a malpractice suit, and a variety of colorful physical symptoms ranging from agoraphobia, hyperventilation, and vertigo, to an imagined brain tumor. The therapeutic team manages to circumvent these ploys with equally inventive counterploys and skillfully averts catastrophic violence.

The dialogue, reading like pages from the theater of the absurd, mirrors the eccentric premises of the family.

Joel Bergman and Gillian Walker. Senior Faculty, Ackerman Institute for Family Therapy, New York, New York.

This case was challenging, not only because of the intractability and chronicity of the symptom and the frightening level of violence in the family but also because of the ferocious contest between therapeutic team and family for control of the therapy. The therapist was Joel Bergman and the members of the consultation team were Gillian Walker, Anita Morawetz, and Paul DeBell.

Seth, a 34-year-old agoraphobic who had accumulated many diagnoses and an impressive list of therapeutic failures in his 15-year career as a mental patient, lived in a continual state of warfare with his mother and father. The initial phone call was from the father, who complained that both he and his wife had to stay with their son at all times because the son got panicky and had violent outbursts when they left him alone. The mother stayed with the son all day, and the father relieved the mother by staying with the son all evening. The father was fed up with this situation and wanted help.

Upon hearing that the son had extensive prior psychotherapy, the intake worker referred the family to the Brief Therapy Project. After the therapist had made the first appointment with the family but before the first session had taken place, a woman called the therapist. She refused to give her name, referred to herself as a "significant other" in the family, and asked the therapist whether she should attend the first session. The therapist thanked her for her interest and said that she might be called on at a later time but that just the family would be seen for the first session.

First Session

The family, an educated, middle-class Jewish family, lived in the New Jersey suburbs, 20 minutes from New York City. Both parents were in their middle to late 50s, and their agoraphobic son, Seth, was their only child. Mother was dressed in a lumber jacket, pants, and hiking boots. She wore her hair in a 1930s bun, smoked Marlboro cigarettes, and cleaned her nails with a matchbook. Father was more conventionally dressed but had the peculiar habit of dozing off several times during the initial interview.

Seth, a powerfully built young man, was wearing a T-shirt, dungarees, and dark glasses. He carried a thermos containing orange juice, which he drank for sugar boosts; Valium, for anxiety attacks; and a brown paper bag into which he hyperventilated during moments of stress. He also took his pulse continually throughout the session. Despite the severity of the presenting problem as described by the father during the intake telephone call, the mood of the session was sleepy, almost dreamlike, marked by occasional eruptions of anger that dissipated quickly.

During the first session, the therapist asked specific questions about the presenting problem, its duration, and the cycle of interaction in which it was embedded, while the team behind the mirror watched analogic cues in order to understand the structure of the system and to assess the family's resistance to change.

SETH: I never go outside because I can't leave the house . . . it's typical agoraphobia. I panic whenever I leave the house, or on a subway or in an elevator or something like that. Around five or six years ago it became constant. And now it's total. And in some way it connected to my mother— I'm also afraid to be away from her. I'm not sure if "afraid" is the right word; it's more complicated than that. There's a lot of anger invested in the fear, is what I'm saying. There's as much magical—schizophrenic, I guess is the right word—schizophrenic magic, you know: her being around, I won't die. But there's also anger: I'm going to die, she's going to see it. She killed me all my life, she's going to see me actually die. So there's that combination of that really psychotic magic . . . really primitive magic, in that anger.

THERAPIST: You were in private therapy 15 years?

SETH: On and off.

THERAPIST: If it's 15 years on and off, how much was on and how much was off?

SETH: About eight or nine on.

THERAPIST: Eight on. Okay.

SETH: At least . . . drug therapy at one time.

THERAPIST: Drug therapy? What kind?

SETH: Any kind you can think of. Okay, we tried Librium and Valium. Valium takes the edge off, it doesn't do much else. Stelazine and Thorazine . . .

THERAPIST: Stelazine, Thorazine?

SETH: . . . didn't work. I had an atypical reaction, got anxious.

THERAPIST: Right. And you were hospitalized?

SETH: Yeah, I went into a day–night center.

THERAPIST: For how long?

SETH: Eight weeks.

THERAPIST: What is the present situation where you're staying in the house?

SETH: Disastrous.

THERAPIST: That's too vague.

SETH: Everybody's at everybody's throats.

THERAPIST: What's the arrangement?

MOTHER: We've been staying in his house.

THERAPIST: Both of you at the same time?

MOTHER: All three of us in his house.

THERAPIST: All three of you staying together in one house?

SETH: Yeah.

THERAPIST: All through the day and night.

FATHER: No, no, I go to work in the daytime.

THERAPIST: (*To mother.*) Okay, and you're with . . .

MOTHER: Twenty-four hours.

THERAPIST: Okay; with Mom in the house during the day, you don't panic and you're okay?

SETH: Unh-unh. Used to be that way.

THERAPIST: But now it's all right?

SETH: Now I panic even with her in the house.

THERAPIST: You panic with her in the house?

SETH: And in fact I don't have home territory anymore. I'm an agoraphobic.

THERAPIST: Well, it's your parents' house.

FATHER: It's his own apartment.

SETH: No. (*All talk.*) I'm trying to explain home territory in terms of agoraphobia. That usually means you come back to your place. Whether you live there or not, you feel safe there. (*Seth "one-ups" the therapist—teaching him about the dynamic theory of agoraphobia.*)

THERAPIST: So you don't have a safe place.

SETH: I don't have a safe territory; I'm constantly in a sort of controlled panic.
THERAPIST: When Dad is home, do you also feel the same thing, or is it different?
SETH: No, it's the same. Sometimes my mother can take the edge off it, but most of the time there's no relief.

As the first session unfolded the team believed that the most important communication from family to therapist was Seth's covert challenge: "I am the expert on my condition and know more about it than anyone else. Other experts have failed, and so will you." Seth's tone was triumphant and challenging as he described his long psychiatric history. The parents' seeming boredom and sleepiness was also a message: "The situation is hopeless. This therapy will be no different, but if it humors him."

In the following section, Seth and his mother described their interaction matter-of-factly, almost without affect. In fact, the parents took turns dozing off. The therapist did not comment on analogic material but attempted to gather information and to bond with the family.

THERAPIST: How can she take the edge off?
SETH: By her presence, her magical thing.
THERAPIST: Just your presence? Do you hold him, caress . . . or comfort him?
MOTHER: No, not really. No, no.
SETH: Yes, she does when I threaten her. I have to threaten her.
THERAPIST: What do you do? Do you throw things, do you yell things?
SETH: All the things you can think of: I throw things.
THERAPIST: Horrible words?
SETH: Yeah, all those things like that.
THERAPIST: Murderous . . . ?
SETH: Yeah.
THERAPIST: You name it. How do you react when Seth says things like that? What do you do?
MOTHER: Depends. Sometimes I scream back at him. Depends on what level it's reached.

THERAPIST: Let's say it's reached . . .
MOTHER: When he hits me, I . . .
THERAPIST: How much does he hit you?
MOTHER: I don't like it. Lately, not too much.
THERAPIST: Slap? Punch?
MOTHER: No. When he hits, he hits hard.
THERAPIST: Where—in the face?
MOTHER: Anyplace.
THERAPIST: Anyplace? Does he knock you over?
MOTHER: Oh, he's knocked the breath out of me.
THERAPIST: Hurt you?
MOTHER: Oh, he's hurt me. I had a bloody head.
THERAPIST: And then she gives you attention.
MOTHER: Then I don't give him attention, I give myself attention.
SETH: No, it doesn't get that far, if it's somewhere in the middle, I think it's somewhere in the middle.
MOTHER: I mean . . . I'm afraid to go near him when he's that way because I don't know whether he's going to sock me if I don't touch him right or not.

The first edge of resistance that the family presented was the contest over who was in charge of the therapy. After a consultation break, the therapist/observation team decided to respond to the family's challenge, "We are desperate but cannot be helped by you or anyone else," by neither accepting it nor refusing it. Instead, the team shifted the contest to a different level by scheduling a consultation session with "world-famous experts in agoraphobia and similar conditions" who would be visiting our institute. By so doing, the team was able to leave it ambiguous as to whether or not the visitors could be of any use to the family and to divert some of the family's rage to the foreign experts. Seth at once countered by asking if the expert was "that man from Philadelphia," and when told that the experts would be Mara Selvini Palazzoli and her associates from Milan, he nodded, smiled, and said that he had heard of her. Since the Milan group was at that time virtually unknown in America, Seth's statement should be seen as his instinctive move to regain control of the therapy.

Five minutes before the scheduled second session, which was to be conducted by the Milan therapists, the "significant other" called to cancel the session for the family. The Milan team saw the cancellation as a powerful symmetrical move by the family to take charge of the therapy. In this family, the most powerful response that one could make was the threat to leave the field. To regain control of the therapy, the Milan team therefore instructed the therapist to telephone to the family to inform them that the family's hour-long session would be spent in consultation with the experts in their absence. Seth, who answered the telephone, was told to stay by the phone so that the results of the consultation could be shared with him.

The Milan team then gave us a written intervention based on their viewing of a video tape of the first session and their thoughts about how to handle the cancellation of the second session. They suggested that the therapist read the intervention to the family at the end of the next session. Four hours after the consultation, the therapist called Seth to say that the information obtained from the consultation was too important to share over the phone and would be shared with the family at the next session, which was scheduled for two weeks later.

Second Session

Of course, the family was too curious not to attend. Seth's response to the team's "one-up" position of having conducted a session even though the family had chosen not to be present was interesting. He arrived for the next session with the "significant other," Annette. Everyone who has ever been to the theater knows that the entrance of a new character at least momentarily distracts the audience from whatever else is going on, for a new character always provides new information. By introducing Annette at this point, Seth was attempting to disclaim the importance of the Milan consultation to the family and the therapy. In fact, during the session, the family showed indifference to the results of the consultation . . . almost amnesia about its existence.

Furthermore, Seth attempted to delay the session by panicking on the stairs and thus being unable to get to the fourth floor video room even with the help of the "significant other." But the therapist began the session with father and mother while the team received bulletins from the amazed receptionist of Seth's progress up and regress down the stairs.

During the second session the parents sought to make an alliance with the therapist by enthusiastically and graphically describing their victimization by their mad son. The team began to see that the parents were bonded by their sense of victimization by Seth. The parents' attitude of helplessness in response to Seth's outrageous actions, their tone of complacent defeat, and the overall lack of anxiety as they described the situation were analogic cues that convinced us that any structural move on the part of the therapist to help the parents set limits for Seth would fail.

FATHER: You say something, he doesn't agree with you; then you say something, he doesn't agree with you, then he blows his top. Usually he's been blowing his top in this particular apartment by taking a glass of water . . .

THERAPIST: This is your apartment?

FATHER: That's right—throwing it on the ceiling and throwing it on the walls and . . .

MOTHER: And all the cabinets.

FATHER: And all the cabinets, and then . . .

MOTHER: All over everything. That's . . .

FATHER: So she gets upset, I get upset; then she cleans it up and we go through the same routine all over again.

THERAPIST: How does that come out, your upsetness? How does that . . . ?

MOTHER: I yell at him.

THERAPIST: You yell at him. Things like?

MOTHER: I just yell at him for doing it.

THERAPIST: You just scream at him for . . . throwing water?

MOTHER: I'm exhausted. I've been up all night with cramps in my leg and I have to climb on the ceiling and move cabinets that're so heavy that a truck can't move them.

THERAPIST: Right. Right.

MOTHER: Two cabinets, one on top of another, and they're falling.

FATHER: And I want to tell you one thing. The reason why he threw the water this time is that she [mother] has been . . . slaving herself getting his apartment in order. Most of the time that she's been slaving . . . When I've come home at night, after she's given me supper, then about nine or ten o'clock he takes her up to his apartment; she works up there all night till about seven or eight o'clock in the morning.

THERAPIST: He takes her to his apartment?

FATHER: That's right.

THERAPIST: To work on his apartment.

MOTHER: He sleeps all day.

FATHER: He sleeps all day.

MOTHER: So I have to be up all day and up all night.

FATHER: And then, while she's up in his apartment, most of the time he's lying in bed and watching television. Now I haven't gone up there the last three times because I've been exhausted and I just couldn't do it anymore.

In the next section, notice how mother detoured the therapist from the question of Seth's violence. No, she says, the only problem is that he has me working too long hours. The moment the therapist attempted to isolate one behavioral problem that can be addressed in therapy, the family "disappeared it."

THERAPIST: Why do you do it for him?

MOTHER: Because if I don't do it for him . . .

THERAPIST: What happens?

MOTHER: He throws things . . . has temper tantrums.

THERAPIST: He starts getting . . .

MOTHER: I don't mind doing work. I just mind doing it this way. See, I don't mind . . . I like to paint, I like to make furniture, I like to sew, I like to do things like that. But he doesn't let me do it at what would be a normal rate for me, or normal hours for me. If I could work all day, and then come home in the evening and rest, it would be fine. But one day . . . last week, I think it was, he had me up for 48 hours working!

THERAPIST: How does he do that?

MOTHER: He insists it has to be done, and if you don't do it it's . . .

FATHER: He's not going to let you sleep, anyhow.

MOTHER: You have no choice, because if I don't do it, he'll have one of these fits and I'll have to work anyhow.

Ten minutes into the session, Seth arrived on the arm of the "significant other." Annette was an attractive young woman of about 30. She had a pleasant, open face, well-cut, short, red hair and was elegantly dressed. As the session proceeded Annette gave a clear useful description of family interaction and of her function in the system.

ANNETTE: I have to make clear why I'm here. I came basically to help Seth get down here. I have been used . . . I think primarily my function is to be a buffer when he goes places with his parents because they all . . . jump on each other.

THERAPIST: These two jump on each other, or they jump on Seth, or who's jumping on whom?

ANNETTE: What I noticed in the basic interaction is mother or father jumping on Seth, Seth jumping on them; it goes both ways. I'm not saying they don't argue between each other. But in the car or when I've been with them or whatever, it's they're angry at Seth or Seth's very angry at them, and it's tremendous rage and frustration on everybody's part that's coming across. Now, over time . . . I mean I've sort of been in it more and more. It seems like I've been asked to be involved more and more, demanded to be in it more and more by Seth. I guess he feels a need for me to be there. I'm not in here because I want to be here; I'm uncomfortable being here; I'm not part of this family. I know his mother and father are angry at me for being involved at all. (Laughs.) I think [the father] is extremely angry with me, the way I know it for sure . . .

FATHER: I think you're wrong. I mean I'm not angry with you. As a matter of fact, if you really want to know, you've been helpful when he's been in these rages. We haven't been able to handle them ourselves. At one time we were able to use his uncle. Now you've taken over the . . . you've been really helpful to him. I couldn't be angry with you.

ANNETTE: Well, uh, what's happened is that I get middle-of-the-night phone calls a lot from Seth when there's . . . some rage and storm going on. According to what Seth tells me, he's beat up on. I do hear screaming in the background to the point where I don't . . .

THERAPIST: By whom?

FATHER: By his father. His father beats him up. He kills him so that . . .

THERAPIST: Is that what you hear?

ANNETTE: That's what I hear. And of course . . .

FATHER: And you're supposed to be a witness, if he's killed, that I murdered him.

ANNETTE: Right. Now what I hear in the background, sometimes I can't even decipher the words, everybody's screaming. *Every*body's screaming.

THERAPIST: All three, huh?

ANNETTE: To the point where I'm so jarred I . . . I freeze. I mean I don't know what to do.

Although the family and Seth left it unclear as to whether Annette was a girl friend to Seth or a professional who had become attached to his case, we were clear that her important role in the family was as a stabilizer who prevented any one of the feared escalations from reaching a crisis point where the system might either break down or find a different kind of organization. Annette's presence "calmed things down," but it also posed a threat to Seth's parents, for she could have provided an exit for Seth from his family that would then leave a void in the parents' relationship.

Later in the interview we asked about the parents' families of origin—a standard procedure that always gives useful information. We learned that both parents came from upwardly mobile, success-oriented families. In each family there was much academic and professional success. Only Seth's parents were failures. During this part of the interview, we heard the first hints of marital dissatisfaction based on the fact that Seth's father, who had failed to achieve what mother's family wanted for her in a husband, hinted that mother put father down, and father raged at her and felt the humiliation acutely. In the past, when mother had not been able to handle Seth, she had brought her brother in as a mediator.

During the team consultation, which took place shortly before the end of the session, it was decided that when the therapist delivered the Milan intervention, he was to take a neutral position, neither agreeing nor disagreeing but saying in effect that the family's actions would prove the Milan team right or wrong. The letter left by the Milan group was then read to the family:

> We have had a 100 percent success rate in 28 cases of treating agoraphobia where the agoraphobic was an only child. The common denominator in the cases treated was that the agoraphobic was an only child who prior to treatment had stayed at home even until the age of 50 or 60 out of fear that without his presence his parents would fall into a state of intolerable loneliness. While we were successful in treating the symptoms of all of the 28 agoraphobics, in 10 percent of the cases we were not successful in preventing the parents from falling into a state of intolerable loneliness. We were therefore relieved when this family chose to stay at home for this consultation because we felt that Seth had an uncanny sense that his family would fall into that 10 percent.
>
> Respectfully yours,
> The Milan Center for Family Therapy

The Milan intervention addressed the resistance of the family to therapy. Leverage was gained by refusing the family's invitation to play by its rules, that is, by not responding symmetrically, for example, "You did not come to the session, you are resisting and that is a bad thing to do." Instead, the Milan team both conducted the session in the family's absence and in the intervention agreed on a metalevel with Seth's decision to keep his family away from the session. The Milan intervention redefined in a circular fashion the structure of family relationships. Although at first glance, the parents showed the most helplessness, and Seth by his behavior seemed to control them, the Milan team implied that in fact he was controlled by their need for him to control their relationship. Statistics were used as evidence of the experts' great power, while the tone of the letter suggested that this was a boringly ordinary case, where, as in so many others, the survival of the family system required the persistence of symptoms. By recommending the continuation of the status quo, the Milan team positioned itself above the struggle and placed the family in a therapeutic bind. The only way the family could continue their familiar pattern of symmetrical escalation, which is how they related to each other and to outsiders, was to one-up the team by proving them wrong. To defeat the Milan team, Seth had to improve, and the parents had to show that their marriage did not need

Seth's presence; but, to do so would have been to admit that they were playing by the team's rules and that admission in itself would have been a defeat.

The family's first response to the Milan team's powerful intervention was to cancel the next session five minutes before it was to have begun. We did not comment on this cancellation but scheduled the next session for two weeks later.

Third Session

The therapist focused his questions on the bizarre relationship of Seth, Annette, and the long-suffering parents. There seemed to be no limit to what the parents and Annette would do for Seth.

ANNETTE: I wasn't aware of all the problems at the time. Seth made me aware that there were problems, but to me it was all very intellectual. It didn't hit me that things could be so seriously bad. It was very much out of my realm of experience. So . . . even he used the word . . . "I might be schizophrenic," he said. But I didn't know what . . . I didn't really know what that meant.

THERAPIST: That *he* might be schizophrenic?

ANNETTE: Yeah. To me they were just words. I didn't know what everything entailed. I didn't know he was phobic, I don't know if he was at the time. He was keeping a lot of secrets from me. I didn't know. Now, looking back in perspective as to how things are now, my guess is he was doing an awful lot of coming to see me with his parents in the car or parked around the corner.

SETH: In the first year I saw her all on my own, basically; in the second year, my parents would come sometimes.

THERAPIST: They would stay in the car and you would visit Annette and they'd wait in the car?

SETH: Yeah.

THERAPIST: (*To father.*) How was it for you waiting in a car while he was . . . ?

FATHER: Very, very, very difficult.

THERAPIST: It must have been hard, huh?

FATHER: (*Laughs.*)
THERAPIST: What did you do in the car? I mean . . .
MOTHER: We sat.
THERAPIST: Did you play cards? Sounds boring as hell.
MOTHER: We talked.
THERAPIST: You talked.
FATHER: I fell asleep.
THERAPIST: You fell asleep.
MOTHER: I listened to the radio. Tried to do crossword puzzles in the dark. Have you ever sat in a car for ten hours?
THERAPIST: It's hard, isn't it? Particularly in the wintertime.

The therapist was careful not to bring up the Milan letter, for that would have indicated that the team had an investment in the family's response. Instead, he waited for the family to bring it up.

In the following section, in response to the therapist's question about how the parents have tried to help Seth, Annette hinted that she agreed with the Milan team in that she believed that the parents had an unconscious fear of Seth's getting better. Seth sensed the danger that in a conflict of loyalties, he might be forced to side with his parents and that a rift might open between him and Annette. He was therefore forced to open the subject of the letter in order to disqualify the Milan team's interpretation and to take charge of the issue.

ANNETTE: Based on my intellectual knowledge of things, I would say that there is consciously a desire that Seth get better, but unconsciously they're very afraid of it.
MOTHER: (*Laughs.*) I don't know why [everyone thinks that].
THERAPIST: Everybody has a right to their opinion.
SETH: I want to say something. That report.
THERAPIST: Which report is this?
SETH: The one from the Italians. I think that there was a lot of tension after that with my parents.
THERAPIST: Tension in the family?
SETH: Not me, my parents.
THERAPIST: How so?
SETH: Because it was saying they weren't perfect.
MOTHER: I didn't read it yet. (*Laughter.*)

SETH: I don't know if I agree with it. See, I don't know if I would've said, Ah-ha, they fall into that category . . . of that intolerable loneliness . . . My feeling would be if I would disappear in some way that that wouldn't be the problem. They had a good setup before I came in, I suspect. "Good" meaning that it was neurotically right.

THERAPIST: Balanced, you mean?

SETH: And I think I upset that completely . . . I don't think they'll [my parents] fall apart if I disappear. I don't agree with that report for various reasons. I think that I might have feared it based on the craziness I saw. But, in reality, I don't think that that's what would happen. I think it would be much easier for them. When I was a kid, my mother choked herself. I was a witness. But the two of them could've handled that in a different way. I was a witness being hurt by it and screaming about it: "I'm being hurt by this." And, "How come you're not doing anything, daddy?" And none of that would exist if I disappeared, if I died or whatever. But I got my feelings much . . . about the interrelationship is much more self-serving than that is . . . But I really see it in a much more malicious . . . going on on both sides.

THERAPIST: Between?

SETH: Between them and me.

THERAPIST: Is it "them" as a group or . . . ?

SETH: Uh . . . more my mother, maybe, but . . .

THERAPIST: With you?

SETH: Yeah.

THERAPIST: And what's that about?

SETH: That's about getting some place in life, accomplishing something.

THERAPIST: Her concern for you?

SETH: No, her concern that I *don't* do it.

Seth wavered between making an alliance with the therapist and protecting his parents by disqualifying the Milan intervention whenever they signaled their distress with therapy. Throughout the therapy, Seth remained in this difficult, ambivalent position, clearly wishing to join the therapist, for whom he showed liking and respect, and at the same time fiercely loyal to his father, who seemed to be the most openly opposed to the therapy.

Hidden in Seth's ramblings was a plea to the therapist to be powerful enough to release him from the hurt of being forced to take his father's place as protector of his mother. Seth explained a central fear that he had: When mother was choking herself, father did not move, and Seth believed that in fact father really wanted her dead. Seth moved in to protect his mother from the murderousness in the marital relationship. From here on in, murder was an important theme in the therapy. If the therapist failed, Seth implied that the only solution would be for him to disappear, to "suicide." "That which I do not witness"—for example, their unhappiness— "does not exist," is a deeper level of meaning to the more obvious, "They would be happy if I died."

During the consultation break, we planned the intervention based on our understanding that the total family–therapist system was a series of symmetrical struggles for control of key relationships (see Figure 1). Each struggle is like a circuit that is interconnected with all the others. When one circuit becomes overloaded and the system threatens to break down, the family

Figure 1.

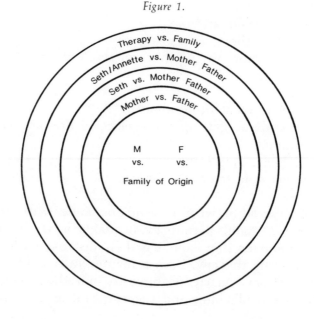

has various mechanisms whereby the overload is switched to another circuit, and another.

At moments of intense internal overload or stress in the family, more and more outsiders or outside systems are "triangled in." Our strategy was to peel off these external stabilizers, working from the outermost struggle inwards, always forcing the stress back into the family, thus creating a crisis that would be resolved in the therapy by the family finding a new, nonpathological organization.

We decided to make an intervention in two parts: the first addressing the family–therapist contest, the second, Annette's stabilizing role in the family. The first part of the intervention countered Seth's disqualification of the Milanese letter and used Seth's statements in the session as evidence of the correctness of their views.

THERAPIST: I'm a little puzzled, Seth, over your disagreement with the letter from the Milan group. When you said that you disagreed with the Milan group, that you thought that you three have stayed together out of spite rather than . . .
SETH: Yeah, I . . .
THERAPIST: Let me finish. And I'm a little puzzled because they talked about how they thought you were sacrificing yourself out of loyalty to your parents, which you disagree with.
SETH: Yeah, there's something . . .
THERAPIST: And yet you told me today that you've had a message or a sense, perhaps unconscious, for a long time from your mother that you'll never amount to anything. That sounds to me like the group was correct in the sense that you have been for a long time very loyal to this sense from your mother that you were never to amount to anything.
SETH: Yeah, yeah.
THERAPIST: And that's much more out of loyalty to your folks and sacrifice to yourself than spite.
SETH: Yeah, I . . .
THERAPIST: You have acted.
SETH: I don't think any of these would be conscious motivations anyway, so . . .

THERAPIST: So my sense is the Milan group was correct in that you are still loyal to your parents because you have picked up the message from your mother not to ever become anything of significance and are still very much, perhaps unconsciously, loyal to that message.

The crucial struggle in these early sessions was for control of the therapy, the contest of family with therapeutic team over the issue, "By whose rules shall this game be played?" The team took charge of the therapy by assuming a neutral posture toward both the family's outrageous behavior and its statements that it wished to change. Instead, the team commented only at a metalevel—that is, at the level of systems organization that includes family and team. By so doing, the team refused the family's dangerous and seductive invitation to "come into its parlor." Were the therapeutic team to have entered into a symmetrical struggle with the family, the contest would have been lost. Instead, the team sent its decoy, the therapist, into the parlor to seem to be seduced by the family. The therapist was the bait that held the family to the game as the family tried to split him off from his colleagues. Had the family been able to do so, by incorporating the therapist into their system they would have restabilized the unstable situation at home that led to the call for help. In severely disturbed families, we frequently find that a therapist has been like a family member for many, many years. That nothing has changed despite the therapist's good efforts is exactly the point.

In the second part of the intervention we made our first move to directly shift the internal structure of the family. Olga Silverstein, who had watched the interview, suggested we prescribe Annette's helping position in order to block her triangulation into the conflict between Seth and his parents.

THERAPIST: (*Turning to Annette.*) The group was very impressed with your investment in helping, and perhaps even an unconscious sense that you're very much needed to keep the balance going in this family to permit what else is operating in this family to occur even though, as you said, you made some sacrifice while being invested in keeping this balance. And they were impressed and touched by what you have done and are doing.

Annette prided herself on her helping role in this family. She mediated the fights between Seth and his parents and believed that she protected all three from the greater danger of unmediated confrontation. In the message, the team therefore redefined her helping behavior as stabilizing the *pathological* balance of the family and thus permitting everyone to continue to act in their terrible ways. We counted on Annette recoiling from her old role once she perceived the result of her efforts differently. If we could get Annette to stop intervening to cool down the triad, Seth and his parents would go into crisis. Such a crisis in that threesome was essential if we were to have access to the key dyad, mother–father. Only if the feared conflict were allowed to take place in the context of the therapy would the myth be dispelled that it needed to end in disaster. Only then would the family have been able to make a leap to a new organization that did not require such massive symptomatology.

Two weeks later the family responded to the move in the third session by canceling the next appointment five minutes before the session. Without comment, the team scheduled the next appointment three weeks later. The family canceled the next appointment, and the team rescheduled a session one month later. As we did so, we commented to the family that their cancellations had been their message to us that the next session should have been spaced at a longer interval. By doing so, we once again refused the family's invitation for a punitive, symmetrical move and agreed with what they were doing.

Seth came to the next session with a brilliant maneuver for control, by which he initially avoided admitting that the therapy was having its effect.

Fourth Session

THERAPIST: We haven't met in some time now because of . . .
MOTHER: Snow.
THERAPIST: Snow?

MOTHER: Storms.

THERAPIST: Storms.

SETH: And a possible brain tumor.

THERAPIST: And a possible brain tumor?

SETH: Um-hmm, namely mine. Uh, I've been having vertigo attacks a long time.

THERAPIST: For how long?

SETH: About three years. And of course whenever it's happened my parents will say, "You're faking it." When you fall down and somebody says that, it makes you angry. So finally the doctor saw it happen in his office. Instead of saying, "You're neurotic," he said, "Better get you to a neurologist. I think you have a neuroma, which is a tumor of the nerve that affects balance."

Vertigo and a possible brain tumor was a brilliant disqualification of all interpretations by parents, therapists, and Annette of Seth's situation. Perhaps, after all, his problems were attributable to vertigo and its organic cause, a possible brain tumor. Of course, Seth was too upset to have the tests that would prove or disprove the tumor's existence.

Later in the session, as the therapist probed, Seth admitted that a change had taken place in the past seven weeks. He was now able to stay with Annette in his own apartment without his parents' presence for as long as five hours "more often and without as much anxiety than there was in the recent past." But for the previous three weeks, since the vertigo, he had spent the remaining balance of his time with Mother and Father in their apartment. It was as if whenever Seth experienced a greater degree of independence and intimacy with an outsider, he had to rebalance the family by developing a symptom. Even though Seth felt freer psychologically from his parents, his physical symptom made him dependent on them for care.

As the therapist explored Seth's greater ability to be alone with Annette, Seth immediately refocused the therapy on his symptom by the following tirade against his parents.

SETH: (*Agitated, almost shouting.*) I've been alone with a possibility of a brain tumor. These two people have been acting basically like this for the last three weeks, not once asking me how do I feel about it, not once asking me, "Is there anything you want to talk about?" not once. . . . That's typical, and, by the way, five years ago, six years ago, when I was in private therapy, I said to the therapist, and I've used it quite often, I said: "If I was dying, my parents . . . my mother would be telling me, 'Why didn't you go to the doctor soon enough?' but at the same time she would have been telling me before that I didn't have to go to the doctor. They'd be yelling and screaming at me; I'd be lying there in bed dying. And it's gonna happen that way."

MOTHER: (*Pacifying.*) First of all, you weren't lying alone, because I was waiting on you hand and foot. You're giving the impression that nobody was taking care of you. Even four o'clock in the morning you were getting food. You didn't care what time it was . . .

FATHER: I want to say something about the way mothers are. Believe me, there is no mother who would stay with him 24 hours a day for the last four years the way she has. If you know any mother like that, Annette, let me speak to her. I'd like to meet her . . .

During the team consultation, we decided to move on three areas:

1. The family–therapy conflict and Seth's vertigo maneuver;
2. Push harder to move Annette out of the helping position;
3. Increase pressure on Mother, requiring her to do even more for her "ill" son.

THERAPIST: Okay, this is the conclusion of the team. I will read it to you and I will send copies of it to you so you can read it more closely. The team feels that Seth misunderstood the implication of our interpretation given at the last session as implying that we expected the family to change. There has clearly been too much change. For example, the absence of his package and the juices and the drugs which he carries right next to him.

MOTHER: It's right there. (*Pointing to Seth's care package of Valium and juice.*)

THERAPIST: Well, usually it's right next to him. His forceful stride as he walked in, and his ability to stay in his own apartment with decreased anxiety. The vertigo, although truly an objective symptom, is an unconscious reflection of Seth's knowledge that change in this family is dangerous.

Since Seth prided himself on his defiance, the team's message defined him as obeying both levels of the team's last message. By misunderstanding the overt level of the message, "Don't change," as actually meaning "Do change," he had in fact complied with the team's covert message, "Change." At the same time, he unconsciously respected the team's overt message that change is dangerous by producing the attacks of vertigo.

THERAPIST: It is very important for mother to redouble her efforts to reassure Seth that he need not be independent at this time. I notice you said that 24 hours of good mothering for the past four years has been a lot. I'm wondering what you can do in the next two weeks that would redouble even more good mothering for Seth.

FATHER: (*Laughter.*)

MOTHER: Oh, I could stop sleeping.

THERAPIST: And attend to . . .

MOTHER: I could stop going to the bathroom.

THERAPIST: Well, he's in bed how many hours a day? Three?

FATHER: Three!

THERAPIST: Eight?

FATHER: Eight!!

MOTHER: Twenty.

THERAPIST: Twenty.

SETH: Twenty.

THERAPIST: Well, 24-hour ministrations. His requests for help. Could you redouble your efforts to meet those requests?

MOTHER: Redouble?

THERAPIST: Yeah.

MOTHER: Impossible. It's impossible!

THERAPIST: Well, I think you can, and what I'm saying may sound kind of . . .

FATHER: Let me . . . I'd like to. (*All talk.*)

THERAPIST: Let me finish. I have to finish this first. All right? Anyway, I think you should redouble your efforts even though I know for the past four years, as [father] said, you have almost given 24-hour coverage, which is a lot. But we'd like you to redouble your efforts even more for the next two weeks.

MOTHER: (*Laughs.*) It's impossible.

THERAPIST: No, it's not. I think you can think of things that you can redouble that you are doing right now, although I grant . . .

MOTHER: I might collapse.

THERAPIST: Well, that . . .

FATHER: Doesn't make any difference. After all, they're behind the television set, behind the mirror there. (*Laughs sarcastically.*)

THERAPIST: What can you redouble? Very quickly, because we have a family coming up.

MOTHER: I don't know.

THERAPIST: Well, we'd like very much for you to redouble. Now Annette must redouble her efforts to be available to help . . . Wait, let me finish, please. Annette, you must redouble your efforts to be available to help Seth accept mother's ministrations . . . you form a balance, as I said before. The more balance you have, the more mother's able to minister to Seth. And father must continue to sacrifice his happiness to help his wife in her task.

MOTHER: (*Laughs.*)

SETH: This *is* satirical.

THERAPIST: I will give you an appointment two weeks from now at six o'clock.

The parents were ordered to assume a one-down position to Seth and by doing so they were told that they would respect Seth's unconscious understanding that change would be dangerous to the family. Annette had to make all this possible by continuing to heed Seth's pleas for rescue. By our prescription, we were only making overt what the parents and Annette were already doing—encouraging Seth's dependence. In addition, we were (1) prescribing that they do it on our orders and (2) that they do more than they have already done. We had, in short, prescribed the system: Seth had to be dependent for his parents, and the parents had to remain Seth's servants so that Seth could remain dependent on them.

The family canceled the next appointment and we gave them another appointment a month later. They then canceled the next appointment, and the therapist asked to talk to the mother on the phone. We learned from the phone conversation with the mother that she had moved back to Seth's apartment. She said that he was impossible, that he was beating her up more than ever. Annette didn't talk to him when he called her, and things were more tense. She was working on his apartment, and he constantly criticized her for not speeding up the work. She rambled on about how she had put five coats of paint on his cubes and he didn't like the paint job so she had to remove the coats. She said she had to take little catnaps to stay awake while working on Seth's apartment. After the phone call with mother, we sent the following letter to her:

> The team feels that you have indeed redoubled your efforts, as evidenced by your move back to Seth's apartment and by painting cubes with five coats of paint. The team also realizes that getting yourself beaten up more by Seth is a final sign to us of your intense motherly devotion to Seth and willingness to fulfill the team's request that you redouble your efforts to help your son.

We then gave the family an appointment a week later. The next session was canceled by a call from Annette, who also requested a session just with her and Seth. We told Annette this was not possible and we would call to give the family the next appointment. We were planning to wait two weeks before giving the family their next appointment, but father called twice asking the therapist whether he agreed with the team and also asking for an appointment. We gave the family their next appointment one month later. During this month interval, we received a letter from Annette asking for an earlier appointment than the one given because she was leaving town for a week. With all the rage going on in the family, she was afraid of what would happen to the family in her absence. We then sent Annette the following letter:

> The team was impressed by your letter and the tremendous sacrifice you're making to help Seth fulfill his mother's wish that he never amount to anything of significance. We agree with you that Seth's progress is premature for the family. Therefore, despite the tremendous progress you have made to stabilize the situation, it is imperative that you do not leave town at this time to make sure that nothing dangerous happens in this family.

Following the letter, we received more calls from father and Annette asking for a session before Annette left. We told father that we would see the family if it were an emergency, if they thought we could be of help, and if they would wait until the day of the session for an appointment since we could only see them if there was a cancellation that day. We then called the family at noon the day of the session and gave them an appointment for five o'clock, P.M.

By the fifth session the family was at a crisis point where substantial systems reorganization had to occur or the family would have successfully reestablished the old balance. Much depended on how the therapist–observer team handled the session.

During the first four sessions the therapeutic team had managed to neutralize the family's attempts to organize the therapist into a position that would have maintained the stability of the family system with Seth as patient. At the same time, some small changes in internal structure of the family had begun to occur. A prescription blocked Annette's helping role, and as she began to pull out Seth was torn between following her in an age-appropriate way or remaining in the child–patient position with his parents. The therapist then had to deal with the violent eruption in the triad as Annette pulled out and Seth became more independent; and he had to expose the dangerous and hidden symmetrical struggle for control between husband and wife that we believed Seth's behavior had detoured. If the therapist could gather evidence in support of the team's paradoxical hypothesis that a sacrificial murder or suicide may be required for the system to survive, then we could block the threatened violence by our prescription.

As the session began there was tremendous tension in the room. Seth was unshaven, bleary eyed; father edgy, explosive. Only the therapist, who had worked for many years with chronic psychotics, remained calm. His stance was that of a detective whose job was to figure out who would be the murder victim before the crime took place. Whereas the family's analogic message to the therapist was, "*You* better do something to stop this violence, (but of course we won't let you)," the therapist's analogic message to the family was, "You will do what you have to do, my job is only to understand your system." The therapist's neutral, relatively unemotional stance had the effect both of gradually reducing the tension in the room and of forcing the family to reassume responsibility for controlling its own behavior. At any point when the family's emotional state threatened to engulf the therapist, the team knocked, pulled the therapist out, and redirected him to gather more information. By the end of the session, the team was convinced that actual violence had been averted.

Fifth Session

THERAPIST: This is an emergency session, and in their [the team's] minds the only emergency that would bring you in, since you've canceled in the past, is over the issue that someone's going to die if you [Annette] were to leave [town]. And I'd like to spend some time today finding out some clues to the mystery of who's going to die . . . Annette, let's start with you. I'd like you to share with me your fear or sense of who might get killed.

ANNETTE: I think there's a potential for any one of the three to get killed. I really do. I think that there's enough rage between the three of them to blow up the city . . . There is a contagious feeling of danger induced in me, a feeling of terrible rage when I'm around them. Lately, more and more I am feeling like I want to be physically violent when I interact.

THERAPIST: Toward whom?

ANNETTE: Well, it's toward Seth, and I get it from Seth when he's having the worst trouble with his parents. In other words, it's just transmitted down the line. So when he's having fights with his parents, he feels he can't let his rage out toward them because it's unacceptable. In other words, even if you tear up a newspaper because you don't want to kill someone, that's like a terrible crime. So therefore, he lets his rage out on me because he feels he has no other place to let it out on. And I'm a good person because I haven't figured out how not to let him let it out on me. So then what happens to me is I want to kill. And the person I want to kill at that moment is Seth, and I know it's being handed down the line, so it's like a circular thing. And what's happened is I'm getting violent

and the violence is toward myself because I can't handle
it. I often want to do something to myself because I find
it unacceptable to hurt people . . .
THERAPIST: So you might die?
ANNETTE: I might die in the process.

The therapist next explored with Seth who he thought
would be most likely to die. Seth stated that his parents would
be most in danger of being killed by him, or he by his father. He
raged at his mother for thwarting his struggle for independence
and at his father for supporting his mother against him.

THERAPIST: So, Seth, in your mind, then, if your mother kept
    you from developing toward independence, she would be
    the one who would get killed; and if your father criticized
    you or agreed with your mother—
SETH: No, I didn't say *criticize*. I said if my father yells at me
    when my mother throws a tantrum, and then my response
    to it is: Well, if she can do it, why can't I do it? Then he
    starts yelling at me. Then I get enraged, yeah. I don't
    understand why, but I do.
THERAPIST: And how do you think each of them might get
    killed? What would be the form it would take?
SETH: It's impetuous, impulsive.
THERAPIST: Could it be beating, stabbing . . . ?
SETH: No, it would escalate from, let's say, I would tear up a
    newspaper and I'd get yelled at . . .
THERAPIST: It would escalate up.
SETH: It would escalate up.
THERAPIST: How do you think the killing would eventually take
    place? What form? Beating to death? Or—
SETH: Uh, my mother probably choking.

The therapist asked whether fights took place that only
involved the marital pair and excluded Seth. Our hypothesis
was that Seth's behavior had detoured a bitter struggle between mother and father, and that his moves toward greater
independence, together with Annette's movement away from
her helping role, had precipitated this crisis. If Annette could
leave, Seth could follow; and the anxiety in Seth and his parents
was that, without Seth, the old battle between the parents

might reemerge. The therapist asked Seth specifically for information about conflicts that occurred between the parents. Seth said there were no more fights between his parents at this time.

SETH: Going way back to the past, I think the same kind of fights that I now have with my mother, my father had with her then; the kind of thing where he would—as I must have brought up before—he would wash dishes and then she would come in and inspect them and find that they weren't perfectly done. And she was not trying to do it maybe antagonistically—

MOTHER: Inspect them. You're using the wrong word.

SETH: —or put them away or whatever, but she wouldn't just turn away; she would look for stuff. He was not in the room. She wasn't doing it to provoke him, necessarily. And he would get mad about it because he felt like he had done something that not only wasn't appreciated but was being redone, and he would get furious about it.

THERAPIST: Would he stand up to her?

SETH: Yeah. Then . . . that was a long time ago, and it usually involved him. I don't remember him standing up to her in relation to what was happening with me and her, or too often . . .

THERAPIST: What about father standing up to mother about issues between them having to do with you?

SETH: Very rarely.

THERAPIST: Only over the dishes.

SETH: I mean she's a hypercritical nag! And every once in a while he would stand up to her.

THERAPIST: And during those years when that was going on, who would have been in danger of getting killed?

SETH: There was physical violence sometimes in those fights.

THERAPIST: Between the two?

SETH: I felt then that my father was controlling himself, where I think he would throw her on the bed or something and try to get out of the room, you know. In other words, her verbal assaults are very aggressive, not . . . You know, here she's so quiet and so . . . They're not the way they seem. She doesn't mention that every time I'm on the phone, she manages to pick up the phone. I mean I think

Annette can remember that practically every time I'm on the phone, she—

FATHER: (*Raging.*) You know, Seth, you're . . . I've just got to say one thing. How you can say that every time you're on the phone she picks up the phone is really . . . it's really . . . I mean I . . . it's unbelievable!

THERAPIST: All right, all right. Let me get this information. All right. Seth, so when they were having tension then, who do you think would have been in danger?

SETH: I think, uh, my mother . . . although my mother sometimes did take a weapon to protect herself, like a knife.

THERAPIST: Your mother.

SETH: My mother.

THERAPIST: And what's your feeling about your dad's standing up and not standing up to your mother?

SETH: I think I'm furious that he didn't in the past. I'm probably still furious about it now. But my father's furious about my tantrums and he's totally indifferent to hers. My mother will do something in front of everybody . . . like, let's say, throw the coffee on the floor. And then she will say, "I didn't throw it on the floor." My father, who has seen her, knows she threw it on the floor; and every once in a while he will say to her, "You did throw it on the floor," but that will lead to a fight, by the way. So most of the time he doesn't. And I come out and say, "Didn't she just throw it in front of my eyes on the floor?! How come it's okay?" My reality gets shook up. I don't have any witnesses, usually. That's one of the reasons that I end up calling Annette *a lot*. If I throw a tantrum and say I didn't do it, he would jump on me.

The therapist pushed harder for evidence as to under what circumstances conflict between the parents could reemerge. In the next section, Seth did not answer the therapist's question directly but suddenly gave an account of recent changes he had made. These changes coincided with the increase of tension in the family that Annette reported and with her decision to take a trip.

THERAPIST: In the event your Mom and Dad would start fighting, let's say in the absence of Annette—okay?—what form would it take and who do you think would get killed?

SETH: (*Long pause.*) I think we've missed the boat, and I have to say this. Around two or three weeks ago I was feeling like I was going to start doing things, and certain things happened, like I was staying in the apartment, my mother wasn't in it.

THERAPIST: You were staying in your apartment?

SETH: Yeah, and my mother wasn't. My father was there, my mother wasn't there for the first time in about a year. The response to it was to not notice it, to not say there was any change, to not encourage her, but to be mad because it wasn't allowed to happen every . . .

THERAPIST: I'm not following what you're saying.

SETH: I'm saying that I haven't stayed in my apartment without Annette or my mother for a year, and in the last month or two I started staying in my apartment without my mother.

THERAPIST: Without your mother but with Annette?

SETH: Without my mother or my father. And that had not happened certainly in well over a year.

When the therapist pressed Seth as to whether, if he were to leave, his parents might resume their old fight, he said, "They might be too tired to fight." Then he reassured the therapist that he didn't need to worry about violence erupting in the family because he had decided to give up his independence and return to bed.

SETH: I don't plan on doing anything; I don't plan on trying to go to plays, I don't plan on continuing exercises; I don't know if the danger is as great as it was a week ago since I accepted the fact that if I stay in bed most of the time and don't try to do anything, then there's a little less tension in the house. I mean I haven't accepted it all the time, but I might change my mind next week and not accept it: that's a problem. Right this minute I feel like, okay, it's better if I stay in bed.

In this family we heard numerous hints from Seth that the relationship between the parents had once contained murderous violence. From this, we hypothesized that when the contest between the parents threatened to escalate to a point where the system might have broken down or a member left the field, as signaled by mother's psychotic rages and withdrawals, father's murderous counterattacks, the family switched to the contest of Seth against his parents. The onset of Seth's symptoms during late adolescence most probably coincided with the threat that he might leave, for Seth was an extremely bright young man. Seth's threat to move out of the system unbalanced a marriage that had been stabilized by the presence of a child. The emergence of Seth's symptoms enabled him to prevent the parents' struggle from escalating by blocking both parents from obtaining the upper hand. In other words, if mother made some potentially devastating remark to father, Seth held her in check by wearing her down until father attacked Seth to protect his wife. If father became too angry with his wife, Seth drew father's fire onto himself and pushed mother to father's side. As the years had passed, the cues necessary to set off these behavioral responses had become more and more minimal; a raised eyebrow, the tone of a remark, was shorthand for a scenario that might have ended in murder and mayhem but that was immediately halted by a symptomatic response on Seth's part.

Since no parental battle ever got beyond these initial moments, the fear of what could result were it to do so increased, as did the intensity of Seth's need to control what was going on. The more Seth controlled the parental battle, the more the parents were joined together in their sense of being victimized by their son and the more desperate they became. Yet the parents could never agree on joint action to control Seth because any attempt they made to cooperate with each other immediately uncovered the marital conflict, which, of course, was a signal for Seth to escalate his behavior once more.

When the struggle between parents and Seth increased to an intolerable level, once again threatening the breakdown of the system (mother might become psychotic, Seth might commit suicide, father might kill Seth), Seth pulled in an outsider, Annette, the "significant other." Annette's entrance made the contest more even—Seth and Annette versus mother and father—with Annette mediating both sides, and thus restoring the system to an uneasy balance by preventing the contest, Seth versus his parents, from escalating to an extreme.

Time once again became a factor that, by forcing the evolution of the system, pushed toward a new instability. A relationship between two young people will usually ultimately break up if it cannot evolve to a new stage. In this family, normal evolution was blocked as tension increased in the relationship between Seth and Annette. At the same time, as we learned in later sessions, Annette was bound into the relationship with Seth by difficulties in her own family of origin. At times, the relationship between Seth and Annette was stabilized by escalations in the relationship between Seth and his parents, with Annette defending Seth against his parents; at times, the relationship between Seth and his parents was stabilized by a fight between Seth and Annette. Yet there was always the threat that Annette would leave. As things escalated in all relationships, tension became unbearable. This increasing internal pressure forced the family to turn to outsiders, not so much to resolve the issues, though there was some dim hope of that, but to restabilize the situation by transferring the internal family struggle to another circuit, a symmetrical struggle in the relationship system of family and therapist.

At the end of the fifth session, the team consulted and decided to point the intervention to the central triad, particularly, to the violence in the marital pair. We felt that we were at the heart of the therapy and that we had to challenge both the triad—Seth and his parents—and the dyad—mother-father—to prove the team wrong by proving themselves able not to be violent.

THERAPIST: The team agrees with Seth that he has not been acknowledged in this family. The team believes that Seth has been willing to sacrifice his life even to the point of risking either killing or being killed in order to protect mother against father's rage and protect father against the psychological death of being humiliated by his wife. Clearly, if mother and father were to admit their role in their son's imprisonment, Seth would be released from his role as guardian of the marital peace.

FATHER: (*Sarcastic laughter.*) I must laugh because—you can finish, but I'll repeat it again—(*Pointing to the team behind the mirror.*) The Cuckoo's Nest.

THERAPIST: All right. All right. Since that admission is clearly not ready for conscious awareness by father and mother, the team commends Seth for his return to bed and his postponement of the steps he was taking (*father laughs*) for his release.

FATHER: Do you want to come again, Seth?

THERAPIST: I will send you a copy of the letter and give you an appointment on May 5.

The family was again pressed to prove the team wrong by proving itself able not to be violent. The team's letter was aimed at Seth, who, it is felt, had most control of whether or not violence actually occurred. The letter defined either killing or being killed as a sacrifice to the greater good of the family system and in fact the ultimate proof that the team was right. A third alternative was offered to Seth: that he retire to bed and make no further effort to change.

In reviewing the tape of the consultation, it was interesting to see that the crisis in the family created an isomorphic crisis in the team that influenced the subsequent intervention. The team's message negatively connoted the parental relationship by referring to mother's humiliation of father and father's rage. Furthermore, Seth alone was described as devoted and self-sacrificing. The team clearly allied itself with one part of the system (Seth) and opposed the other (the parents), a move that created the danger that the family might withdraw from therapy in order to restore family cohesiveness. In retrospect, the negativity of the intervention was due to two factors: (1) the team's lack of experience in reframing all interactions positively, even ones that seemed most highly charged with anger and violence, and (2) the pressure of the family crisis on the team. Despite our error, the intervention was effective and after this session, the family attended each of the following sessions that were scheduled at one-month intervals.

Sixth Session

SETH: The past three weeks basically, as far as I can tell, I'm pretty good, which is strange.

THERAPIST: What does that mean?

SETH: I don't think there was a particularly strong amount of tension compared to other times. I didn't get anything accomplished particularly, but I didn't lie in bed: I kept on doing my exercises. I did start going out alone. *Alone.*

THERAPIST: You started . . .

SETH: Going out into the street *alone*, meaning across the street. But that is big cause that hasn't happened for a year and a half.

THERAPIST: Right. Uh-huh.

SETH: Uhh. (*Sighs.*) Maybe just because I'm contrary, you know. (*Laughs.*) The letter said stay in bed. So I didn't.

The next two sessions were split, with a half-hour session devoted to Annette and Seth and the remaining half hour to the parents. The split sessions were arranged both because of a request by Annette and to obtain personal information from the twosomes that might not be readily available from the foursome. Seeing the parents separately was also an analogic message to Seth that the parents can be alone together without danger, and seeing Seth and Annette together tacitly defined them as an adult young couple.

During the split sessions, we learned that Annette's family had learned of her relationship with Seth. Religious people, they were outraged that she had a lover, considered her a sinner, and threatened to disown her. Annette attempted to break off the relationship with Seth, and each time she did so, Seth threatened to kill himself and his agoraphobia increased. Because of her shame, Annette maintained to her family that she was no longer seeing Seth. She was terribly afraid that if she were indeed to leave him he would punish her by revealing to her family the extent of their relationship.

In the seventh, eighth, and ninth sessions, changes in Seth's behavior continued as Annette continued to pull out and become more independent. She even considered breaking up with Seth and becoming involved with another man; and she decided to go to Europe for a two-week vacation. At that point, however, Seth became agitated and threatened suicide as a way of pinning her down.

SETH: I plan completely, one, to do one simple thing: I plan on killing myself before she goes to Europe. I plan on sending the letters [sent by the team] to Dr. _____ for Medicaid certification and also somebody I know well, and let him decide if they have anything to do with my suicide. It's as simple as that.

Ninth Session

The team consulted and decided to send a letter to Seth and his parents that shifted the original intervention and saw the whole family as acting in the service of Annette. The aim of the intervention was threefold: (1) we felt it would help Annette consolidate her shaky moves for independence; (2) we knew the last thing the parents could tolerate was to be seen as serving Annette, whom they cordially detested, though needed; and (3) although it was obvious that Seth's agoraphobia did keep Annette pinned down, we felt it would be intolerable to him to be defined as "sacrificing himself" for her.

THERAPIST: Let me share with you the team's report. They just handed it to me. The team has always been puzzled by the mystery over who is the real prisoner in this family. But in the last three sessions the answer has become clear to us.

FATHER: Seth is the prisoner.

THERAPIST: It is Annette who is in the most dreadful dilemma. As once before in the past when Annette decided to leave, this family has unknowingly provided her with the perfect solution. Annette is by nature a helping person, and yet she's also a sinner, having brought great shame on her family. Mother and father are willing to seem to be tyrants of the worst order to their only and beloved son to allow Annette the possibility of expiating her sins by performing the role of the helping angel. By cooperating with his parents in seeming to maintain a constant state of terror, Seth has thoughtfully and sacrificially provided a penitentiary for Annette, knowing that as a sinner . . .

FATHER: (*To mother.*) You're free. (*Laughs.*)

THERAPIST: . . . knowing that as a sinner she feels she must do penance, perhaps forever. Therefore, Seth and his parents must continue to help Annette by keeping her the prisoner of their family.

Four days after the ninth session took place, a telephone message was left at the institute by a lawyer for Seth. The lawyer indicated in the message that he was canceling the next appointment for the family, canceling all future appointments, and bringing malpractice charges. The following day Annette called the institute for Seth and left the message that "there had been a change of mind, and the family would like the next appointment which someone had canceled."

Later, we found out that the lawyer who called was Seth himself.

Tenth Session

In the 10th session, Seth detoured the therapy by launching on a tirade against his mother, accusing her of entering his room while he was masturbating. Everyone in the family followed his cue and became embroiled in a battle. When the therapist settled the family down, he proceeded to ask about changes that had taken place.

THERAPIST: Let me ask you how things shifted once Annette came back [from her summer vacation].
FATHER: He's on the phone with her. I want to tell you what happened the other night: I was up there on Tuesday night and I was watching television. [Mother] was downstairs. All of a sudden, I heard him screaming on the phone: "You slut, I'll kill ya," this, this, this. I thought he was speaking to his mother. He wasn't speaking to his mother, he was speaking to Annette on the phone. For two or three nights this week he's been with her on the phone with this sort of talk and hysteria. I don't know what she's been telling him and I don't know what he's been telling her. The only time I hear is when he starts screaming and you can hear it through the door. He comes out of the room: "You've got to drive me downtown, I'm going to kill her." He said that to me. So I said to him, "Unless you tell me what's going on, I'm not going any place with you." And then he quieted down a little later after that. This happened about three times this week.

THERAPIST: And he wouldn't tell you?
FATHER: No, he wouldn't. This happened three times this week.

Until this session the team had only sent the family messages prescribing the symptom and the system. At this point we believed the family was ready to ally with the therapist against the team in the direction of change. The therapist negotiated a small behavioral task with the family while the team reiterated the belief that the family was not yet ready for change and would therefore fail at the task. Note that this family had already successfully defeated many therapists who had attempted to give such sensible advice. Only when the family had built up a huge head of angry steam at the team were they ready to accept a simple commonsense structural move.

THERAPIST: I am going to give you the following task, but I warn you that the team does not believe you can carry it out. Seth, in order to begin taking steps toward independence, you are to stay by yourself for a certain period of time each day. During the session you suggested an hour, but I feel that this may be too long. You therefore should determine the period of time which you feel is tolerable for you to stay alone. Each day I suggest that you increase the time alone by no more than five minutes. You may feel tempted to test yourself with longer periods of time away from stressful situations, but under no conditions should you do so. You must keep a log of your attempts, noting date, time, and what you did and how progress was acknowledged by your parents.

[Mother], you are not to enter Seth's bedroom unless you are directly invited. You may feel that Seth is sending you indirect signals for motherly help, but you must resist the temptation to be a loving and helpful mother.

Mother and father, you are to log Seth's small steps toward independence and commend him for them. I must warn you again, however, that the team disagrees with me completely. Due to the reasons stated in the last letter, they are convinced that the family must not change, and therefore will find itself unable to do the task.

Eleventh Session

The following session was the last of the therapy. Although we had counted it as the 11th session, the family had clearly followed our statement that the Milan consultation was a session in and of itself and had correctly counted this as the 12th and last session of the 12 originally contracted for. There was much tension in the family, clearly about termination, and Seth had made some calls to the clinic administrator to ask about this peculiar therapy.

SETH: If I had known that . . . that there was any possibility of getting, first of all, family sessions not too regularly and then of getting letters from one part of the group and from another part of the group, I never would have gone into it. I'm not saying this in retrospect, I've been saying it all along. But the thing that's angering me about it is that I did; I was curious to find out if this was conventional, because as far as I knew . . . even though my gut told me this couldn't be the only . . . the main method of family therapy. When I called up to find out, you know, what is . . . is this normal? I asked them. I'm not going to lie to you. I called up and said, "Look, what do you normally give?" And they said, "Normally, it's once a week with one therapist." Because I . . . I . . . I said, "Well, I'm getting all of this," and then she said, "Well, talk to your therapist about it."

The tirade against team and therapy continued until the team decided to interrupt the session with a message that would put Seth in another bind. The team instructed the therapist to tell Seth that "we are relieved that he has decided to spend the session discussing the therapy because we were afraid that he would publicly humiliate our colleague, Dr. Bergman, by proving his optimism about change wrong, and thus validating the team's position."

THERAPIST: The team called me up to tell me that they would like you to continue talking about your criticism of the therapy and all the problems with this kind of therapy to avert from discussing what was happening with the agoraphobia because they were concerned that you might say things that could prove that I was wrong compared with what the team thinks.

SETH: Compared with what the team thinks, you're right, because I've been getting better and . . .

Okay, I'll tell you the changes very quickly. I'm not going to go into them in detail. Stayed alone without having, you know, telephone contact with my parents.

THERAPIST: For how long?

SETH: Only an hour and a half or an hour.

THERAPIST: Without anyone?

SETH: They were in the street. I saw . . . knew where they were, but I didn't have telephone contact with them. Stayed alone a few times more since I talked to you on the phone . . . you know, where I did have telephone contact.

THERAPIST: Yeah.

SETH: Uh, went to, uh . . . went up to the 12th floor in the elevator in the Vocational Rehabilitation—not alone, but I went up—and I got tense and I . . .

THERAPIST: You went up with whom?

SETH: I went up with . . . with my parents, my mother and Annette. Went to a movie.

THERAPIST: By yourself?

SETH: No, not by myself. With Annette.

MOTHER: Without us following. Been a lot . . .

SETH: Without them following. I went on dates. I mean, you know.

MOTHER: He drove downtown alone in the car.

SETH: But I was followed.

MOTHER: . . . with us following in another car.

THERAPIST: Alone, without anyone in his car?

SETH: Without anyone in the car.

MOTHER: With nobody in the car.

SETH: There were a lot of . . .

THERAPIST: How far away were you following?

MOTHER: We were right behind.

THERAPIST: Right behind him.

MOTHER: . . . but, you know, sometimes cars get inbetween. But he was all alone in the car and it's the first time in years that he's done that.

During the team consultation we decided that as a final message the team should once again advise the family to slow down. We also decided to ask the family to reread the team's letters since the letters from the team had had such a powerful effect in mobilizing the family to change.

THERAPIST: Here's the team report. "The team was alarmed that Seth and his parents acknowledged that the family was changing. They refer them to the team's letters and warn Seth of the dangers to his family, and particularly to Annette, should any member of this family change."

FATHER: What is this? (*Laughter.*)

SETH: Paradox. It doesn't work if everyone is onto this.

FATHER: Yeah.

THERAPIST: Let me finish. "Furthermore, in all justice to the family, the team must warn them that we believe Dr. Bergman is being deceived by an apparent flight into health on Seth's and his parents' part."

FATHER: A flight into what? Say that . . .

THERAPIST: Health.

MOTHER: Health.

THERAPIST: "From our reviewing of the tapes, together with our extensive work with severe phobic symptoms, we conclude that Dr. Bergman is being naively optimistic about change. We still believe, with the Milan team, that Seth and his family are in the 10 percent of families who must learn to live with their unhappy situation. Dr. Bergman expressed to us his interest in continuing working with Seth and his parents even though the 12 sessions initially contracted for have ended. The team urged against this, citing Seth's behavior in this session as evidence that *he* knows best when progress should be stopped and false hopes should not be raised."

The session ended with the therapist offering the family the opportunity to continue treatment despite the team's pessimism. Seth said he'd think about it and call when he had decided. One month later Seth left a message on the therapist's telephone answering machine requesting that the therapist call him between seven and eight in the evening, since he wouldn't

be home except for that time period; and that he wished to continue family therapy. When Seth's call was returned between
seven and eight, no one was home or cared to pick up the
phone. We then waited. Two weeks later Seth left a message
on the therapist's answering machine saying it was common
courtesy to return people's phone calls. The therapist then
tried to call Seth several times without being able to reach him.
A few weeks later Annette called and asked for the name of a
family therapist who could see Seth privately. The therapist
told Annette to tell Seth to call the therapist so we could
discuss the issues related to a referral. Seth has yet to call since
that message was given to Annette.

Follow-up two years later was fascinating. First, a member
of the team attempted to speak with father. Father's rage at
the team was as intense as it had been at the last session, and
the team member had to use every strategy known to keep him
on the phone. After raging at the team and the therapy, he let
slip that Seth was greatly improved but that it had nothing to
do with the therapy but rather with his wife's efforts on behalf
of their son. The family had not had further therapy since
termination, nor had Seth been in individual therapy. Father
betrayed his investment in our therapy when he added, rather
resentfully, "I don't see why I should talk to you now [almost
two years later] when nobody cared enough about us to follow
up earlier." He then added that although he would not give
further information to a team member, he would be delighted
to talk to Dr. Bergman who, in contrast to the team, was a
good and caring person who could have helped the family if he
had been allowed to see them without the team.

We were reminded of a case of Milton Erickson's where a
woman who is hallucinating is instructed to leave the figures
she hallucinates in Erickson's closet where they will be safe. So
father's anger lay safe with the team that freed him, his wife,
and, above all, Seth. Father, however, still attempted to split
Dr. Bergman from the team, perhaps as the good son he
wanted, perhaps as a gentle father who managed to care about
the family and had the courage to stick with them through
fearful times.

Bateson tells a lovely fable about the relationships between
a porpoise who must be trained in new behaviors, a trainer

who must teach him, and a supervisor who must be responsible for planning the strategy of the training program. Bateson's point is that the porpoise continues to learn in very frustrating situations because of his relationship with the trainer who, out of sympathy for the mammal's difficult and arduous task, breaks the rules set by the supervisor and gives unearned fish. The supervisor remains stern and unyielding and absolute in his insistence on the rules. His skill sets the strategy for learning, but the trainer's steady affection for the porpoise is the essence of the teaching. Bateson's fable is the paradigm for the therapy we do.

One other point: It is important to us that the family gives the therapy little credit for change and, in this case, that father instead gave all the credit to his wife. For, in the end, it is the family, not the therapist, that has found its own unique way out of its dilemma.

A call to Annette revealed that she had finally broken up with Seth about three months after the termination of therapy. Although she still feared that some violence would occur, she felt that there would be greater danger to herself were she to stay. Nothing terrible happened; in fact, Seth, without Annette, continued to improve. He went out more without his parents accompanying him, took art courses and completed them, was able to visit Annette on a friendly basis, and began to make other friends.

Failures and Pitfalls

It is impossible to assess all the elements that go into effecting change because of the complex, unpredictable qualities of human systems. The therapist can set the stage for change but can never predict how it will take place or *if* it will take place because of the random and circumstantial elements over which the therapist has no control—or even sometimes no knowledge. It is, therefore, impossible in retrospect to know for sure what didn't work, why it didn't work, or indeed *if* it did work. Sometimes little or no change occurs during the course of therapy but unexpected shifts take place afterwards (which may or may not be related to the therapy). People have been changing for thousands of years without the benefit of mental health workers, which indicates there are many different routes to transformation. Such questions as how the family would have responded to a different intervention, to different timing, to a different assessment of the problem, can only be speculative.

This chapter is not being written so that others may avoid making the same errors as described here (each therapist must learn from his/her own mistakes) but to correct any erroneous impressions that this approach always leads to change. Change in this context means the elimination or substantial modification of the presenting problem. If the presenting problem remains the same, though other positive changes take place in the family during therapy, the outcome is considered to be less than successful.

Perhaps one of the reasons that failures are not often written about is that the process of retracing one's steps is painful and frustrating, accompanied by the inevitable, "How could I have missed what now seems so obvious" or "If only I had done such and such everything would have turned out differently" or "Why did this intervention, which I planned so carefully and thought so brilliant, fall flat, while that other one which was hastily formed and makeshift produce a marked change?" But then again, what one thinks produces change may not be what actually produced it.

This was brought home to me when I was a beginning therapist at the Ackerman Institute many years ago. At that time I was working under the assumption that if one understood why one did what one did, one would stop doing it (commonly referred to as insight). In an attempt to help a mother change her behavior toward her children I said, "You know, Dorothy, you are a very intelligent woman and so I'm sure you can see that you are treating your children in the same way that your mother treated you. She pushed you because she was afraid you wouldn't live up to your potential just as you are now pushing your children in the same way." Her eyes lit up and she replied, "I have never made that connection before—but—yes, you are right. Oh thank you, Mrs. Papp, this has been very helpful."

The following week Dorothy came to the session with a glowing face and reported she had had a wonderful week. The tension had left the house and she had stopped fighting with her children. I sat secretly congratulating myself on my brilliant interpretation until the end of the session when she turned at the door to ask, "By the way, Mrs. Papp, what was that you said last week about my mother and me? All I remember was 'Dorothy you're an intelligent woman' and all week I've been saying to myself 'Mrs. Papp thinks I'm intelligent, Mrs. Papp thinks I'm intelligent' and it's made me feel wonderful." That experience left me eternally humble about what produces change. And yet it is important to speculate as it increases the therapist's awareness of the therapy process.

Reported here are some speculations on what went wrong in some particular cases around some particular issues. Rather than definitive conclusions being stated, questions are raised. The reader is invited to speculate also and his/her speculations may be quite different from mine.

Most of the failures in the Brief Therapy Project were connected with inconsistencies in overall policies. Because the guidelines for making these policies were not clear, the therapy that followed mirrored the confusion. Inconsistencies surrounding absent family members and an outside therapist were responsible for two of our major failures.

Coping with Outside Therapists

Many difficulties have arisen in connection with cases in which an outside therapist has been involved. In a high percentage of cases referred to our clinic, one or more family members are currently in individual treatment outside the institute. We have vacillated in our policy concerning this issue, dealing with situations in different ways with varying degrees of success. In some cases we accepted the continuance of the individual therapy and treated it as part of the system. Rather than asking the family to relinquish someone in whom they had made a large emotional and financial investment, we incorporated the therapist into our interventions. For example, in the case of a 13-year-old delinquent who had been seeing a psychologist for two years, the therapist told the family we would leave the son's deeper intrapsychic problems to the psychologist to resolve and would only deal with problems related to the family. (They did not elect to come to family therapy on their own but were referred by the hospital where the mother was taken after a suicide attempt.) The parents had skillfully avoided coming to terms with other threatening issues by becoming obsessed with their son's behavior. During the sessions, whenever the parents attempted to obscure these issues by haranguing the son, the therapist would interrupt to ask if they thought his behavior was connected with something going on in the family. They inevitably replied it had to do with something inside the boy. By telling them that in that case they should discuss the son's behavior with his individual therapist, the therapist blocked their torrent of complaints and compelled them to talk about the issue that had driven the mother to attempt suicide. Her husband, after a recent heart attack, had decided he wanted to uproot the family and move across the country to live next to his parents. The wife, wanting to stay near her family and friends, felt helpless to make her desperation known other than through a suicide attempt. When it became evident to the family that the son was caught up in trying to resolve this crisis between his parents through his frenetic behavior, the parents voluntarily stopped the son's therapy. His behavior was then dealt with as part of the family process. This would have been complicated if the son had been attached to the therapist, but in this case he was simply complying with his parents' orders.

We sometimes used this same approach with couples in which one spouse was in individual therapy. We left the diagnosed symptoms of "low self-esteem," "chronic depression," "free-floating anxiety," and "unmet dependency needs," up to the individual therapist to resolve while we dealt with the problems between the couple. The "patients" often voluntarily quit their individual therapy when it became clear that their individual symptoms were part of the marital interaction. Even when this did not happen and they continued in individual therapy, it did not always interfere with a successful treatment of the marital problems. However, in other cases, we found ourselves working in direct opposition to the outside therapist and the treatment was seriously undermined. Occasionally, it was possible to work in tandem with the individual therapist but only when this therapist accepted the marital therapy.

After several frustrating experiences, we instituted the policy that unless the person in individual treatment gave it up for the duration of family therapy, or unless their individual therapist agreed to join us in sessions, we could not accept the family. This policy produced new complications as the person sometimes gave up the treatment reluctantly at the insistence of the family, felt coerced into coming to the sessions, and refused to participate. With one such family, we made the decision to discontinue therapy after three sessions. The father had pulled his 21-year-old son out of a four-year psychiatric treatment against the wishes of both the son and the psychiatrist. The son agreed with the father that he had not improved, but he still had faith that one day the psychiatrist would help him. He reluctantly agreed to come to the family sessions, but it soon became apparent that he had struck a secret bargain with his psychiatrist never to change with anyone but him. The reason given the family for discontinuing was that if the son should improve in family therapy he would put his psychiatrist in a bad light and would consequently feel disloyal to him. Until the son had paid his debt to the psychiatrist by improving, family therapy would not be helpful.

Absent Family Members

Another policy about which we have been inconsistent is whether or not to accept a family if one or more members refuse to come to the sessions. Our decision making has been complicated by our having achieved a variety of results by following different courses. In certain cases we have managed to involve the missing person after therapy has begun. In "The Daughter Who Said No" the father who had refused to come initially was later engaged and became a regular participant. Although we began the first session with only the mother and the identified patient, we were convinced that the other three members of the family would follow. This was based on our impression of the family as being highly involved in garrulous athletics, which would preclude any one member not putting in his/her two cents. This initial impression was quickly validated.

In other cases, we have managed to bring about change with one member missing throughout the entire course of therapy. This has usually been the symptomatic child whose refusal to participate was part of his/her general pattern of rebellion. For example, in a family treated by Olga Silverstein, the delinquent behavior of a 21-year-old son was changed without his ever attending a session. The rest of the family was seen for regular appointments and letters were sent home to the son after each session, supporting his staying away on the basis of what had transpired during the session. If, for example, the parents had a fight, he was congratulated for having had the foresight to anticipate this and to know they would only have been sidetracked by his behavior had he been there. Or if the focus of the session was on his sister, the letter stated how much the family appreciated his allowing the spotlight to be on his sister who had been neglected recently. Or that he would not have agreed with all the things that were said in a particular session and he had thus avoided an unpleasant scene for the whole family. He was constantly referred to as "the guardian of the home" who remained behind to preserve the old way of life while the family sought to change.

After three months the family reported a marked lessening of his rebellious and abusive behavior; he eventually obtained a job and moved out of the home. The only way he could prove the therapist wrong was to either come to therapy or to move out of the home that the therapist instructed him to guard.

The Golden Thread

In another case, however, our agreeing to see the family without the father handicapped the therapy severely. The father remained incommunicado, neither answering our telephone calls nor reading our letters. The absence of a parent is sometimes a more serious problem than the absence of a child whose leaving the family is a natural occurrence in the life cycle. This does not hold true of a parent. In the following case, our frustration in not being able to involve the father caused us to press for change in nonproductive ways. After several sessions, feeling we had reached a dead end, we terminated the case. We later wondered if this termination had not been premature and if there were not other alternatives available to us. During the process of writing this chapter, this question was reopened and left me wondering if perhaps our mistake had been in assuming that we could not have proceeded without the father. I will leave this to the reader to think about.

In this case the mother had requested therapy because her 38-year-old daughter, Christina, had recently been hospitalized for bizarre behavior—hearing voices, writing notes on doors and windows, scattering money about, and leaving the door of her apartment open. Mother stated she also had a marital problem of 40 years with her husband who was "violent and paranoid" but would not join them for therapy. She claimed she had tried to involve him many times over the years but he was suspicious of the entire mental health profession. The therapist at first refused to see the family unless the mother could persuade her husband to join them, but after repeated desperate calls from the mother, who suggested her husband might follow if the rest of the family came, the therapist relented, hoping to involve him later.

The mother and her three children appeared for the first session. Christina, 38, a tall, willowy blonde, waltzed into the room in a wide-brimmed hat with the elegant air of someone out of a Tennessee Williams play. Robert, 35, married and living away from home, was cautiously guarded and looked like he didn't want to be there. The younger brother, Clyde, 27, in contrast was open and articulate and seemed eager to have something done about the family. He lived at home with his mother and father and was involved in starting his own business. The mother, descended from an aristocratic European family, spoke with a heavy accent. She looked shopworn, like a faded beauty who had fallen on hard times.

Robert and Clyde had come only to help their sister, Christina, who felt she had no problems and had come only to help her mother. Christina's most flagrant symptoms had disappeared and she was living quietly in her own apartment, earning a living walking dogs and causing no problems. The brothers were concerned she might get "sick" again. Christina was concerned about her mother's "fragility of soul" and was worried she might have a nervous breakdown or a serious accident because she was so preoccupied with her marital problems. The brothers confessed they were also worried about this, and it soon became clear that all three were deeply involved in trying to resolve their parents' unhappiness.

During this session we learned that both parents came from wealthy, titled families, had met and married in Europe where the father had been a respected musician and the mother, his doting student. They came to this country after being driven from their home during World War II and losing all their property and money. Father was never able to establish himself in this country and mother had supported him and the family by teaching and arranging music. Father returned to Europe several times in an effort to reestablish himself there but, each time failing to do so, returned home to rely on mother's support. Although it was her work that brought in financial remuneration, he set himself up as the maestro and connoisseur, constantly criticizing mother's technique and style. According to the family, he maintained the air of a courtly, old world gentleman in dress, manner, and habit. Mother complained about father's exploitation of her, claiming he criticized and humiliated her, never appreciated her supporting him, and often indulged in uncontrollable outbursts of rage. But she stated she couldn't leave him because, "I still believe in him—in his talent—and keep hoping one day he will change."

Mother constantly relayed her distress to the children, particularly to Christina whom she called frequently to unburden herself. Christina's response was to try to talk her mother out of her "romantic illusions" concerning father and convince her he was not going to change. "She is so optimistic, she makes me sick." Christina tried to convince mother to leave father, to live with her temporarily so father would appreciate her more.

The event that seemed to have precipitated her recent "psychotic episode" was a fear of her parents separating. Following a violent argument, father threatened to leave. Hearing of this, Christina called her parents at midnight and demanded they come over and stay with her because she was afraid to be alone. When they arrived she said, "Just sit there and don't say anything." She kept them the whole weekend and spoke of having dreams in which trains were derailed.

The children also worried about their father's unhappiness and made efforts to comfort and support him. Robert was described as being the closest to him, the one most like him who understood him best. However, again it was Christina who seemed to bear the major burden for looking after his physical and emotional well-being. She took him to the eye doctor, arranged for him to have physical check-ups, discussed music with him, and remembered to send birthday and Father's Day cards.

The family agreed that father should be involved in the sessions, but all proposals in this direction led to an impasse. When the therapist suggested she herself might call or write extending an invitation, she was told father refused to answer the telephone and would probably not open any mail addressed to him from us. (This was validated when our telephone calls went unanswered and our letters to him were returned unopened.) Although we speculated that the family must in some way be collusive in keeping father away, it was not clear to us just how they were doing this or for what reason. What was clear was that Christina's problems were connected with the gigantic job she had taken upon herself of trying to keep her parents together and happy.

Mother kept her involved in this job by playing the victim to father,who seemed to be making up for his lost prestige by lording it over mother. This way both mother and father preserved their master–student relationship from the past. The therapist and team felt hampered in forming a hypothesis without the input from father. Any hypothesis made with half of the marital equation missing is bound to be half-formed and lopsided. In our experience, a single description, devoid of any rebuttal or on-site observation of interaction, always requires extensive revision with the appearance of the other spouse. We therefore decided not to address the marital problem but to focus our attention directly on trying to help the children extricate themselves from their involvement in it. We did this by prescribing a ritual that included only mother and the children. It was decided that the therapist and group would agree on the ritual but the group would take a dubious position regarding the children's ability to follow through on it and would suggest mother help them by testing their resolve.

The therapist told the family that she had come to the conclusion that it was time for the children to bury their expectations for their parents' happiness and that they should have a ceremony to commemorate their giving up. They were to write down on a piece of paper their fondest dreams and hopes over the years and all the ways they had tried to bring these about. They were to read them to each other and then bury them in the backyard under the tree where Christina often sat to meditate. It was suggested this be done on Thanksgiving when the family was planning to convene, and Christina was put in charge of following through on the ritual. They were told that although the group agreed with the therapist that this would be a good idea, they thought it would be difficult for the children to do. They suggested mother could be helpful in testing their resolve by telephoning every day and complaining about her great unhappiness. Christina commented, "It will solve our separation—that we are not married to our parents."

We were hoping that this ritual would begin the process of disengagement by dramatizing the hopelessness of the children's efforts to resolve their parents' difficulties and that mother would recoil from the prescription to call her children more often to test their efforts to become less involved. Although we realized this direct push for change might be premature, we knew we had the option of backtracking and prescribing homeostasis if they did not follow through on it.

Robert was absent from the following session, giving his work schedule as an excuse. The family did not follow through on the task; Christina stated, "It was a good suggestion but I analyzed it myself and parts are missing. My father is not here." Discussing it afterwards, we realized that the ritual would have been looked on as an act of great disloyalty toward father as he had not been present in the session and was not made part of it as mother had been. Robert, his representative, expressed his disapproval by not coming to the session, and Christina, who always spoke in metaphors, spent this session talking about "the golden thread of love that holds the family together and which can never be broken." These were distinct messages to us that we had moved too quickly to sever the golden thread. The groundwork for disengagement had not been prepared through a positive reframing of the parents' relationship that would provide the children with an incentive for extricating themselves. For example, we might have said that the children should not interfere in their parents' relationship because it was important for the parents to maintain their romantic illusions about one another—for father to continue to act tyrannical and critical and for mother to continue to act helpless and subservient because this kept father in the position of the supreme maestro and mother in the position of the admiring student. The parents were willing to pay any amount of unhappiness in order to preserve their remembrance of things past, and therefore the children must not interfere with their devotion to their unhappiness.

We did not use this formulation of the problem at the time because we were preoccupied with trying *not* to deal with the marriage. In retrospect, it seemed obvious that to extricate the children from the futile game they were playing with their parents without first defining the name of the game, the rules by which it was being played, what the stakes were, and why they could never win was impossible.

During the next session, mother spent a great deal of time talking about father again and wondering what to do about him, while Christina and Clyde kept trying to give her helpful advice. Christina described her mother as having a "blind spot" in relation to her father. "Every time she thinks that the relationship is harmonious, it turns out not to have changed— still she maintains her blind faith." Clyde supported mother, saying it was because she did not believe that anybody was either all good or all bad and always believed in the positive. He often interceded on behalf of mother during father's violent outbursts.

In consultation, we decided to backtrack from our premature push toward change and, instead, define and prescribe the impasse created by mother and the children in trying to figure out what to do about father. We did this by defining the repetitious circular pattern (mother not knowing what to do, the children giving her advice, mother ignoring their advice and continuing not to know what to do, etc.) as the golden thread that kept mother and children forever involved. It was decided the therapist would take a neutral position in relation to the message and give Christina credit for understanding it since it was her metaphor. The message read as follows:

> The group believes that it is very important that you do not know what to do about your husband and that you continue not to know what to do because this keeps your children involved in trying to help you to know what to do. If you were to find out what to do it would break the golden thread which holds the family together. We apologize for not having understood this sooner.

The therapist continued, "I am not sure I understand the message, but the group said Christina would understand it." Christina's reaction was, "It's going on the right track but there are a few cars missing." Still a reference to the missing father. A copy was sent to Robert.

This is an example of a definition of the problem that deals with the periphery rather than the vortex of the situation. The never-ending game that mother played with the children was a result of the never-ending game she played with her husband. By avoiding a reference to that game we avoided the central problem and missed the mark. Again, it was the absence of the husband that prompted this avoidance.

Neither Clyde nor Robert appeared for the next session, which was attended only by mother and Christina. Clyde sent a message that he had the flu and Robert sent a message he would not attend any more sessions as he didn't think they were helpful. When a family member drops out of therapy it can mean many different things and can even be a good sign in certain situations. We considered the possibility that Clyde and Robert might be reacting to our messages by pulling back and becoming less involved with their parents' problems, but from what was reported by Christina and her mother this did not seem to be the case. More probably they were reacting to our being off the track.

In this session mother revealed how she colluded with father to keep him away from therapy and thus preserve their mutual illusions. She spoke of how upset she was because her husband had accused her of stealing a piece of music and selling it and stashing the money away somewhere. "It gets my molecules out of order and I feel like breaking things," she stated. "But if I leave him alone he is O.K. If you rip it open it makes a big blow. It's like a package pushed under the bed—if you open it and he would see that he has to take responsibility for his failure it would be a big shock. It's better to keep it closed."

It now seemed clear that mother was protecting father. By treating him as someone who was too fragile to face reality and take responsibility she continued to preserve his illusion of being the great maestro. In doing so she also protected her position as the one on whom he was totally dependent, the only other person who shared this illusion. The package under the bed was filled with fantasies, pretenses, memories, and illusions that kept both tied to each other and to the past. The father's absence was the parents' way of making sure the package stayed untied and of preserving a precarious balance between them. But the children were left in a state of constant apprehension and foreboding that this precarious balance might suddenly and disastrously collapse.

At this point we decided that the package under the bed had to be untied and that father's presence was essential to this process. We believed we were perpetuating the system by going along with his absence. The therapist told mother that after thinking it over she had decided it was not a good idea for mother to continue not to know what to do about father as the group had suggested but that it was time for her now to know what to do and that she had to find a way to bring father to the session. If he did not come she felt she could no longer be helpful to the family and would have to terminate therapy. The group sent in the message doubting mother would be able to convince father to come because she was too protective of him and didn't want the package under the bed opened.

We set an appointment time with a provision that mother was to call and cancel in the event she failed to persuade father to come. After mother canceled two appointments we sent a letter to each member of the family informing them that we could no longer work with mother and Christina as the primary couple in the family and that we would resume therapy if at some future date the entire family was interested in participating.

Six months later we learned from the hospital that Christina had been readmitted. This raised questions in our minds as to what the alternative to termination might have been. Was it really necessary to involve father or could we have found a way to change the family's perception of the marital relationship without his presence? For example, we might have taken the position that it was good that father had not come in because if he had there was a danger that the package under the bed might be tampered with. We could have argued that it should be left alone as it contained the precious things that kept father and mother tied together and tied to the past and that under no circumstances should Christina or any of the children try to rob their parents of their unhappiness because this was the price they gladly paid for keeping the package under the bed.

Such an approach might have diminished Christina's intense involvement in her parents' relationship. However, since this was her only way of maintaining contact with them, this involvement would have been difficult for her to give up.

The question that remains unanswered is if we had managed to break the golden thread would the family have found another way of holding themselves together in time to prevent Christina's rehospitalization?

The Great Mother Tradition

The following case came to an abrupt and violent end after six sessions. We believe there were a variety of factors that contributed to this, including confusion over the initial referral, an ill-advised intervention, faulty timing, and the family's powerful investment in keeping the identified patient in the patient role.

This was a family whose many previous bouts with therapy had failed (always a seductive challenge for a therapist who hopes to succeed where others have not.) The previous therapies included eight years of individual therapy for the identified patient, Eric, an adopted son, following a four-month hospitalization eight years earlier; two attempts at couples therapy for the parents; and two attempts at family therapy that ended with both family therapists referring the family elsewhere.

The referral to our institute was made by Eric's individual therapist who had become a convert to family therapy and was extremely anxious to have the family seen because of the extraordinary and increasingly explosive degree of tension and violence in the home. This therapist was planning to relocate in another city, necessitating her terminating therapy within three months. She requested that we see the family during this process of termination, and we agreed to do so under two conditions: (1) that she would attend the family sessions until her departure, and (2) that she would make arrangements with the hospital under whose auspices she worked to transfer responsibility for Eric's treatment to the institute. This would mean Eric's dispensing with his monthly visits to the hospital psychiatrist for medication. The therapist agreed to these conditions, and we saw the family for three evaluation sessions under the assumption that the conditions would be met. However, the therapist found it impossible to coordinate her schedule with ours, and the hospital refused to turn over the responsibility for Eric's treatment to us. We realized we had made a mistake in starting to see the family prior to these arrangements having been put into effect and dismissed them after four sessions. Six months later, having terminated treatments with the hospital and individual therapist, the family reapplied to our institute and we saw them for two more sessions.

During the first four sessions we obtained a history of the problem, the crux of which was summed up in the opening dialogue:

MOTHER: We don't get along.
FATHER: My son has a problem.
ERIC: My father has a problem.
MOTHER: Both of them have problems.
FAY [21-year-old sister]: It is between my father and Eric but it involves the whole family. My mother takes my brother's side. It is just horrible. I don't take anyone's side. I try to stay out of it.
GEORGE [23-year-old brother]: I agree with Fay. I more or less break up the fights by physically stepping between my father and Eric.

The family went on to describe a typical sequence of interaction. Eric, who was not working nor going to school, would become upset about something at home and would go on a rampage in which he would vandalize the house—smashing in doors, breaking furniture and dishes, throwing garbage around, and so on. Mother would try to calm him down but would only make things worse and they would end up screaming at each other. Father, hearing mother screaming at the top of her lungs, would come rushing in to stop Eric, and he and Eric would become embroiled in a violent fight. This was George's cue to come in to separate father and Eric and stop them from killing one another.

Father called the police once to press assault charges against Eric, but when they arrived mother protected Eric by saying they were both assaulting each other. Father had ordered

Eric out of the house several times, and he had slept in the car until mother later let him back into the house. Father, while ranting and raving about mother's overprotectiveness, would always back down and accept the situation.

During the second session, mother stated she had to stay home from work for three days following the first session because she became so anxious about having the whole family come in. She had wanted family therapy because she felt caught in the middle and was afraid of the mounting violence. A heavyset woman, always out of breath, she complained about assuming the responsibility for rounding the family up to come here as they were all giving her a hard time. Fay was irritated as she had difficulty getting off from work. George looked bored and said they had been this route before (referring to family therapy) but that he was willing to give it another try. Father sat with eyes bulging, his face purple with rage, saying it was his wife's idea but it was probably better than nothing. Eric stared into space, claiming he felt detached and depersonalized.

In this session we learned the following history: After mother had had a stillborn she could not conceive again, and the doctor told her that the only way she could get over her "mental block" was to adopt a child. Eric described himself bitterly as "just a prescription" to help his mother conceive and said he had always felt different. He claimed he never knew he was adopted until he was hospitalized, when it had come out in the family sessions. Mother insisted she told him when he was 5 by giving him a book about the "chosen child" that made the family happy but Eric claimed he never understood. He referred to himself as a "professional mental patient." He stopped going to college after three days eight years earlier and currently spent his days sleeping, smoking pot, going to therapy, and sometimes playing sports. He had been on heavy doses of prescribed drugs, at one point taking as many as 40 milligrams of Valium a day, but was now down to five. Recently the doctor prescribed Librium but he flushed it down the toilet because he feared he was becoming addicted to drugs.

Father believed that Eric had been spoiled because he was their first child and adopted and they had bent over backwards to make him feel loved. "He was put on a pedestal and treated like a prince. Everything was done for him—and she still does everything for him." He believed that Eric would never learn to take care of himself because his wife always gave in to him. "She treats the whole family that way—she does everything for everybody." George agreed, "My mother treats us all like children but it doesn't affect my sister and myself as much because we are more independent and out of the house." (George was working, going to school and had a steady girl friend; Fay was working and engaged to be married in eight months.) Mother agreed, "I am too good to all of them but not to my husband because of the fights over Eric."

Both parents stated they had had a perfect marriage with no problems until eight years ago when Eric began giving them difficulty. Now there was constant tension between the two of them but only over Eric. The children described an extremely dependent relationship between their parents, reporting that when their father had to work late and was not home mother was miserable. Eric was the most sensitive to mother's loneliness stating, "I hate to see her unhappy and moping around. I feel bad and don't like to see her left alone. But sometimes I go out anyway."

When father declared Eric should be working and living away from home, Eric said he would not move more than 10 blocks away from home. He had tried to find an apartment but all the apartments within 10 blocks were too expensive. Mother, defending Eric, stated, "Eric can stay as long as he doesn't have the confidence to live alone. He does need someone. I know that." Father felt his hands were tied because if he intervened he was afraid his wife would have another heart attack. She had suffered one four years earlier and had been hospitalized for eight weeks. A year later she had had angina again and had been hospitalized for four weeks.

The maternal grandmother who had died 10 years ago had lived upstairs for her last 12 years with her husband. This grandmother doted on Eric as the first male grandchild, and whenever his parents tried to discipline him he would run upstairs where she would protect him. Despite this the whole family worshipped her and spoke of her as though she were a saint. Father stated with tears in his eyes, "She was great— nothing was ever too much for her. She was a beautiful person and very giving of herself. With my wife it is the same. She has the same kind of great mothering instincts—but let's face it, grandma never had such problems." And Fay stated, "Grandma would have kept Eric with her. She would have accepted it. That's the way she was. She accepted everything and everyone." Mother, who cried every time grandma's name was mentioned, agreed with Fay. "She would try to calm him down. That's what I do. But one thing is different—grandma would never have approved of anyone leaving home until they were married—and I would."

Grandfather, who still lived upstairs, seemed to play a minor role in the life of the family and wasn't mentioned except in relation to grandmother's death after which he had been hospitalized with gastrointestinal disorders.

Based on this information, our initial hypothesis centered around the great mother tradition in the family and the connection between this tradition and Eric's symptomatic behavior. Grandma was deified as a great earth mother who had sacrificed herself uncomplainingly to nurture others. Ten years after her death everyone cried at the mention of her name. Not only did mother seem to be struggling to carry on grandma's tradition by taking care of everyone in the family, but she was intent on carrying out grandma's injuction to keep Eric the special child. If she took a firm position with him she would run the risk of desecrating grandma's memory.

Father, who was extremely sensitive to mother's anxiety, colluded with her in keeping the great mother tradition alive by never taking a definitive step to challenge it. He had much to gain from it personally and condoned and stood in awe of this "great mothering instinct" both in grandma and in his wife. He only complained about it when it got out of hand with Eric. Mother's heart condition had been used to control father over the years, but his sensitivity to her anxiety must have predated her heart condition.

We speculated that after grandma's death, mother had increased her caretaking of all the family members both as a means of dealing with her own depression and of proving her loyalty to grandma. She focused a large portion of this caretaking on Eric as both Fay and George seemed on their way to becoming self-sufficient through jobs and educations and had formed romantic attachments outside the family. (It remained to be seen if George's role of mediator would deter him from leaving home.) Increasingly Eric had been left to keep mother company and fill up her emptiness when father was working. He must have picked up signals from mother that he was needed and responded by becoming a drop-out. Having been treated as a special child from the day he was adopted, he learned to manipulate and intimidate the family through violent and crazy behavior. The family setup was fertile ground for this as no family member related to Eric independently, on their own terms, but in reaction to one another—mother in reaction to grandma, father in reaction to mother, Fay and George in reaction to the relationship between the two parents. This left Eric feeling detached and "different."

In considering the consequences of change, we concluded that if Eric were to function responsibly and leave home, mother would be left with no one to lavish her mothering instincts on but father since Fay and George were on their way out of the family. This might be overwhelming for father since mother would probably start making more demands on his time with no one else around to fill it up. We decided to reframe Eric's behavior as serving to protect father from being the sole recipient of the great mother tradition should all the children leave home. The group took the position that Eric needed to continue to protect father by remaining at home with mother, but the therapist opposed this, saying the burden was too heavy for him to shoulder alone and suggested it was only fair for Fay and George to share it with him. They should do this by taking turns keeping mother company when father wasn't there.

The family first validated our description of the problem and then denied it. Fay exclaimed she did try to relieve Eric by "baby-sitting with mother," but it was very tiresome. George complained that the last time he had tried to do this, mother had driven him crazy. The therapist was appealing to their sense of fair play when mother interrupted to ask if we could provide individual therapy for Eric since his therapist was leaving. Father agreed with mother ("Eric definitely belongs in individual therapy"), and Eric asked if we could not combine individual and family therapy. The therapist said the group must be right because the best way to make sure that no change would take place was for Eric to remain in the role of the patient. However, it was again made clear that we would not be providing individual therapy at the institute.

When one person in the family has been slotted into the patient role through individual therapy over a long period of time, it is extremely difficult for the family to reverse their perception of the problem and accept the concept of family therapy.

Mother telephoned before the third session to say that Eric was sick and she wanted to know if they should come without him. Eric requested to speak to the therapist on the phone and yelled into the receiver: "Help, help, I'm going crazy!" The therapist said that was a good reason to come to the session, but he said he couldn't.

The parents appeared alone: Fay sent a message she had to work late, and George claimed he had to write two term papers. It turned out that Eric had merely wanted to watch a hockey game, and mother insisted she could not get him to come.

The parents reported a great improvement in the home atmosphere. For the past two weeks, there had been "something like a beautiful calm in the house." Eric was in a different frame of mind, was opening up, coming out of his room, speaking with them, and even eating dinner with them. He even kissed mother's relatives. Mother ascribed this to his new medication, but father thought it was the result of our sessions. However, today, Eric had given them a hard time and they felt discouraged again. Eric had called mother at work and said he did not feel well and wanted to watch the Rangers game rather than attend therapy. Mother refused to give in to him and told him he had to come. He called her a second time, saying he had lost all control of himself and that he was going to smash everything in the house. Mother went home and found him crying and feeling detached. He smoked pot to calm himself down and then threw a temper tantrum, flinging garbage all over. For the first time, mother made him pick it up. She said she had begun to wonder if she shouldn't be stricter with him. She then blamed his actions on the fact that his therapist was leaving and again requested individual therapy for him.

During this session, mother also began to complain for the first time about taking all the responsibility for what happened in the family. Besides working part-time, she cleaned up after the children, did all their wash, all the cooking, and the whole family took her for granted. She was fed up and was considering not doing anything—but found she couldn't stop herself. Father agreed that she was under a lot of pressure but said she took it upon herself. "She feels she can do everything better and faster than anyone else." He insisted he would be happy to help her, but every time he tried, she did it herself instead.

The consultation team discussed the marked change that had taken place in the family: Eric had behaved differently for two weeks until the day of the appointment when he had felt compelled to prove to his family and to the therapist that he was still the patient. Mother had set a limitation on his behavior for the first time, forcing him to clean up his mess and had begun to question the way she had been handling him. It seemed Fay and George had found a way to avoid our asking them again to share Eric's job. The group sent no message at the end of this session, saying they would wait until the rest of the family was present.

Between this session and the next, we learned that the hospital had refused to turn over responsibility for the case to us, insisting that Eric remain under the care of their staff psychiatrist and receive monthly medication. We decided we could not continue to see the family until Eric had terminated treatment both with the hospital and his individual therapist, and the family was told of this decision. They were confused and disappointed, and Eric stated he wished to continue in individual therapy and perhaps they would assign him another therapist at the hospital. Mother spoke of Eric's difficulty in leaving his therapist, "His whole world is coming to an end." He was back to his destructive rages, had broken a door, and thrown a glass at the wall. The first time Eric called, mother ran home, but the second time he called she told him she was too busy in her office and that she would be home at five and expected him to have his mess cleaned up by that time, which he did.

These changes were encouraging and we regretted having to terminate at this point. However, both the team and therapist agreed it was the right decision under the circumstances.

With an outside psychiatrist administering medication and an outside therapist involved in the termination process, we would have had no control over the case. Whenever medication is used in the Brief Therapy Project, it is done after a consultation with our staff psychiatrist, Dr. Robert Simon, who determines how and when medication should be prescribed. It is then integrated into the treatment plan and becomes part of an overall strategy. For example, in one case in which the identified patient was insisting we give him medication in order to control his violent outbursts, Dr. Simon concluded that medication would have little effect. He suggested we tell the patient that the doctor would only prescribe medication after he had proven to us that he could control himself and behave responsibly because it would be very dangerous to place medication in the hands of an irresponsible person. This put the patient in the position of having to prove to us he could control himself, after which there would be no need for medication.

Eric's family reapplied for family therapy six months after we had terminated and were given an appointment. Before they appeared for the first session, Eric called the therapist to again request that he be seen in individual therapy in conjunction with the family sessions. He was told we would discuss this in the session. In a presession consultation with the team it was decided that the group would take the position that his desire to continue in individual therapy was commendable as this would protect the parents from the many difficulties that would arise between them in family therapy; and that also as long as Eric remained the patient neither of his siblings would have to stay behind to make sure his parents were okay. It was agreed that the therapist would continue to support Eric's moves toward independence, suggesting some small steps that he might take in that direction.

In retrospect we believe this was where we made one of our major mistakes. The therapist was supporting change in the wrong part of the family. It was virtually impossible for Eric to take unilateral steps toward change while the parents remained locked into their same intransigent positions. A wiser decision would have been for the therapist to keep challenging the parents' relationship around the issue of the great mothering tradition. Would mother feel she had betrayed grandma if Eric left home before he was married? Would she lavish father with more mothering? How would father respond? How much mothering could he tolerate? We also failed to realize that by supporting Eric's increasing independence, the therapist would be seen as siding with father against mother since it was father who kept trying to push Eric out of the home. A third error was in our not anticipating that Eric might resort to violence within a session as a means of proving he still needed individual therapy. We might have forestalled this if the group had predicted it. Eric would probably have gone to great lengths to avoid following the group's prediction.

These miscalculations, together with the family's intense investment in keeping Eric the patient, precipitated an explosion. In the following session, in which Fay was not present, Eric perceived that the therapist was siding with father and reacted to the implication that he should grow up and leave home, by launching into a tirade against both the therapist and group, using obscenities and threats. The therapist countered these by saying the group must have been right—that change was too frightening, whereupon Eric accused the therapist of being in cahoots with his father and suggested they run off together. At this point George walked out of the room, saying he had had it with this family. The parents used the fracas to validate their positions. Father screamed at mother, "Now do you believe what I have been telling you for eight years. He belongs in a hospital. You'll never learn. I've given my time, thank you. You can stand on your head, cry all night, carry on, get depressed. I'm not coming back here." Mother responded by screaming at the group: "Now maybe you will all believe Eric needs to be in individual treatment. See how sick he is!" Eric, returning from the hallway where he had injured his hand banging on the group's door, screamed yes, he was sick, but so was his father, only he didn't admit it. They began to fight physically, and the therapist interceded and told them to take Eric home and call for another appointment if they decided they wanted one. Each stated they would never return.

The mother telephoned the following week, apologizing for Eric's behavior and asking for a referral for individual therapy. The therapist referred her back to the outpatient department of the hospital where they were known, apologizing for not having heeded the group's warning about change. Mother stated Eric had been calm since the session and she had seen very little of him, since he was out of the home a great deal.

While the last session seemed to have temporarily calmed things down, Eric still remained in the role of the patient; we had been unsuccessful in getting him out of that role.

Reviewing failures raises intriguing questions concerning broader issues related to therapy and change. One such question is, why do the same errors have serious consequences in one case and not in another, similar case? Many of the so-called mistakes described in the above two cases had been made in varying degrees in other cases—poor timing, mishandled referrals, unsystemic interventions, and oversights; in many of these cases, however, successful results were achieved despite therapeutic mishaps. A case that is considered a failure reveals, in retrospect, errors at every turn; yet, had the case turned out differently, these same errors would have been overlooked, considered inconsequential, or given a theoretical justification.

Another question that is raised is, at what point should the therapist change his/her approach if it appears not to be working? Because families usually go through a number of crises in the process of changing, how does the therapist know if the crises are a natural reaction to this process or the result of ineffective therapy? We have held many postmortems in the middle of therapy to declare a case a failure; asked ourselves, like guilty parents, what went wrong; planned a new strategy— only to have the family appear the following session to report startling changes. Would these changes have taken place if we had shifted our approach prematurely?

In one instance, we decided to change our tactics because there was no evidence of progress being made. Before we could implement our new approach, however, the family canceled their next appointment because the two sons who had been depressed and dysfunctional were both working and unable to attend the session. What were the currents of change that had been quietly taking place, carefully concealed by the family?

At other times, we have congratulated ourselves on a particularly elegant strategy, confident the family would never again be the same, only to later discover they had managed to remain totally impervious to our artistry.

While certain guidelines may be offered in conducting family therapy, there are no hard and fast rules, no absolutes, no certainties. It is difficult to comprehend the many currents impinging on the family, both from within and without their system; it is impossible to control random events or to predict the family's response to the therapist, the therapeutic messages, or the presence of the consultation team. It is this very unpredictability that makes the study of human behavior and human systems endlessly fascinating. One never has all the answers and is never sure of the answers one thinks one has.

B I B L I O G R A P H Y

Bateson, G. *Steps to an ecology of mind*. New York: Ballantine Books, 1972.

Bateson, M. *Our own metaphor: A personal account of a conference on the effects of conscious purpose on human adaptation*. New York: Alfred A. Knopf, 1972.

Bloch, D. A. (Ed.). *Techniques of family psychotherapy: A primer*. New York: Grune & Stratton, 1973.

Bowen, M. *Family therapy in clinical practice*. New York: Jason Aronson, 1978.

Carter, E., & McGoldrick, M. (Eds.). *The family life cycle*. New York: Gardner Press, 1980.

Castaneda, C. *Journey to Ixtlan*. New York: Simon & Schuster, Pocket Book Edition, 1972.

Dicks, H. V. *Marital tensions*. New York: Basic Books, 1967.

Dell, P. Beyond homeostasis: Toward a concept of coherence. *Family Process*, 1982, *21*, 21–41.

Duhl, F., Duhl, B., & Kantor, D. Learning, space and action in family therapy: A primer of sculpture. In D. Bloch (Ed.), *Techniques of family psychotherapy*. New York: Grune & Stratton, 1973.

Ferreira, A. J. Family myths. In I. M. Cohen (Ed.), *Psychiatric research reports 20*. Washington, D.C.: American Psychiatric Association, 1966.

Framo, J. *Explorations in marital and family therapy*. New York: Springer, 1982.

Frankl, V. Paradoxical intention: A logotherapeutic technique. *American Journal of Psychotherapy*, 1960, *14*, 520–535.

Freud, S. Charcot (1893). In *Standard edition*. London: Hogarth Press, 1962.

Haley, J. *Strategies of psychotherapy*. New York: Grune & Stratton, 1963.

Haley, J. *Uncommon therapy*. New York: W. W. Norton, 1973.

Haley, J. *Problem solving therapy*. San Francisco: Jossey-Bass, 1977.

Haley, J. *Leaving home*. New York: McGraw-Hill, 1980.

Hess, R. D., & Handel, G. *Family worlds*. Chicago: University of Chicago Press, 1969.

Hoffman, L. *Foundations of family therapy*. New York: Basic Books, 1981.

Keeney, B. P. *Aesthetics of change*. New York: Guilford Press, 1983.

Madanes, C. *Strategic family therapy*. San Francisco: Jossey-Bass, 1981.

Minuchin, S. *Families and family therapy*. Cambridge, Mass.: Harvard University Press, 1974.

Mittelmann, B. Complementary neurotic reactions in intimate relationships. *Psychoanalytic Quarterly*, 1944, *13*.

Mittelmann, B. The concurrent analysis of married couples. *Psychoanalytic Quarterly*, 1948, *17*.

Nadelson, C. C. Marital therapy from a psychoanalytic perspective. In T. Paolino & B. McCrady (Eds.), *Marriage and marital therapy*. New York: Brunner/Mazel, 1978.

Napier, A., & Whitaker, C. *The family crucible*. New York: Harper & Row, 1978.

Paolino, T., & McCrady, B. (Eds.). *Marriage and marital therapy*. New York: Brunner/Mazel, 1978.

Papp, P. Brief therapy with couples groups. In P. Guerin (Ed.), *Family therapy, theory and practice*. New York: Gardner Press, 1976. (a)

Papp, P. Family choreography. In P. Guerin (Ed.), *Family therapy, theory and practice*. New York: Gardner Press, 1976. (b)

Papp, P. (Ed.). *Family therapy: Full-length case studies*. New York: Gardner Press, 1977.

Papp, P. The use of fantasy in a couples group. In M. Andolfi & I. Zwerling (Eds.), *Dimensions of family therapy*. New York: Guilford Press, 1980.

Papp, P., Silverstein, O., & Carter, E. Family sculpting in preventive work with well families. *Family Process*, 1973, *12*, 197–212.

Reiss, D. Varieties of consensual experience. 1. A theory for relating family interaction to individual thinking. *Family Process*, 1971, *10*, 1–28.

Rohrbaugh, M., Tennen, H., Press, S., & White, L. Compliance, defiance and therapeutic paradox; guidelines for strategic use of paradoxical interventions. *American Journal of Orthopsychiatry*, 1981, *51*, 454–467.

Rohrbaugh, M., Tennen, H., Press, S., White, L., Pickering, R., & Raskin, P. *Paradoxical strategies in psychotherapy*. Paper presented at American Psychological Association meeting, San Francisco, 1977.

Sager, C. *Marriage contracts and couple therapy*. New York: Brunner/Mazel, 1976.

Satir, V. *Peoplemaking*. Palo Alto, Calif.: Science & Behavior Books, 1972.

Selvini Palazzoli, M. *Self-starvation*. New York: Jason Aronson, 1978.

Selvini Palazzoli, M., Boscolo, L., Cecchin, G., & Prata, G. *Paradox and counterparadox*. New York: Jason Aronson, 1978.

Selvini Palazzoli, M., Boscolo, L., Cecchin, G., & Prata, G. Hypothesizing–circularity–neutrality: Three guidelines for the conductor of the session. *Family Process*, 1980, *19*, 3–12.

Simon, R. Sculpting the family. *Family Process*, 1972, *2*, 49–57.

Sluzki, C. Marital therapy from a systems theory perspective. In T. Paolino & B. McCrady (Eds.), *Marriage and marital therapy*. New York: Brunner/Mazel, 1978.

Tomm, K. The Milan approach to family therapy: A tentative report. In D. Freeman *et al.* (Eds.), *Treating families with special needs*. Ottawa: Canadian Association of Social Workers, 1982.

Watzlawick, P. *How real is real?* New York: Random House, 1976.

Watzlawick, P. *The language of change*. New York: Basic Books, 1978.

Watzlawick, P., Beavin, J., & Jackson, D. *Pragmatics of human communication*. New York: W. W. Norton, 1967.

Watzlawick, P., Weakland, J., & Fisch, R. *Change: The principles of problem formation and problem resolution*. New York: W. W. Norton, 1974.

Winch, R. F., Ktones, T., & Ktones, V. The theory of complementary needs in mate selection. *American Sociological Review*, 1954, *19*.

Wolin, S. J., Bennett, L. A., & Noonan, D. L. *Ritual myth and family identity*. Unpublished manuscript.

Woolf, V. *To the lighthouse*. Middlesex, England: Penguin Books, 1964.

I N D E X

versus structural approach, 121
Paradoxical intervention: defiance based,
    33–35
  Brief Therapy Project, 33
  case study, 34, 35
  defined, 33
  versus individual therapy, 35
  systemic paradox, 33, 34
Parent–child relationships, pediatrics, 122
Patten, J., 2n.
Paul, N., 7
Penn, P., 2n.
Philadelphia Child Guidance Clinic
    (PCGC), 3, 121, 123
Pickering, R., 31, 242n.
Prechange tests, 144–146
Press, S., 31, 242n.
Prata, G., 1, 22, 242n.
Private practice, 65, 66
Psychotherapy
  ambiguities, x
  group as therapeutic tool, x, xi
Public opinion poll, 52, 53

R

Raskin, P., 31, 242n.
Reciprocal arrangement, marital therapy,
    140
Reciprocal overadequacy and inadequacy
    patterns, 140
Reciprocity
  bilateral, 140
  central theme, 141
  historical context, 140
  in relationships, 141
  systems terms, 140
Reiss, D., 15, 242n.
Resistance, x
Reversals: compliance and defiance
    based, 37–45
  couple, 42–44
  defined, 37, 38
  individual, 44, 45
  family, 41, 42
  motivating, 38, 39
  renegotiating, 40, 41
  sustaining, 39, 40
  uses, 38
Rohrbaugh, M., 31, 242n.
Ross, J., 2n.

S

Sager, C., 140, 242n.
Satir, V., ix, 142, 242n.
Selvini Palazzoli, M., ix, xi, 1, 7, 9, 22, 178,
    242n.
  systems paradoxes, 7
Setting terms for therapy, 27–45
  Brief Therapy Project, 30
  contradictions in presenting requests,
    27
  direct interventions, compliance based,
    32, 33
  family's definition of problem, 27
  hidden agendas, 27
  interventions, classification of, 29–31
  paradox, designing of, 35–37
  paradoxical interventions: defiance
    based, 33–35
  reversals: compliance and defiance
    based, 37–45
  therapeutic contract, 27
Sibling subsystem
  anorexia case presentation, 89–93
  as example, 37
Siegel, S., 4, 60–63
Silverstein, O., xi, 22n., 4, 142, 242n.
  absent family members, 219
  consultation team, 56, 67
  reversals, 42
  three-way debate, 60–63
  violence case presentation, 190
Simon, R., 242n.
Sluzki, C., 16, 242n.
Stability, theory of, 12
Stepparenting, 111
Structural approach, intervention, 121
Suicide, 111
Supervision, 64, 65
Support groups, 51, 52
Surprise and confusion, produced by
    group, 53, 54
Symptom formation, 9–11
  coping patterns, 10
  evolutionary function, 10
  homeostatic function, 10
  reciprocity, 10
  symptom, occurrence, 9
Symptoms, connection with family
    system, 73–75
Systemic paradox, 33, 34
Systems theory, 6, 7